Contents

Introduction

This book has been written to support students who are studying for the single award AS level GCE using the course structure set by OCR. The book is designed to support the three AS level units:

Unit 1   Promoting Quality Care
Unit 2   Communication in Care Settings
Unit 3   Promoting Good Health

This book has been organised to cover each of these units in detail. Headings are designed to make it easy to follow the content of each unit and to find the information needed to achieve a high grade. As well as providing information each unit is designed to stimulate the development of the thinking skills needed to achieve an advanced level award.

Assessment

Each unit will be assessed by coursework or by an external test set and marked by OCR. Detailed guidance for coursework assessment and external test requirements can be found in the unit specifications and at OCR's website. This book has been designed to support students to achieve high grades as set out in the guidance from OCR available during 2004/2005.

Special features

Throughout the text there are a number of features that are designed to encourage reflection and to help students make links between theory and practice. In particular this book has been designed to encourage a depth of learning and understanding and to encourage students to go beyond a surface level of descriptive writing.

The special features of this book include:

Think it over   Think it over...

The feature is designed to provide thought provoking questions that will encourage reflective thinking, or possibly reflection involving discussion with others.

Did you know?   * DID YOU KNOW?

These are interesting facts or snippets of information included to encourage reflective thinking.

Scenario   SCENARIO

We have used this term in place of the more traditional term 'case study' because the idea of people being perceived as 'cases' does not fit easily with the notion of empowerment – a key value highlighted by government policy and by OCR standards. Scenarios are presented throughout the units to help explain the significance of theoretical ideas to Health, Social Care and Early Years settings.

Consider this   Consider this

Each author has designed a 'consider this' feature at the end of each section of each unit. Each 'consider this' involves a brief scenario followed by a series of questions.

Key concept   Key concept

Because the authors believe that the development of analytic and evaluative skills requires the

ACADEMIC YEAR
2005 – 2006

ACADEMIC YEAR
2006-2007

Afreen AHMED

CENTRAL RESOURCES

R45328J0430

AS Level for OCR

Health & Social Care

Series editor

Neil Moonie

www.heinemann.co.uk
✓ Free online support
✓ Useful weblinks
✓ 24 hour online ordering

01865 888058

Heinemann

Inspiring generations

Heinemann Educational Publishers
Halley Court, Jordan Hill, Oxford OX2 8EJ
Part of Harcourt Education

Heinemann is the registered trademark of
Harcourt Education Limited

Text © Neil Moonie, Jo Irvine, David Herne 2005

First published 2005

British Library Cataloguing in Publication Data is available
from the British Library on request.

ISBN 0 435 45369 6

Copyright notice
All rights reserved. No part of this publication may be reproduced in any form or by any means
(including photocopying or storing it in any medium by electronic means and whether or not transiently
or incidentally to some other use of this publication) without the written permission of the copyright
owner, except in accordance with the provisions of the Copyright, Designs and Patents Act 1988 or
under the terms of a licence issued by the Copyright Licensing Agency, 90 Tottenham Court Road,
London W1T 4LP. Applications for the copyright owner's written permission should be addressed to the
publisher.

Edited by Neil Moonie
Designed by Lorraine Inglis
Typeset by TechType, Abingdon, Oxon

Original illustrations © Harcourt Education Limited, 2005

Illustrated by TechType, Abingdon, Oxon

Cover design by Wooden Ark Studio

Printed by Edelvives

Cover photo: © Photonica

Picture research by Ruth Blair

Acknowledgements
Every effort has been made to contact copyright holders of material reproduced in this book. Any
omissions will be rectified in subsequent printings if notice is given to the publishers.

ability to use concepts, the authors have identified key concepts and offered a brief explanation of how these terms might be used.

Key issue

Key issue

The authors have identified key issues students should be aware of and consider.

Assessment guidance

At the end of each unit there is a 'how you will be assessed' section that provides either sample test material for externally assessed units or outline guidance and ideas designed to help you achieve the highest grades when preparing internally assessed coursework.

Glossary

This book contains a useful glossary to provide fast reference for key terms and concepts used within the units.

References

There is a full list of references used within each unit together with useful websites at the end of each unit.

Author details

Neil Moonie, former Deputy Director of the Department of Social Services, Health and Education in a College of Further and Higher Education. Chartered Psychologist, part-time lecturer and contributor to a wide range of textbooks and learning resources in the field of health and social care. Editor of Heinemann's GNVQ Intermediate and Advanced textbooks on health and social care since 1993 and editor of the 2000 Standards AVCE textbook.

Jo Irvine has worked in health visiting and nursing and in further education for a number of years. She currently works as a consultant in health, social care and childcare.

David Herne works as a public health specialist for the Chorley and South Ribble Primary Care Trust.

UNIT 1

Promoting Quality Care

This unit contains the following sections:

1.1 Attitudes and prejudices

1.2 Rights and responsibilities of service users and providers

1.3 Facilitation of access to services

1.4 Care values

Introduction

This unit explores aspects of quality, and what this means in a care environment. Quality is an essential characteristic of care work, and refers to the standard of the services which are delivered. This unit begins by exploring issues concerning the values and attitudes of care workers towards vulnerable people. A fundamental principle of providing care is the recognition that everyone has rights as individuals and as human beings, and it is the responsibility of care workers to promote and protect the rights of those they care for. The rights and responsibilities of those using services and service providers are explored, as well as different ways in which individual rights can be promoted, and the interaction between rights and responsibilities. The values that apply to care work and work with children are also explored, together with the concept of safe working practices.

The range of health care provision includes preventive services, diagnostic services, general medical and surgical services, therapies, specialist services for adults, children, people with learning difficulties and mental ill health. These services are provided either in hospital (acute services) or in the community through Primary Health Trusts (preventive, long-term and rehabilitation services). Social care services support adults and children who are vulnerable due to life circumstances and unable to manage daily life without support of some kind, or who are at risk of harm or abuse. Such support may be offered at different times and be short- or long-term, depending on individual circumstances.

Children's services are concerned with the care, learning and development of all children, not just those who are ill or have special needs or those at risk of harm.

Children's services are delivered by a wide range of organisations, including private nurseries, childminders, playworkers, and classroom assistants.

When considering care services, there are two main aspects that it is helpful to take into account when examining quality, namely, what is delivered and how it is delivered.

What is delivered

Examples include specific services, treatments or interventions. Interventions are activities carried out by health or care workers.

How it is delivered

Service delivery may be focused on patient or user-centred care, which involves service users in decision-making, or task oriented care, in which the individual has little or no say in the arrangement or delivery of care and treatment.

How you will be assessed

The unit will be assessed through a 90-minute test.

Section 1: Attitudes and prejudices

Because care work involves working closely with people, it is important to develop trusting relationships between workers and service users. Therefore, the attitudes and values of care workers are of great importance. We all hold a range of attitudes that we may not have ever explored. Attitudes begin to develop from our earliest years, through values and beliefs that we pick up during the process of **socialisation** (see page 4), but it is important to note that socialisation is an active process that takes place throughout life and that attitudes can change as a result of experiences.

Attitudes

Attitudes involve beliefs and values. Beliefs and values concern issues which are considered to be of fundamental importance, such as the importance of family or religious beliefs, or the importance of independence or personal wealth. Every culture also has certain expectations of what is acceptable or unacceptable behaviour (**behavioural norms**), which reflect a particular culture's values. Attitudes and values provide the basis for all social interactions with other people, and the world around us.

Britain is a multicultural and diverse society in which there are many different customs and values. People from different cultures hold a variety of different views and beliefs, which can often be reflected in their behaviour. For example, in some social groups it is polite to shake hands on meeting, in other cultures a kiss on both cheeks is an acceptable greeting. Within a multicultural society it is important that a diversity of views and opinions is seen as a positive quality.

We all make unconscious judgments about people, based firstly on initial appearance, body language and expression. These initial opinions may be either confirmed or modified, once we begin to talk to others and get to know them better. We often instinctively prefer people similar to ourselves, because similar backgrounds and circumstances often lead to shared values and beliefs.

Prejudices

Prejudice means, literally, to pre-judge something or someone, and refers to preconceived opinions or attitudes held by individuals towards other people or groups. A prejudiced person may have a favorable attitude towards groups with whom they identify and a negative attitude or prejudice towards other groups, who are seen as different: such preconceived opinions are usually based on stereotypes.

> ### ✳ DID YOU KNOW?
>
> The word *stereotypes* (stereo meaning two) originally referred to a printing stamp that was used to make multiple copies from a single model or mould.

Stereotyping

Stereotyping can be defined as a simplified or generalised image or idea, which is applied to individuals or groups. When applied to human beings, stereotyping is like 'stamping' a set of fixed and inflexible characteristics to a whole group of people, even though few members of the

FIGURE 1.1 *Stereotyped thinking can result in discriminatory behaviour*

group may have these characteristics. We all recognise stereotypes from the language used to describe them, which is often unflattering and has negative associations. Stereotypes are frequently based on limited and inaccurate information; they become embedded in cultural thinking and are difficult to eradicate. It has been said that stereotyping is a lazy way of thinking, because it requires both awareness and effort to ignore one's prejudices, suspend judgement and see others as individuals. When you hear someone talking about a particular group of people and they start a sentence with the words 'they all...' , it often indicates stereotypical thinking.

Think it over...

Divide into two groups, or several smaller paired groups. One group should write out the name used to identify people or groups on cards or the board. The other group has to think of as many words to describe this group as possible. Here are some to start with:

* Teenage mother   * Homeless person

* Old woman   * Rapper

* Youth

1. Do these words conjure up a mental image of the people named?

2. Do you think the descriptions are true of all people in these groups?

3. Think carefully about where your information has come from. Is it from personal experience? When discussing these issues, you need to be aware that people can have strong feelings about their values and beliefs, especially if they are challenged.

Primary socialisation

Socialisation is the process in which young children learn the cultural values and **norms** of the society into which they are born, primarily from their parents. Therefore **primary socialisation** refers to the child's growing understanding of the language, customs and practices of their particular family. Socialisation

Think it over...

'Our government, politicians and the media sanction discrimination and disadvantage through perpetuating the belief that teenage mothers are at best, ignorant and at worst, irresponsible and incapable of being good parents.'

Director, YWCA Charity, the *Guardian*: 8 September 2004

This quote suggests that there is prejudice against teenage parents, particularly mothers.

1. Debate this statement in two groups, with one group supporting the statement and one group arguing against it. You will need to carry out research into the issues faced by teenage parents and young mothers in particular. You should find out about access to financial services, including benefits and banking facilities, housing options in your local area and the extent and availability of educational, health and social services.

2. Is access to services and facilities different for this group of people? If you consider that it is, explain in what ways?

3. What stereotypical assumptions are made about teenage mothers?

starts from birth, with the process known as bonding, and it is now understood that the infant is an active participant in this process.

Because infants and young children have little experience of the outside world, what they experience in the home environment, or care environment, is accepted as normal. In other words, young children expect that their experiences are the same as everyone else's. Children also learn about how to behave, i.e. find out what is acceptable and unacceptable behaviour, from how adults and children with whom they have regular contact behave towards each other, and from the rules that are in place in the home or care environment. Examples of these include: whether it is normal to eat together sitting around the table as a family; whether there are routines, for example, at bedtime; and saying, 'please' and 'thank you'. However, it is important to note that in addition to the parents' values and beliefs, any prejudices the parents may hold will also be transmitted to the children, and accepted as a given truth because young children do not have the experience to form their own views and opinions.

One example of primary socialisation is the way in which children learn what it means to be male or female, which starts with children using parents as **role models** for appropriate behaviour. This is known as **gender socialisation** and in order to understand this concept, it is important to recognise that sex is biologically determined and therefore fixed (except in the case of developmental abnormalities). Gender on the other hand, is socially determined with behaviour, which is based on sex differences. The concept of gender behaviour and characteristics can be thought of as a continuum along the line from male to female, with people (men and women) being located somewhere along the line.

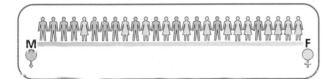

FIGURE 1.2 *Concept of gender behaviour and characteristics*

For example, some men demonstrate what are often thought of as more 'feminine' qualities such as sympathy, kindness and sensitivity, whereas some women display more 'masculine' qualities,

Think it over...

Make two lists, one of masculine traits and behaviours and one of feminine, using the following words:

Brave Temperamental Compassionate Adventurous Rational Thoughtful Sympathetic Enterprising Gentle Dainty Logical Sensitive Aggressive Assertive Resolute Careful Gallant Intuitive Decisive Elegant

such as self-confidence, boldness and independence. Such behaviour can challenge assumptions about what is considered 'normal' behaviour for their gender, and people may experience prejudice and disapproval from others.

Sociologists such as Ann Oakley (1974), put forward the theory that gender roles are learned behaviour, because boys and girls are socialised differently according to adult views on what is acceptable and unacceptable social behaviour for different sexes. One of the first questions parents ask at the birth of their baby is whether it is a girl or boy. Oakley argues that, from then on boys and girls are treated differently according to the expectations of gender behaviour held by the parents, reflecting the cultural norms of masculine or feminine within their particular society. For example, the cries of baby boys may be described as 'lusty' or 'hearty', whereas girls may be expected to be quiet. This is regarded as 'good' behaviour and usually praised: in other words, children are conditioned to display gender appropriate behaviour. Boys may be expected to be active explorers of their environment: activities such as climbing on furniture are more likely to be tolerated in boys than girls.

Think it over...

1. Can you identify different ways in which adults may respond differently to boys and girls, starting from birth?

2. Think of examples of acceptable and unacceptable behaviour for girls. Does this differ from boys, and if so, in what way?

3. Listen to the way in which parents speak to their children or describe them to others – can you identify words or phrases that are more commonly associated with one sex or the other?

4. What conclusions can you draw about gender roles within society?

Research has now established that gender development is more complex and the stereotypical gender behaviour that young children demonstrate at around 2–3 years of age is thought to be a way of simplifying and making sense of complex social behaviour. (for more information see the Open University website supporting *Child of Our Time* which can be found at www.open2.net/childfourtime/2005)

The development of socialisation can be observed through the way in which young children play. Children's play gradually becomes more complex and formal, with defined sets of rules. This is true of play that is invented and initiated by the children themselves. Children are helped to understand the purpose of rules, and ideas about fair play through participation in team sports such as hockey and football.

Secondary socialisation

Secondary socialisation refers to the process in which the child comes to understand the social norms of a wider society. Although the parents or carers are the most enduring influence on a child's attitudes and behaviour, the child's assumption that everyone's family is the same, and that all families behave in the same way as their own is gradually challenged by contact with the wider world, and the different influences that they are exposed to. This process, which generally started at school age, now often starts earlier as increasingly more children go to nursery school and come into contact with different children and adults. It is particularly important therefore, that childcare workers and educationalists acknowledge, accept and positively value cultural diversity and understand different social customs and norms. Some of the key influences affecting secondary socialisation are discussed below.

Education

When children enter school, they encounter adults and children from other family backgrounds – teachers and other pupils – and learn what is expected from them in the school setting, in addition to the formal curriculum. These expectations are based on social and cultural values of the society and community in which the school operates: they may be similar to what children and young people are accustomed to at home, or they may be very different; this can cause conflict. The social and behavioural norms are transmitted through school rules, and

disobedience may be punished by sanctions, such as detention. In this way, children learn to behave in a socially acceptable way, with the school operating as a social institution. Sociologist Pierre Bourdieu (1977) referred to this as 'social reproduction'. This process of socialisation within the school is sometimes referred to as the 'hidden curriculum' because it is not concerned with formal school subjects. Schools are also involved in **gender socialisation**. Mairtin Mac an Ghaill in *The Making of Men* (1994) argues that schools are institutions in which such things as subject allocation, disciplinary procedures and student-teacher interaction serve to construct gender relations which reflect Western industrialised society and are based on traditional relationships and nuclear families, in which females tend to take a secondary or passive role. There is some evidence to suggest that this may be changing, reflecting the growing awareness of the importance of the contribution of educational institutions to socialisation.

Peers

A significant aspect of secondary socialisation concerns learning to understand and manage relationships with others, particularly peer-group relations. These relationships are different to those previously experienced within the family group, in that they are based on what each can do for the other, rather than the unconditional mutual loving relationships within the family. The child gradually realises that others have rights, wants and needs of their own, which may conflict with theirs. In addition, peers either reinforce or undermine the child's internal view of themselves through such social relations, for example, whether they are sporty and good at games, and whether they are popular. Children begin to measure their value as individuals through the way in which other children relate to them and the number of friends they consider themselves to have. In extreme cases, where the child experiences bullying, self-esteem can be cruelly damaged. Once the young person reaches adulthood, this process of socialisation continues in the workplace, through relationships with work colleagues.

The media

The television is an especially important influence in the process of secondary socialisation. Young children often have difficulty in differentiating between fact and fantasy in terms of what they see on television. Children may see TV characters as role models, and there has been much discussion on the influence that television has on children's behaviour, especially programmes which have violent or abusive content. The way in which families and different groups within society are portrayed on television also influences children's perceptions of the world around them, and their understanding of their own place within it. This can be particularly damaging to a child's developing self-esteem if he or she belongs to a group that is not represented accurately on television, not represented at all, or is portrayed in a negative light. In this way, the media can be responsible for perpetuating gender stereotypes, especially through marketing and advertisements. For example, adverts convey the relative power and social status of men and women by showing men as bigger and positioned physically higher than women. Similarly, whilst women are often shown averting their gaze from men, men only avert their gaze from a superior, such as their boss. Men are sometimes portrayed as inferior and incompetent when doing household or caring tasks, i.e. 'women's work'. Advertising sends out strong messages about the differences between boys and girls, men and women and the sort of behaviour that is acceptable; for example, adverts are likely to show boys as strong, independent, athletic and in control, whereas girls are shown as giggling, gentle, affectionate and concerned with their appearance.

Books and magazines are another influential source of information, especially when children are learning to read. The characters and illustrations in books can reinforce stereotypes or provide an alternative view of the world and other cultures.

Think it over...

1. Look carefully at both the programmes and adverts you see on TV for a week. Make a note of how the people in them are portrayed.

2. How many men on TV are like the men you know personally, for example, your father, friends, relations, and teachers?

3. Why does the perpetuation of traditional gender stereotypes disadvantage both men and women?

Religion

For some people, their religious beliefs are very important and their socialisation is directed by the behavioural codes found within their holy writings. Some religious practices, such as fasting or wearing special clothes, clearly identify members of a particular religious group, who may then become the focus for the prejudiced attitudes of others. Such religious intolerance is usually based on misinformation and stereotypical views. There are many different religions practised in Britain, and care workers should be familiar with the basic principles and practices of most of these in order to provide appropriate care.

It is through the process of socialisation that we develop beliefs about what is 'normal' within their society. These beliefs become 'internalised', i.e. they become subconscious and we do not even think about them. However, whether we are aware of them or not, they guide our behaviour and inform our attitudes to others. Adolescents and young adults often choose to break conventional social norms; this is a normal part of developing an individual identity. Adolescents who do things

FIGURE 1.3 *How many things linked to socialisation can you spot?*

1. In groups of two or three, select one religious or cultural group and carry out research into the cultural characteristics of the group. This must be a group *other* than the one with which you most identify.

2. Find out about:

   Festivals and celebrations
   Music, songs and dance
   Food and diet
   Personal hygiene
   Religious practices
   Clothes and fashion
   Family traditions
   Family roles
   Leisure and pastimes
   Death and dying.

3. Prepare a presentation for the rest of your group, using a range of images, handouts and visual aids.

socialisation is a process through which an individual comes to understand the social rules and normal expectations of behaviour in their society. Socialisation carries on throughout life as people are exposed to different circumstances and different cultures. It is important as it provides the basis for attitudes, values and beliefs which inform the way people behave towards others. It is important to remember that these attitudes, values and beliefs are internalised; however, they can be changed through experience.

continuing throughout life, such as, each time individuals come into contact with a new group of people, or when visiting different countries on business or on holiday, they will be exposed to a different set of social and cultural norms and values. Attitudes and beliefs will continue to change as we have new experiences.

Health and well-being

Human beings, all have a number of basic needs, which they need in order to stay healthy. Most people manage to meet their own needs through work, home life and leisure pursuits.

differently may become the focus of disapproval because of the way they dress, or act.

An individual's identity and sense of self, including a sense of self-esteem is either made stronger or changed through feedback from others. So secondary socialisation can be seen as

BASIC NEEDS OF A HUMAN BEING	
The need to give and receive attention.	Human beings are social creatures designed to live in groups and interact with each other, forming intimate relationships and social connections. This is why solitary confinement is seen as a punishment, and infants deprived of appropriate attention fail to thrive.
The need to take care of the body.	Includes the need to provide the body with healthy food to enable it to prevent disease, grow new cells and repair existing cells, also to maintain structures and functions through sufficient rest and exercise.
The need for stimulation and challenge.	This is constant throughout life, as the human brain needs exercise. If intellectual functions are insufficiently stimulated by external stimuli, such as new information, the brain will turn inwardly to the imagination in order to prevent boredom. However, even the imagination needs something to work on and without stimulation, mental health is at risk.
The need for meaning and purpose.	People need to have goals to aim for, in order to feel a sense of achievement. This sense of achievement is linked to feelings of value and self worth, particularly if these goals involve helping other people, i.e. they are outwardly directed.

FIGURE 1.4 *A summary of the basic needs of a human being*

These requirements can be summarised and are shown in Figure 1.4.

The effects of attitudes and prejudices on the health and well-being of service users when these needs are unmet can be profound. The effects of discriminatory actions are both physical and psychological. When prejudiced attitudes affect the way individuals behave towards other people, this is known as **discrimination**.

> **Key concept**
>
> *health and well-being* is maintained when individuals are able to meet all their physical, social and intellectual needs, preserving good physical and mental health.

Discrimination

To discriminate means to show preference, or to choose. It is important to understand that discrimination can be in favour of someone or something as well as against. Care work is concerned with anti-discriminatory practice, which means not treating any person or group more favourably than another. Discrimination is defined by Giddens (2001) as 'activities [or actions] that deny to the members of a group resources or rewards which can be obtained by others'.

It is important to recognise that although prejudice is linked to discrimination, not everyone who is prejudiced behaves in a discriminatory way. In other words, people who discriminate are usually prejudiced, but not all prejudiced people discriminate.

Discrimination can occur because of the differences between people, as shown in Figure 1.5 overleaf.

Consider the following famous people, Christy Moore, author; Helen Keller, teacher; Stephen Hawking, scientist; Nelson Mandela, lawyer and activist; Amelia Earhart, aviator; Wayne Sleep, dancer. All these people have several things in common – they can be considered disadvantaged in some way. They belong to groups that are often discriminated against; they do not fit conventional stereotypical roles and, most importantly, they became famous because of their achievements, not because of their disadvantages and for the most part they regarded themselves as ordinary people.

Discriminatory actions include those shown in Figure 1.6 below.

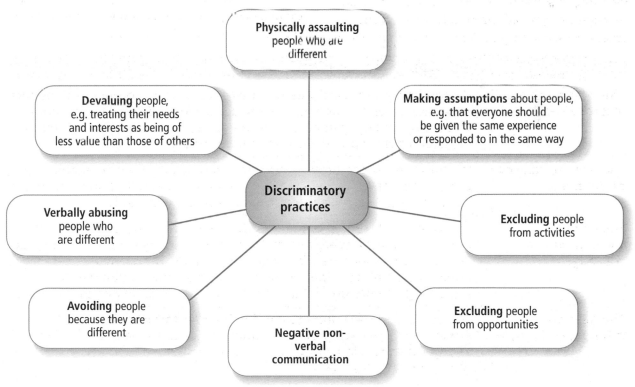

FIGURE 1.6 *Types of discrimination and abuse*

DIFFERENCES BETWEEN PEOPLE	
Ability	Individuals who have some form of physical or mental disability, e.g. wheelchair users, people with cerebral palsy, people with speech difficulties, people who talk to themselves, people with learning difficulties
Appearance	People with physical disfigurements, e.g. birthmarks, burns, unusual features including stature
Age	Older people or very young people can be prevented from participating in activities, sporting activities for example, based on assumptions about their competence and physical skills
Ethnicity or culture	People from different parts of the country or another country within the UK may be discriminated against because of the way they speak, for example
Gender	Women and men may be discriminated against if they do not conform to stereotypes of male or female role behaviour; some resources may be denied to individuals on the basis of gender or preferential treatment may be given to one sex over the other
Marital status	Within many societies, the expectation is that adults will marry in order to raise children. Certain financial advantages are therefore made available to married couples that are not available to single people, or single parents
Race	Racism is the term used to describe prejudice based on physical distinctions such as skin colour. Such a prejudice is based on the belief that some races are superior to others – usually white superior to others. There is a growing awareness of the extent to which racism is systemic within British society, that is, institutions within society such as the health and social services, the police and the education system promote policies, customs and practices that favour some groups more than others. The Macpherson report (1999) into the handling of the murder of black teenager Stephen Lawrence concluded that racism was institutionalised and there was a 'collective failure... to provide an appropriate and professional service to people because of their colour, culture or ethnic origin. It can be seen and detected in processes, attitudes and behaviour which amount to discrimination through unwitting prejudice, ignorance, thoughtlessness, and racist stereotyping which disadvantage minority ethnic people.' Following this report, the Race Relations Act was amended in 2001 (Section 19B) so that all public bodies now have a duty to prohibit race discrimination. Public bodies include the police, local government, mental hospitals, prisons and courts
Religion	Although many Western societies are secular and religion is of less importance to many people, some religious groups are returning to the fundamental principles of their religion in response to what they interpret as the declining moral values of Western society. For example, there are fundamentalist movements within both Christianity and Islam. In addition, there are differences between religious groups such as Protestants and Catholics, Muslims and Sikhs. Discrimination by one religious group against another is not uncommon, and has arguably been one of the most enduring causes of human warfare.

FIGURE 1.5 *Some of the differences between people that may give rise to discrimination*

SCENARIO

Tariq is a young man aged 17 years, who, due to cerebral palsy affecting his legs, needs to use a wheelchair to get around outside. Tariq's other difficulties include occasional uncontrolled movements of his head and sometimes his speech can become difficult to understand, especially when he is angry or upset.

Tariq lives at home with his parents and older sister, but intends to move into independent living accommodation once he has finished his studies; he is currently studying business at college.

Tariq is making preparations for a party he intends to hold at a local hotel to celebrate his 18th birthday. He has arranged to go shopping for new clothes with two friends from college, Adam and Yousuf. In the local shopping mall, they go into a branch of a high street chain which sells fashionable clothes for young people. As they browse through the racks of clothes, they become aware that the assistants are watching them closely and talking quietly to each other.

With the help of Adam and Yousuf, who find the right size and reach up to fetch the clothes down from the rails, Tariq eventually chooses a shirt, trousers and jacket. However, when they go to the assistants to ask if Tariq can try them on, two of them walk away and one turns his back on the three boys and starts to price up some new stock. Undeterred, the they head towards the changing rooms to help Tariq out of his chair so he can try on the trousers, only to be approached by the senior assistant who tells them that only one person at a time is allowed in the changing rooms. He addresses his remarks to Adam.

When Tariq tells the assistant that he will manage by himself and call for assistance only if he gets into difficulties, the assistant turns to Adam and tells him that the changing rooms are unsuitable for wheelchairs due to access difficulties.

What legal rights protect people from this kind of discrimination nowadays?

1. **Read through the information above and identify the different ways you think Tariq is being discriminated against.**
2. **What would have been a non-discriminatory experience for Tariq?**
3. **How do you think this incident might affect Tariq?**

Prejudice can lead to discrimination and lack of respect for individuals, preventing them from having their needs met. In some cases, this can lead to bullying behaviour which culminates in abuse of vulnerable individuals, especially children and older people, by those who are in positions of power over them. In the care setting, this can result in the mistreatment of people, including elder and child abuse.

The effects of attitudes and prejudices are:

* prejudice
* discrimination
* disrespect
* bullying
* abuse.

In order to be an effective carer, workers need to examine their own attitudes honestly, work hard to overcome any prejudices and maintain respect for individuals as human beings with equal rights. This is called anti-discriminatory practice.

The effects off anti-discriminatory practice are:

* open mindedness
* fairness
* respect
* consideration
* care.

Abuse can take many forms, some of which are shown in Figure 1.7.

MISTREATMENT OF PEOPLE	
Physical abuse	Slapping, hitting, burning, scolding, pushing, inappropriate restraint, inappropriate use of medicine, withholding medicine as punishment, lack of consideration, roughness when handling or treating people, e.g. helping them to the toilet or when changing dressings. (An estimated 20 per cent of reported cases of elder abuse involve physical abuse.)
Psychological abuse	Shouting, swearing, frightening someone, threatening someone, withholding or damaging something with emotional importance to someone, and failing to deal with people with respect and dignity (35 per cent of reported cases)
Financial abuse	Stealing and fraud, especially from elderly people (20 per cent of reported cases)
Sexual abuse	Including inappropriate touching, unwanted sexual attention, making sexual remarks designed to make someone feel uncomfortable, and rape. (2 per cent of reported cases)
Neglect	Such as failure to provide food, heating, adequate care or attention to hygiene, such as helping with bathing; neglecting treatment, e.g. prevention of pressure sores (10 per cent of reported cases)

FIGURE 1.7 *Examples of some forms of abuse*

Source: House of Commons Health Committee Second Report on elder abuse, 2004
Note: Although the figures in brackets refer to elder abuse, these forms of abuse apply to all vulnerable individuals, including children.

Discriminatory and abusive practices damage individuals, both physically and psychologically as a result of the stress they cause. Stress has physical manifestations such as negative thoughts that affect sleep patterns, causing anxiety and depression. Associated physical symptoms include high blood pressure, comfort eating/drinking and other compulsive health-damaging behaviour. When a person faces a stressful situation, the body's response includes flooding the system with stress hormones such as adrenaline in preparation for what is known as 'flight or fight'. Normally, once the stressful situation has passed, physical exercise helps the body to excrete the stress hormones quickly. However, if individuals are unable to remove the stress hormones from the system, for example, if they occur in a working situation or a person is physically unable to exercise, the stress hormones continue to have a physical effect, keeping the body in readiness for action.

Physical injury and exclusion can affect access to economic resources and access to social opportunities, which results in the individual becoming isolated and financially vulnerable.

When individuals have been physically attacked, they may continue to feel unsafe because of the threat of attack, including intimidation and verbal abuse. Avoidance, devaluing and exclusion leads to people feeling that they do not belong and a predisposition to depression.

Self-esteem and empowerment

Discriminatory actions resulting from uninformed attitudes and prejudice have a significant impact on an individual's self-esteem. Self-esteem is concerned with the ability to have belief in oneself, confidence in one's abilities, a sense of self-assurance and self-respect – in other words, positive self-regard. Discriminatory actions undermine an individual's self-esteem. When individuals are suffering from low self-esteem they often feel that they have no control over their own life and cannot achieve anything. They have expectations of failure and stop trying to influence events in their lives. This blocks personal development and can lead to depression and in extreme cases, self-harming behaviour.

The negative effects on self-esteem and sense of empowerment for service users who are ill and experience prejudice and discrimination can delay the healing process because psychological health and well-being are an integral part of care. Service users are likely to feel a sense of helplessness and hopelessness, which will affect their ability to be independent and contribute to their own care; they may feel unable to ask for help for fear of recrimination, afraid of being perceived as a 'nuisance'. If they are not consulted about their care and treatment, they are likely to feel devalued.

> ### Key concept
>
> *empowerment* refers to the process through which individuals exercise choice and make decisions about their lives. Individuals can be disempowered by lack of information, lack of money, fear of consequences (e.g. bullying behaviour directed at them) or belonging to a group that is marginalised in society (e.g. homeless people). It is the responsibility of care workers to ensure that service users are empowered as equal partners in their care and treatment, for example by ensuring they have sufficient information on which to base a decision.

Direct and indirect discrimination

Direct discrimination

This occurs when it is obvious by the words or actions of individuals that they are deliberately disadvantaging another. For example, refusing to consider a black person or a woman for a job interview even though they have the required qualifications and experience would be discriminating on the basis of race or gender. Name calling and nicknames based on race, ethnicity, gender, age, and size, for example, are all forms of discrimination. Within care services, giving preferential treatment to some groups or denying appropriate treatment to other groups is discriminatory.

'Discrimination may be seen to occur where people are treated differently, and either do not receive the service, or it is delivered to them in an inappropriate way.

Unfair discrimination can occur on the grounds of age, class, caste, colour, creed, culture, gender, health status (e.g. HIV status), lifestyle, marital status, mental ability, mental health, offending background, physical ability, the place of origin, political beliefs, race, religion, responsibility for dependants, sensory ability, sexuality or other specific factors.'

(Tossell and Webb, 1994)

Indirect discrimination

This is much less obvious. It occurs when certain conditions are in place that demonstrates preference for some people over others. Examples could include not providing female toilets, and not providing toilet facilities that children or disabled people can use. As the Macpherson report (1999) concluded in relation to racism in the police and criminal justice system, the way in which health, care and childcare services are provided and delivered can contribute to indirect discriminatory practices. In 1992 the National Institute of Social Work's Race Equality Unit published a report entitled *A Home from Home – the Experiences of Black Residential Projects as a Focus of Good Practice*. The report stated that:

'On the one hand, those members of the black community who have received mainstream residential care have experienced prejudice and racism which has denied them their cultural reality, racial pride, self-dignity and black identity. On the other hand, myths and stereotypes of black families such as "they look after their own" and "residential care is not part of their culture" have worked against the interests and welfare of their members in need of residential care.'

The report concluded that health and social services agencies had not fulfilled their duty of care to black families and their communities because they had either not provided services, or provided poor quality services in which a discriminatory culture was present.

Summary

The way in which care workers treat the people they care for can have a marked effect on their health and well-being. A positive, respectful and considerate approach can improve the rate of recovery from illness and enable older people to maintain their mental alertness and enjoy a higher quality of life for longer. Negative attitudes and stereotypical thinking among care workers will be apparent to service users, whether or not these are consciously demonstrated, and will have a significant effect on the emotional and physical health of those they care for.

When working with children, care workers need to recognise that they become part of the process of socialisation and can influence the development of positive or negative attitudes, values or prejudices in the children they care for. Care workers therefore have a responsibility to examine their own views and be open-minded if they are to deliver high-quality, anti-discriminatory care.

Section 2: Rights and responsibilities of service users and providers

All members of our society have fundamental human rights that are grounded in moral, ethical and philosophical ideas, such as the principle that all people are of equal value and the sanctity of human life.

These universal rights are protected by laws (legislation) concerning human rights and the right to equal treatment; they are intended to protect individuals from physical and emotional harm and exploitation.

In addition to the laws protecting the rights of all individuals, there are also particular laws in Britain to safeguard those considered to be vulnerable or at risk.

Many of these laws were influenced by European Union Law, for example, Article 141 of the Treaty of Rome (1957): the founding document of the European Union, states:

'Each Member State shall ensure that the principle of equal pay for male and female workers for work of equal value is applied.'

After joining the European Union in 1973, legislation was passed outlawing discrimination against men or women on the grounds of sex: the Sex Discrimination Act 1975.

Sex Discrimination Act 1975

The Sex Discrimination Act (SDA) covers discrimination in the following areas;

* All areas of *employment*, including job advertisements, with some particular exemptions, such as where it would be detrimental to have a member of the opposite sex in a particular job, e.g. men being employed as counsellors for women survivors of rape or sexual assault. Any contract of employment, which contravenes the Act is invalid.

* All *educational establishments* designated by the Secretary of State for Education, except single-sex schools and colleges. Single-sex competitive sport is allowed, if women's physical strength would put them at a disadvantage. In practice, this is often been used to exclude girls from certain sports at school.

* A wide range of *goods, facilities and services* come under the Act, including clubs, cafes, restaurants, hotels, transport, banking, insurance, hire purchase, recreation and entertainment. However, there is also a wide range of exceptions, including private clubs, political parties, religious bodies, hospitals, prisons, hospitals and care homes, charities and non-profit making organisations that were set up to provide for one sex only.

* *Housing*, including renting, managing, sub-letting, or selling accommodation. Single-sex housing associations are exempt.

The Act makes the distinction between direct and indirect discrimination.

Direct sex discrimination

This occurs when a person is treated less favourably in the same circumstances than someone of the opposite sex, just because of their sex. For instance, charging women more than men for the same service, for example, mortgages or pensions, or offering an educational course in childcare to women only. Sexual harassment is also a form of direct discrimination. Sexual harassment, as defined by the European Commission code of practice is 'unwanted conduct of a sexual nature, or other conduct based on sex, affecting the dignity of women and men at work'. This includes unwelcome and repeated physical, verbal or non-verbal conduct, including ridicule, comments about appearance, requests for sexual favours and in extreme cases, physical assault. Both men and women can suffer from sexual harassment.

Indirect sex discrimination

This happens when, despite the same criteria, service or provision being applied to both sexes, far fewer members of one sex can take advantage of it. For example, if a Housing Association excluded single parents it may be indirectly discriminating against women, because the majority of single parents are women.

Indirect discrimination is against the law if it cannot be shown to be justified, irrespective of sex, and if the discrimination has caused disadvantage or distress to an individual.

The Sex Discrimination Act also protects people from being victimised by taking action under the Equal Pay Act or the Sex Discrimination Act; examples include making a complaint, or helping someone else to make a complaint, giving evidence at a court or tribunal, or accusing someone of breaking these laws. Indirect discrimination may occur, for example, where an employer refuses to give a reference on behalf of the employee, because he or she brought proceedings against him under the Act.

Strengths of the SDA

* The Act applies to both men and women, although in practice, women have probably benefited more, since they were discriminated against in more areas, particularly in relation to housing and financial services. For example, before the Act, women were not allowed to have a mortgage in their own right, denying their home ownership.

* The 'burden of proof' lies with the perpetrators not the victims; this means that although individuals have to demonstrate that their treatment appeared to be discriminatory, the employers or providers of services (perpetrator) have to prove that their action or omission was not intended to be discriminatory.

* The Act covers both actions and behaviour, such as, for example, harassment. It is unlawful for someone to assist, coerce or persuade someone else to carry out a discriminatory act. The law also protects people who have used the Act from victimisation by those who have been accused of breaking the law.

* In a significant development aimed at securing equal treatment for gay men, lesbians, bisexuals and **transgendered** people, the Act

has recently been amended to bring discrimination against **transsexuals** within the scope of the Act. Although there is no legal definition of transsexualism, the term 'gender re-assignment' is used to cover such situations.

* One important issue is that employers are liable for discriminatory acts (or omissions) carried out by their employees during the course of employment, whether they were aware of it or not. It is therefore the responsibility for employers to provide equality training for their staff and have an equal opportunities policy that is monitored regularly. The employers may escape prosecution providing they can demonstrate that they took reasonable steps to ensure their employees were offered appropriate training and took action such as ethnic monitoring of the workforce to ensure the employees were aware of the law.

Weaknesses of the SDA

* There are important areas not covered by the Act, such as income tax, social security benefits, immigration, and nationality, including asylum seekers.

* Although it is unlawful to discriminate against married people in the areas of employment and training, this does not apply to the other areas of the Act listed above.

* The status of single people is not covered by the Act in the same way, and discrimination against them because they are not married, is lawful.

* It is not a statutory requirement under the Act for local authorities to eliminate unlawful sex discrimination and promote equal opportunities.

* Although the law is reasonable and clear, legislation does not change deeply held attitudes and values of individuals; only time and experience can encourage people to reflect on their attitudes. The law may prevent the more open examples of discrimination, but to be truly effective individuals have to be prepared to use it. Sex discrimination does still occur, for example, around maternity rights.

However, women often fail to challenge employers because they are afraid of losing their jobs. Others are unaware of their rights and are not provided with information by their employers. In other cases, people have suspected discrimination but have been given other reasons for their treatment. For example, women who are passed over for promotion may be told they are not suitable, or their performance is not up to standard. Even where indirect discrimination is suspected, it can be difficult, time consuming and expensive to prove.

Equal Opportunities Commission

Compliance with the Sex Discrimination Act is currently overseen by the **Equal Opportunities Commission**, whose aims are shown in Figure 1.8.

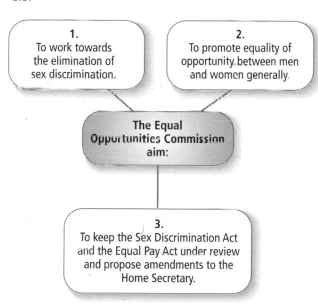

1.
To work towards the elimination of sex discrimination.

2.
To promote equality of opportunity between men and women generally.

The Equal Opportunities Commission aim:

3.
To keep the Sex Discrimination Act and the Equal Pay Act under review and propose amendments to the Home Secretary.

FIGURE 1.8 *Aims of the Equal Opportunities Commission*

The Commission has the power to undertake formal investigations into discriminatory practices on behalf of individuals and provide financial support to individuals complaining about discrimination. The Commission publishes codes of practice on employment, which may be used as evidence in an employment tribunal. It is therefore important that employers are aware of such codes of practice and comply with them. The Commission undertakes research and keeps relevant government policy areas under review; social security, taxation and maternity rights, for example.

Individuals who believe they have been discriminated against, can contact the Commission directly for advice. (www.eoc.org.uk). Information is also available through local branches of the Citizens Advice Bureau, and other welfare rights organisations. Financial assistance with bringing a discrimination case may also be available in certain circumstances.

FIGURE 1.9 *The commission undertakes employment tribunals*

The Race Relations Act 1976 (amended 2001)

The Race Relations Act 1976 (RRA) shares many of the features of the Sex Discrimination Act in that it covers employment, education, goods, facilities and services as well as housing. The Act identifies, direct and indirect discrimination – the concept of treating someone less favourably because of their race. There are four types of discrimination covered by the Act:

* Direct discrimination   * Victimisation

* Indirect discrimination   * Harassment

Direct discrimination

Examples of direct discrimination include denying entry to a club, school or other establishment because of race, or operating quotas limiting the numbers of black and/or members of other racial groups. It is also direct discrimination to refuse employment to a person on the basis that customers will not like being attended to by a person of that race. For example, a nursing home manager who refused to employ a black care worker on the grounds that the residents would object would be breaking the law. The Race Relations Act also defines segregation as direct discrimination; for example, providing separate facilities or limiting the job roles of black or other ethnic minority employees to positions where they have no contact with the public, whilst allowing others a full range of job roles.

Indirect discrimination

Indirect racial discrimination is identified in a similar way to indirect sex discrimination; applying criteria which only some people can meet. For example, requiring employees to be clean shaven would disadvantage Sikhs and other groups, whose religious and cultural beliefs require that they wear beards. Special arrangements must be made to allow equal access to the full range of job opportunities. The Act also covers victimisation and harassment. The definition of victimisation is similar to the Sex Discrimination Act, protecting individuals who bring action under the Act; harassment, which was added as an amendment in 2003, is defined as 'unwanted conduct with the purpose or effect of violating dignity or creating a hostile, degrading, humiliating or offensive environment on the grounds of race or ethnic origin' (Race Relations Act (Amendment) 2003). The Act covers similar areas to the Sex Discrimination Act, namely, *employment; housing; education; the provision of goods, facilities and services; harassment and victimisation*.

* In the area of *employment* the Act covers training opportunities, promotion, hours of work and fringe benefits in both permanent and temporary jobs as well as apprentices and trainees, employment agencies and the police. There are exceptions, called 'genuine occupational requirements', such as in restaurants or for drama and theatre productions, or to provide personal care services to a particular racial group. Training organisations are allowed to practice 'positive

discrimination' in situations where there have been few people from different racial groups doing a particular job role during the previous 12 months; this includes specifically targeted training courses, for example. As with other equality legislation, employers are liable for the actions of their employees and need to ensure that they are aware of the law. Most organisations have an Equal Opportunities Policy which should be made available to staff and monitored.

* Following the amendment to the Act in 2000, it is unlawful for the government to discriminate on race grounds when appointing people to serve in public office or on committees. Similarly, trade unions and professional associations cannot refuse to let people join, provide different benefits, facilities or services (e.g. legal representation) or apply different terms of membership. These areas come under *goods, facilities and services.*

* Licensing bodies such as the Director General of Fair Trading (who licenses credit and hire purchase facilities), magistrates or the police cannot discriminate on the basis of race. They are also obliged to take into account any evidence about previous racist conduct on the part of the applicant when considering their character, such as refusal to serve ethnic minority customers.

* The Act covers discrimination between any racial group, including between different minority groups. In many parts of the world there are groups who have been at war with each other, often, but not always as a result of religious differences, for example, in former Yugoslavia, in India and Pakistan and between Greek and Turkish Cypriots. The law provides protection for all these different groups of citizens.

* The Race Relations Act applies to *education*; specifically to schools and colleges maintained by a local education authority, but also to independent and fee-paying schools, special schools and grant-maintained schools and universities. The only exception to this is overseas students, who are not British citizens and may not remain in Britain once they have

completed their course. This allows educational establishments to charge higher fees to overseas students.

* The Act applies to *housing*, including renting from landlords (public or private), buying and selling. For example, it is illegal to discriminate by making members of ethnic groups wait longer or pay different charges. The exceptions to this are small boarding houses or shared accommodation and private sales by owner-occupiers, unless they use the services of an estate agent, in which case the Act applies because this is a service provided by the agent and thus covered by the Act. As with the Sex Discrimination Act, charities acting for a particular group are allowed to provide exclusively for them.

Strengths of the RRA

* The Act is wide ranging in its application, covering most areas of life.

* Following the Macpherson report (1999) into the death of Stephen Lawrence, the Act was amended to extend to the police. This was a key recommendation; in 2000 it was further extended to cover all public bodies such as local government, mental hospitals, prisons and courts.

* The Act applies to all racial and ethnic groups, covering discrimination between minority groups as well as between majority and minority groups.

Weaknesses of the RRA

* The Act has made open racial discrimination socially unacceptable to most people; however, like sex discrimination it occurs in more hidden and indirect forms and can be difficult to prove.

* Legislation does not change deeply held attitudes; however, it can be effective in preventing unacceptable behaviour in the long term.

* Taking action (invoking) the Act requires individuals to know their rights and what options are available to them, including what action to take. Organisations such as Citizens Advice Bureau and other welfare rights organisations can assist individuals with such information and may be able to provide legal advice.

The Commission for Racial Equality

The Commission for Racial Equality (CRE) is the body responsible for monitoring and enforcing the Race Relations Act (RRA) and has wide ranging powers. The Commission's responsibilities are shown in Figure 1.10.

The CRE has similar powers to the Equal Opportunities Commission in terms of investigation,

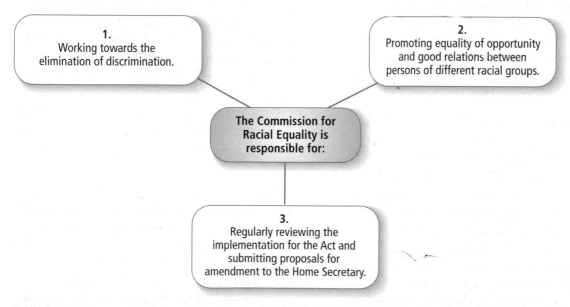

1.
Working towards the elimination of discrimination.

2.
Promoting equality of opportunity and good relations between persons of different racial groups.

The Commission for Racial Equality is responsible for:

3.
Regularly reviewing the implementation for the Act and submitting proposals for amendment to the Home Secretary.

FIGURE 1.10 *Responsibilities of the Commission for Racial Equality*

alleged discriminatory practices and supporting individuals who are bringing action under the Act. It also provides codes of practice, which can be used as evidence in Employment Tribunals. The Commission can carry out a formal investigation into any area, but must give notice of such an intention and draw up the terms of reference, stating the nature and scope of the investigation. The organisation or person will then be required to produce information or evidence. In addition, in situations where it finds that discrimination has occurred, the Commission can issue non-discrimination notices requiring the organisation or individual to make changes, for example to procedures or policies, in order to comply. However, such notices are not legally binding, although they can be used in evidence in individual cases. The Commission is required to give notice to the organisation of its intentions to issue a notice and what they need to do in order to comply; they then have 28 days to make any changes or prepare an appeal, explaining why they cannot or should not need to comply.

The Commission can enforce a non-compliance order by applying to the court (County Court or High Court) to take out an injunction against the organisation or person. An **injunction** is a court order requiring the person or individual to comply; failure to do so is considered to be contempt of court, which can result in fines or imprisonment. It is important to recognise that the Commission has up to five years after the issuing of a non-compliance notice to apply for an injunction.

Consider this

Vincent is a 28-year-old Rastafarian, who has worked at a community home for people with learning disabilities for the last six years. He is the only black person working in the home, although there is a black male service user, aged 17 years, and an Asian girl of 14 years. Vincent gets on very well with his fellow workers, and occasionally goes out for a drink with them, after work.

The new line manager has recently been appointed, following the retirement of the previous post holder, who had been at the home for 10 years. The new manager seems to have taken a dislike to Vincent and has begun to follow him around whilst he undertakes his duties, making critical remarks about the quality of his work. He has been overheard making racist comments, particularly about Rastafarians, in the staffroom, and is critical of Vincent and his work in front of the other staff. He has suggested that Vincent should get his hair cut and remove his Rastafarian dreadlocks, even though he keeps them tied back whilst on duty.

The new manager has also introduced a new work rota, allocating Vincent most of the cleaning duties that are not undertaken by the housekeeper. None of the other staff have been given extra cleaning duties.

Recently, Vincent was late for work on two occasions, due to his car breaking down, although his timekeeping is usually excellent – his colleagues rely on him to make the tea on the early shift and tease him about being unable to sleep. The manager gave Vincent a verbal warning on the first occasion and a written warning on the second. He has been informed that if he is one minute late for duty in future, he will be disciplined.

At the annual performance review, Vincent was given a particularly poor score and informed that he would not be getting a pay rise, although previously his reviews have been excellent, particularly in relation to his communication and relationships with the service users. All of the other staff received good reviews, and all have been awarded pay rises.

Using concepts can you identify?
1. What types of discrimination are evident in Vincent's treatment by the line manager?
2. What effect might this have upon Vincent?

Go further – can you analyse using theory?
3. What are the different ways in which the law protects Vincent's rights?
4. What action might Vincent take using the law?

Go further – can you evaluate, using a range of theory?
5. How might the line manager's attitude affect the residents, particularly the two non-white residents?

The Disability Discrimination Act 1995

The Disability Discrimination Act 1995 is concerned with the equal treatment of disabled people and outlaws discrimination against disabled people solely on the basis of their disability. In this respect it differs from the Sex Discrimination Act and The Race Relations Act, which apply to all people, and are general equality acts. There are proposed changes to the Act currently passing through the parliamentary process in the form of the Disability Discrimination Bill 2003.

The Act sets out the definition of a disabled person or person who has had a disability. There are four main criteria as set out in Figure 1.11.

* The Act covers similar areas to other equality legislation; *employment, trades unions and trade associations, goods, facilities and services, housing and education*. In addition, this Act includes *public transport*, because disabled people, as citizens, should have the same access to public spaces and transport as non-disabled people.

* Discrimination in *employment* applies to all job applicants, contract workers and employees. The Act covers appointments, contractual terms and conditions of employment, training opportunities, dismissal and redundancy. An employer is considered to have discriminated against a disabled person if he or she is treated less favourably than non-disabled people in the same employment, for reasons related to the disability, and they cannot demonstrate that such treatment is justified. In addition, employers are required to make 'reasonable adjustments' to the working environment to enable disabled people to work. This might include changes to the physical environment, or changes to policies and work practices, so that the disabled person is not placed at a disadvantage. The Act identifies the sort of things that might be considered reasonable adjustments, for example, allocating some of your duties to another person, altering working hours and permitting absences from work for rehabilitation, assessment and treatment. Importantly, it is not necessary for an employer to be aware that the employee is disabled, in order to be guilty of discriminating and failing to make reasonable adjustments. Many organisations now include a section in their job application forms that asks questions about disability in order to prevent such unintended discrimination. As with the other equality legislation, employers are held liable for acts of discrimination carried out by the employees in the course of their employment.

FOUR MAIN CRITERIA FOR DISABILITY	
Physical or mental impairment	Mental impairment includes suffering from mental illness, which is clinically well-recognised. Medical evidence may be required to show whether or not, there is impairment.
The ability to carry out daily activities	Impairment includes difficulties with any one of the following: mobility; manual dexterity; physical coordination; continence; ability to lift, carry or move everyday objects; speech, hearing or eyesight problems; memory or ability to concentrate, learn or understand; perception of risk and danger.
Substantial adverse effect	This means that the impairment must be more than minor, and may get worse over time.
Long term	The impairment must have lasted for at least one year. With progressive conditions such as cancer and HIV, the 1995 Act considers a person to be disabled as soon as the condition becomes symptomatic; however, under the proposed changes, such conditions would be considered a disability as soon as they were diagnosed. This is an important change, because individuals suffering from terminal or life-limiting diseases should not be subject to delays when seeking claims for discrimination under this Act.

FIGURE 1.11 *Definition of a person who has a disability*

* Trades unions and trade associations must be prepared to admit disabled people to their membership and existing disabled members should have the same rights and benefits as non-disabled members, including membership on the same terms.

* *Goods, facilities and services.* This includes services provided by public authorities, as well as private agencies and individuals, whether they are paid for or not. Areas included in the Act include: communications, information services, hotels and boarding houses, financial and insurance services, entertainment facilities, training, employment agencies and the use of public places. Education and transport facilities are dealt with separately. The proposed changes to the Act will also include private clubs, which at present are excluded, unless they provide services to the public, such as hiring rooms for private functions. Again, discrimination occurs when the service provider treats disabled people less favourably for reasons relating to their disability and the treatment cannot be justified under the provisions of the Disability Discrimination Act. They are also required to make reasonable adjustments, so that their services can be accessed by disabled people. Disabled people must be offered the same standard of service, delivered in the same manner, as non-disabled people. The service cannot be provided on less favorable terms to disabled people.

* Discrimination in the provision of *housing* services include refusing to provide premises to disabled people, offering the premises on less favorable terms or treating disabled people less favourably than non-disabled people requiring the same housing facilities. This is very similar to the provision of goods facilities and services in general. The proposed changes will require reasonable steps to be taken to provide aids, for example, handrails or ramps, where these would allow disabled persons to use the premises or facility.

* *Education.* From September 2002 new duties were imposed on schools, which were intended to provide greater support to disabled pupils in mainstream education. The Special Educational Needs and Disability Act 2001 amended the Disability Discrimination Act, preventing discrimination against disabled people in terms of access to education. This includes the duty not to discriminate in relation to admissions, for example by refusal to admit disabled pupils, or the terms in which admission is offered. The education or associated services that are provided for pupils should be equally available to disabled pupils. Local Education Authorities and schools are expected to improve access to education for disabled students, and they are expected to prepare access ability plans, including improvements in access to the curriculum, physical improvements, and the provision of information in a range of formats suitable for use by disabled students, for example, Braille. There have also been some changes to the Special Educational Needs framework which deals with the specific needs of individual children. In particular, the Special Educational Needs Tribunal, which oversees the decisions relating to children with special educational needs, can now decide whether schools or colleges have discriminated under the Disability Discrimination Act.

* *Transport.* The Act covers licensed taxi cabs, and the licensing authority will not be able to grant licenses to taxes, unless the vehicles comply with the accessibility provisions. The Disability Discrimination Act requires taxi drivers to carry disabled passengers while they remain in their wheelchairs without additional charge; to carry the wheelchair if the passenger chooses to sit in the passenger seat; and to ensure that the passenger is carried in safety and reasonable comfort. Taxi drivers are expected to give reasonable assistance to their disabled passengers, including those with guide dogs or hearing dogs. Public service vehicles such as buses and coaches carrying more than 22 passengers are also covered under the Disability Discrimination Act since the accessibility

regulations were brought into force in 2000. Small buses, private hire vehicles and minibuses are excluded, although the proposed changes will end this exemption, requiring all providers of transport services to comply with the regulations. Rail services are also included under the Disability Discrimination Act, as a result of the Rail Vehicle Accessibility Regulations 1998 which required all new vehicles to the accessible to people with disabilities. The Disability Discrimination Act does not state the timeframe in which vehicles will be required to be accessible, and the implementation of disabled facilities on all rail transport is likely to be sometime in future.

Consider this

Read the example of Tariq shopping for clothes on page 11.

Using concepts can you identify?
1. Which aspects of the Disability Discrimination Act apply to this situation?

Go further – can you analyse using theory?
2. What reasonable adjustments could the shop make to enable wheelchair users to access all the facilities?

Go further – can you evaluate using a range of theory?
3. What are the manager's responsibilities in relation to the staff attitudes towards Tariq?
4. What can be done to help staff fulfil their responsibilities under the Disability Discrimination Act?

Opportunities for redress

If any individual feels that they have been unfairly discriminated against, and they wish to rectify the situation or complain, this is known as 'seeking redress '. There are several ways in which this can be done; for example, if the complaint of discrimination relates to employment, individuals would usually use the organisation's policies and procedures and equal opportunity as a means of

changing their situation. Organisations are required to have an equal opportunities policy, which they should make available to all staff, for example through a staff handbook. Line managers and supervisors are responsible for implementing and monitoring equal opportunities for the staff they manage; however, senior managers have responsibility for ensuring the line managers and supervisors understand what is expected by making certain they are properly trained. Senior staff should monitor recruitment and retention to ensure that people are not leaving employment unnecessarily and expect to receive regular reports from managers and supervisors. An Equal Opportunities Policy should provide details on the recruitment, terms and conditions, training, promotion and the procedure for complaints, as set out below.

Recruitment

This will include information for managers and staff on the recruitment process, for example, the content of job advertisements, so that they do not contravene any of the equality Acts and details of any exemptions applicable to the particular job roles of the company.

Application forms should be designed so that the company does not ask for irrelevant information, which may be discriminatory, for example the age of the applicant. It is important, however, to monitor the ethnicity of applicants (ethnic monitoring) in order to highlight any possible inequalities, which can then be investigated and any disadvantage addressed; this will ensure that the composition of the workforce represents all sections of the local workforce. Benchmarks (comparisons) can be used to ensure fair representation, and to provide opportunities for increasing the number of employees from minority groups, for example by an agreed percentage. It is possible to discriminate positively in favour of under represented groups without contravening any law, and information from the Census can be used as a guide. In Scotland, information about ethnic minorities on the census returns is different.

And equal opportunities policy should also provide details of how to conduct recruitment interviews in order not to discriminate, for example by ensuring that all questions are asked of both men and women, and including questions about caring responsibilities. Many organisations now have standardised interview procedures in which the questions are agreed in advance of interviewing candidates.

Terms and conditions

Equal opportunities policies should provide information on the terms and conditions of employment, which will be included in the contract of employment, such as maternity rights, how pay is negotiated, holidays and paid leave, the rights to belong to a trade union, how performance is monitored and under what circumstances employees may be dismissed. This is to ensure that staff are fully aware of their rights and responsibilities and those of their employers before they sign the contract of employment. The policy should include under what circumstances the employee may be disciplined, and provide details of the disciplinary procedures. Employees are entitled to representation during disciplinary hearings, for example from a trade union representative or colleague, who can speak on their behalf and support them.

Training

An equal opportunities policy should state how opportunities for training are provided for all employees. This should include compulsory training, such as health and safety and diversity training. This is particularly important to the care sector, to ensure that employees are aware of their responsibilities not to discriminate. Training opportunities should be available to everyone, and based on individual learning needs, which should be identified from performance reviews.

Promotion

Equal opportunities policies should identify how and under what circumstances opportunities for promotion are provided for staff. It is good practice to ensure that people are encouraged to apply for promotion on the basis of their performance reviews, and that opportunities are offered to the existing workforce before advertising externally.

Complaints

The policy should give clear guidance to managers and staff on how employees can complain about their treatment, including discrimination, harassment, bullying and victimisation. This is sometimes called the grievance procedure, and often has a timescale within which the employee should apply for redress. It is important to recognise that the first step in a grievance procedure is often the individual's line manager, who may be the person that the employee wishes to complain about. The policy should clearly state what the employee should do in such situations.

The first step for employees who feel they have been a victim of discrimination should be to use the organisational procedures described above in order to rectify the situation. If the situation does not reach a satisfactory conclusion, employees may seek advice and guidance from the appropriate Commission, their trade union, the Citizens Advice Bureau or other welfare rights organisations such as the Low Pay Unit. Disputes relating to employment, which are not satisfactorily resolved between employer and employee may be taken to an Employment Tribunal, which will hear the evidence and make judgments. Employers who have been found guilty of discrimination will be obliged to change their procedures, reinstate the employee and sometimes pay compensation. If the employees are victimised on returning to work as a result of bringing such an action, they are entitled to redress for this as a separate case.

If the alleged discrimination relates to other areas covered by the relevant equality Acts, such as the provision of goods, facilities and services, individuals should contact the relevant Commission directly for advice and guidance. Other organisations may be able to provide assistance, for example, the Office of Fair Trading.

The Human Rights Act 1998

The Human Rights Act 1998 (HRA) is the most important significant piece of British legislation protecting human rights and freedoms, and has its origins in the European Convention on Human Rights, drafted after World War II. The countries that have signed up to the Convention make up the Council of Europe, which is separate from the European Union. The European Court of Human Rights is the international court set up to interpret and apply the Convention. The court is overseen by judges who are nominated by each of the countries that are members of the Council of Europe. The Human Rights Act enshrines the rights from the European Convention on Human Rights into a form of higher law in the UK.

The Convention is divided into 'articles' which set out the rights that are protected, and new protocols giving additional rights have been incorporated over the years by the Council of Europe as circumstances have changed. Many of these are incorporated into the new Act. However, it is important to recognise that not all of the rights set out by the Convention and its protocols are incorporated into the Human Rights Act 1998.

The Rights

Article 2: The right to life
The right to life is protected by law, and there are only certain limited circumstances, where it is acceptable for the state to take away someone's life, such as a police officer acting in self-defence.

Article 3: The prohibition of torture
This covers the right of individuals not to be tortured or subjected to treatment or punishment, which is inhuman or degrading.

Article 4: The prohibition of slavery and forced labour
Individuals have the right not to be treated as a slave or forced to perform certain kinds of labour.

Article 5: The right to liberty and security
This means the right not to be deprived of one's liberty, for example 'arrested or detained', except in certain cases, such as where someone is suspected or convicted of committing a crime and this is justified by existing legal procedures.

Article 6: The right to a fair trial
Everyone has the right to a fair public hearing within a reasonable period of time. This covers criminal charges, civil rights and obligations. Hearings must be carried out by an independent and impartial tribunal, established by law. The public may be excluded from some hearings, if it is necessary, for example to protect national security or public order. Individuals accused of criminal charges are presumed innocent until proven guilty according to the law, and have the right to defend themselves.

Article 7: No punishment without law
This covers the protection of individuals who have committed actions that have since become criminal. It also protects people against later increases in sentences for an offence.

Article 8: The right to respect for private and family life
Everyone has the right of privacy and to have family life respected, including an individual's home and correspondence. This right can only be overridden in certain circumstances, for example in the interests of national security.

Article 9: Freedom of thought, conscience and religion
This enshrines the right of individuals to hold a broad range of views, beliefs and thoughts, including religious faiths.

Article 10: Freedom of expression
Everyone has the right to hold opinions and express their views, either individually or within groups. This includes unpopular or disturbing beliefs; however, it can be restricted in certain circumstances, for example incitement to religious hatred, or causing a breach of the peace.

Article 11: Freedom of assembly and association
This includes peaceful demonstrations, trade union membership and the right to associate with other people holding similar views. It can be restricted in a similar way to freedom of expression.

Article 12: The right to marry
Everyone has the right to marry and start a family; however, the national law still governs how and at what age this can take place.

Article 14: Prohibition of discrimination
This means that when the Convention rights are applied, individuals have the right not to be treated differently because of their race, religion,

sex, political views or any other status. This article ensures that the Convention applies to everyone.

Note: Article 13 is not included in the Human Right Act, since the government felt the existing legislation would be sufficient.

The protocols

These are later additions to the Convention.

Article 1 of protocol 1: The protection of property

This means that everyone has the right to enjoy their own possessions in peace. Public authorities are not allowed to interfere with things you own, or the way you use them, except in very limited circumstances, for example confiscation of property for noise pollution or from convicted drug dealers.

Article 2 of protocol 1: The right to education

Individuals must not be denied the right to the educational system.

Article 3 of protocol 1: The right to free elections

Elections for the members of any legislative body (law-making organisations such as Parliament) must be free and fair. They must take place by secret ballot, although qualifications may be imposed on those that are eligible to vote, such as a minimum age.

Article 1 and 2 of protocol 6: Abolition of the death penalty

This article formally abolishes the death penalty. There may be limited exceptions in times of war, but only in accordance with the law.

Compatability of new law and the Convention

It is important to recognise that as a result of the Human Rights Act, every time the government proposes a new law in Parliament, it has to ensure that the new law is compatible with the rights of the Convention. This is the reason that many of our existing equality Acts have recently been amended, particularly in respect of public bodies. The Human Rights Act states that all

public authorities must pay attention to the rights of individuals when they are taking decisions that affect them. Public authorities include the government, civil servants, local authorities, health authorities, the police, the courts and private companies that carry out public functions.

Strengths of the HRA

1. Because the Human Rights Act is now enshrined in British law, individuals with human rights grievances will no longer have to go to the European Court of Human Rights in Strasbourg, but will be able to bring their case to court in the UK. However, it is still possible for individuals to make an application to the European Court of Human Rights under certain key requirements. For example, the individual must be a victim of a violation of one or more of the articles of the Convention, and he or she should generally have pursued any proceedings through the UK courts before making an application. Applications must be made within 6 months of the conclusion of any court proceedings in the UK.

2. Under the Human Rights Act, public bodies are no longer exempt from taking individual human rights into consideration when making decisions. This has considerable implications for the health and social care sector. For example, under Article 2 – The right to life – the State must safeguard life, as well as refraining from taking life. This means that, in theory, patients could challenge their local health authorities if certain drugs were unavailable in their area, but were available elsewhere. (**Postcode rationing**).

3. Some Acts of Parliament give the power to make detailed laws to a government minister. In such cases, known as secondary legislation, the law itself is often set out in regulations with orders. Much social security law is set out in such regulations rather than in Acts of Parliament. Where courts find that secondary legislation is incompatible with Convention rights, all courts have the power not to apply it.

Weaknesses of the HRA

1. The definition of public authorities remains unclear, and will be decided by the courts. For example, the status of a private day nursery remains unclear; even though it is subject to government regulation it provides a private service for which payment is made.

2. Many areas of the Act remain to be tested. For example, asylum seekers could challenge the restrictions introduced by the Home Secretary under the Immigration and Asylum Act 1999 , which leaves many asylum seekers without entitlement to help with accommodation costs.

3. If someone brings proceedings against a public authority for breach of their Convention rights, the authority may argue that it had no choice, because it was required to take action under an existing Act of Parliament. In such cases, the individual bringing the case can only hope for a declaration of incompatibility (this means that an existing Act of Parliament may breach the Convention rights – see page 25). Although the higher courts (the High Court, the Court of Appeal and the House of Lords) have the power to make such a declaration, which is meant to encourage Parliament to amend the law, the courts cannot force the government to amend the law if they do not want to.

The Home Office Human Rights Unit provides a range of guidance, explaining the Act for the public, for public authorities, for civil servants and for the private and voluntary sectors. These can be accessed through www.crimereduction.gov.uk

The Mental Health Act 1983

The Mental Health Act (MHA) is a complicated piece of legislation, because it deals with both the care and control of people suffering from mental illness. The circumstances under which an individual's rights can be overridden are detailed within the Act, which is wide-ranging. It also covers people who commit criminal acts as a result of their mental state.

The Act has 10 main sections:

* Part 1: Application
* Part 2: Compulsory admission to hospital and guardianship
* Part 3: Patients concerned in criminal proceedings while under sentence
* Part 4: Consent to treatment
* Part 5: Mental Health Review Tribunals
* Part 6: Removal and return of patients within the United Kingdom
* Part 7: Management of property and affairs of patients
* Part 8: Functions of local authorities and the Secretary of State
* Part 9: Offences
* Part 10: Miscellaneous provisions

The Act defines different types and degree of mental disorder, which are covered under the regulations. Definitions are as set out in Figure 1.12.

MENTAL HEALTH ACT 1983	
Mental disorder	Mental illness, arrested or incomplete development of mind, psychopathic disorder and any other disorder or disability of mind.
Mental impairment	A state of arrested or incomplete development of mind which includes significant impairment of intelligence and social functioning and is associated with abnormally aggressive or seriously irresponsible conduct on the part of the person concerned
Psychopathic disorder	A persistent disorder or disability of mind (whether or not including significant impairment of intelligence) which results in abnormally aggressive or seriously irresponsible conduct on the part of the person concerned

FIGURE 1.12 *Some definitions of types and degree of mental disorder*

1. Patients may be admitted to hospital against their will – '**sectioned**' – for assessment and/or treatment if they are suffering from a mental disorder that is considered to require medical treatment, because they may pose a danger to themselves or others. The request must be made on the written recommendations of two medical practitioners and a person can be detained for up to 28 days, unless a further order is made, or the individual has consented to remain in hospital. This is known as 'civil admission'.

2. In an emergency situation, where the individual poses as immediate threat to himself or others, an emergency application can be made either by an approved social worker, the police, or the nearest relative. In such situations, a person can be detained for up to 72 hours, unless a further application has been made. This is known as removing the person to a place of safety, which is usually a police station or a hospital.

3. Patients may be granted leave of absence, if authorised by a medical practitioner; this may be accompanied by a member of staff or unaccompanied.

4. In some circumstances, an application for guardianship may be made by the local authority social services department, or a person who is accepted by the local authority social services as a guardian if it is considered to be in the best interests of patient. The guardianship would be effective for the duration of patient's stay in hospital, but can only be made on behalf of patients over 16 years of age, and on the recommendation of two medical practitioners, as before. The person acting as guardian has to agree in writing to act as guardian.

5. If a person has committed an offence, and is either awaiting trial or has been convicted but not yet sentenced, the court can apply for admission to hospital for an assessment of the accused's mental condition (admission via the courts).

6. In certain circumstances, where individuals have committed a serious offence, they may be subjected to a '**restriction order**' by the courts. In such situations, the person will be detained in a secure unit instead of being sent to prison. The Crime (Sentences) Act 1997 provides the court with powers to specify the level of security in which the patient should be detained. The secure unit may be a locked psychiatric ward in a hospital, or a type of special 'medium secure' unit, or a special hospital, such as Rampton, Broadmoor or Ashworth. In such circumstances, only the Secretary of State can permit leave of absence, the transfer of patients, or the discharge of patients.

7. Patients can be treated without their consent if the responsible medical practitioner (usually a consultant psychiatrist) thinks it is appropriate. Exceptions to this include surgical treatment, and invasive procedures such as electro-convulsive therapy (this is not commonly used now).

8. A patient detained under the Mental Health Act, whether detained under civil proceedings or criminal proceedings, can apply to the Mental Health Tribunal to have the situation assessed. Tribunal provides an independent hearing and consists of a legal representative, a medical representative and one lay member. Patients are usually represented by a solicitor, although patients may choose to represent themselves. The Tribunal will decide whether the patient's condition continues to meet the legal and medical criteria for detention under the Mental Health Act, and may order the patient to be discharged.

9. The Mental Health Act requires steps to be taken to ensure that patients understand their rights as soon as possible after their detention has begun. The information must be given both orally and in writing, and includes the section under which the patient is detained, the effect of this section, and the patient's right to apply to the Mental Health Review Tribunal.

FIGURE 1.13 *The Mental Health Act requires that patients understand their rights*

Strengths of the Mental Health Act

1. The Act provides protection for people who might harm themselves or others, primarily through compulsory admission to hospital.

2. People detained under the Mental Health Act have the right to appeal to the Tribunal, which has the power to discharge them from detention in hospital.

3. Under the Act, individuals have the right to receive information, both orally and in writing, explaining why they have been detained and their right to appeal.

4. The Act makes provision for the aftercare and treatment of people who have been discharged into the community.

Weaknesses of the Mental Health Act

1. The Mental Health Act 1983 was put into place at a time when most patients with mental health problems were treated in psychiatric hospitals. Since then, there has been a concerted effort to treat people wherever possible within the community, in order to avoid 'institutionalisation'. People who have spent many years in institutions often lose the ability to live independent lives, because they have become dependent on others to take care of their needs. Therefore, this Act is now out of date, as it no longer meets the requirements of present-day modern mental health practice.

2. The Mental Health Act 1983 makes no provision for people suffering from 'severe personality disorder', who are considered to be untreatable, either with medication or through other methods. Sometimes such people pose a danger to others and this has raised concerns for public safety.

3. Compulsory detention in hospital poses issues for human rights, particularly in relation to consent to treatment. It can also delay recovery, due to its traumatic nature.

4. The Act does not address the stigma and discrimination suffered by people who have mental health problems. The Social Exclusion Unit has found that the biggest problem experienced by people suffering from mental health problems was stigma.

5. The Act makes no provision for people who are suffering from less severe mental illness, such as, for example, anxiety and depression. It has been suggested that patients need to be seriously ill before they are entitled to treatment and that this, in fact, diverts resources away from care in the community and towards hospital treatment.

6. It has been suggested that the Mental Health Act 1983 focuses more on control and containment of people with mental illness, rather than treatment, and therefore increases the perception of mentally ill people as dangerous, adding to their stigmatisation.

7. The current legislation does not adequately cover the needs of those suffering from 'dual diagnosis', such as those with substance abuse and mental illness.

Proposed reforms of the Mental Health Act

In response to the perceived weaknesses of the Mental Health Act 1983, the government has proposed to reform the legislation, and first put forward the Mental Health Bill in June 2002. This Bill was extremely controversial, particularly in its proposal to extend compulsory treatment of those being cared for in the community. This was overwhelmingly opposed by a wide range of people, including professionals, mental health campaigners, charities, service users and carers, who felt that this was both unnecessary and would reinforce the misconception that all people with mental health problems are dangerous.

The Bill was revised and a second draft is currently being consulted on; however, serious concerns remain. Campaigners argue that the new Bill over-emphasises the protection of the public at the expense of service users, that this will further stigmatise mental illness and continue to divert resources into compulsory care at the expense of those who voluntarily seek help. They argue that compulsion should be used as a last resort, and wherever possible people should be treated on a voluntary basis, fully consenting to their treatment. Campaigners maintain that the principles governing the care of people with mental illness should be the same as those for physical care, and argue for people to have a right to assessment and treatment if they feel that they are suffering from a mental disorder. There are concerns that removing the 'treatability' definitions of the existing 1983 Act in order to bring people with severe personality disorder under the legislation (in order to detain them in secure accommodation) means that people who are sexually deviant, or substance abusers would also be liable to compulsory detention, particularly since the definition of 'mental disorder' will be revised to cover 'a disturbance in the functioning of the mind or brain resulting from any disability or disorder of the mind or brain'. Examples of a mental disorder include **schizophrenia**, depression or a learning disability. The Bill is currently being examined by the Joint Scrutiny Committee, which has heard evidence from campaigners. It is likely that further changes will be made to this legislation before it finally becomes law.

The Human Rights Act can protect an individual's rights; for example, judgment has already been given in a case brought before the European Court of Human Rights, concerning a man with **autism** and learning disabilities, who was admitted to hospital treatment for his mental disorder. The man was not formally detained under the Mental Health Act 1983, because although he lacked the capacity to consent to treatment, he did not resist it. The court found that this person had been unlawfully deprived of his liberty under Article 5 of the Convention. The court however, made it clear that an individual's particular circumstances will need to be considered in any future judgments.

Consider this

Ryan is a 21-year-old man, who suffers from schizophrenia. He lives with his mother on a local housing estate and is currently unemployed.

Following a short spell in hospital, Ryan was discharged into his mother's care, and on medication. However, the medication made Ryan feel extremely ill, so he stopped taking it. Recently he has started to hear voices again, but is managing to cope with the help of a local support group for people with mental health problems. Ryan feels that he will eventually get better, and wants to get a job. However, his mother is very worried that he will relapse, and his behaviour will become more erratic and unpredictable.

Using concepts, can you identify?
1. Under which aspect of the Mental Health Act 1983, would Ryan have been admitted to hospital?

2. Can Ryan be forced to take his medication?

Go further – can you analyse using theory?
3. Examples of the type of circumstances under which Ryan's rights might be overridden?

Go further – can you evaluate using a range of theory?
4. How Ryan might be affected under the new proposals in the Mental Health Bill 2002?

The Mental Health Act Commission

The implementation of the Mental Health Act 1983 is overseen by the Mental Health Act Commission, which was established in 1983 and consists of some 100 members (Commissioners), including laypersons, lawyers, doctors, nurses, social workers, psychologists and other specialists. Its main functions are shown in Figure 1.14.

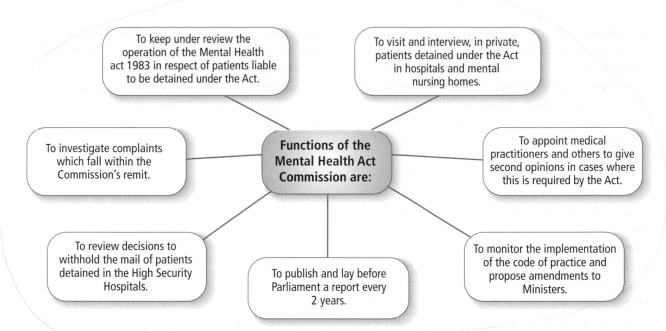

FIGURE 1.14 *Main functions of the Mental Health Act Commission*

In addition, the Commission advises government ministers on policy matters which can within its remit. More information can be found at: www.mhac.org.uk

The Children Act 1989

The Children Act 1989 is the primary legislation relating to the welfare of children. There are a number of very important principles contained in this legislation.

Key principles:

1. The welfare of the child is the paramount consideration when decisions are made by the courts or others in relation to the upbringing of the child. In practice, this means that the parent's wishes can be overridden if these are considered not been the best interests of the child. This is sometimes known as the **'paramountcy principle'**. Although the concept of welfare is not defined in the Children Act, there are a number of factors which are taken into consideration when the courts are making decisions (sometimes known as the 'welfare checklist').

2. Wherever possible, children should be brought up and cared for within their own families.

> **The welfare checklist**
> This includes that:
> * the wishes or feelings of the child shall be ascertained in the light of his or her age and understanding
> * the physical, emotional and education needs of the child shall be considered
> * the likely effect of any change in the child's circumstances should be determined
> * the age, sex, background in any other characteristics the court considers to be relevant, should be considered
> * consideration should be given to any harm which the child has suffered, or is at risk of suffering
> * the capability of the child's parents in meeting the child's needs should be taken into consideration
> * the available powers of the court to take action should be determined.

3. Children in need and their parents should be supported in the upbringing of their child, by the local authority social services department. Local authorities have a duty to:

* safeguard and promote the welfare of children in need

* so far as is consistent with that duty, promote the upbringing of such children by their families.

Children are defined as being in need if they are:

* unlikely to achieve, or maintain, or have the opportunity of maintaining a reasonable standard of health for development without the provision of local authority services. Health includes physical or mental health; development includes physical, social, emotional, intellectual or behavioural development

* their health for development is likely to be significantly impaired, or further impaired without the provision of such services

* the child is disabled. Disabled includes the blind, deaf, dumb or suffering from mental disorder, or handicapped by illness, injury or congenital deformity or other disability as may be prescribed.

The help and assistance provided by the local authority should:

* be provided in partnership with the parents

* meet each child's identified needs

* be appropriate to the child's race, culture, religion and language

* allow for independent representations and complaints procedures

* be provided in effective partnerships with other agencies, including health, welfare and voluntary agencies.

4. Children should be kept safe to be protected by effective interventions, if they are in danger.

5. Courts should ensure that delays are avoided, and should only make on order if to do so is better than making no order at all.

6. Children should be kept informed about what happens to them, and should participate in decision-making, where it concerns their future.

7. Parents will continue to have parental responsibility for their children, even when they do not live with them. They should be kept informed about their children and participate in decisions made about the future.

Where children are involved in separation or divorce proceedings, parents are encouraged to agree about the child's welfare and the continuation of parental responsibility. It is important to recognise that Article 8 of the Convention – The right to respect for private and family life – may affect the decision-making process, in that the court must be aware of the parents' right to family life. However, the welfare principle continues to dominate the view of the courts and has not yet been challenged under the Human Rights Act.

Parental responsibility

Parental responsibility is defined within the Children Act as 'all the rights, duties, powers, responsibilities and authority, which, by law, the parent of the child has in relation to that child and his property'. It is important to recognise that mothers always have parental responsibility for their child. Where the parents are married, the father automatically has parental responsibility; where parents are unmarried, but the father's name is on the birth certificate, he also has parental responsibility. However, if the parents are unmarried and the father is not named on the birth certificate, he does not automatically have parental responsibility and can only acquire it: through marriage to the mother; by entering into an agreement with the mother; by obtaining a residence order (which states where the child shall live); or by order of the court. Other people who cannot obtain parental responsibility for a child include anyone granted a residence order, such as grandparents, or where a guardian is appointed by the court. When a child is taken into care, the local authority shares parental responsibility with the parents, unless the child has entered care voluntarily, in which case the parental responsibility remains with the parents.

As children get older, and gain maturity, they can make decisions about their own future. This is commonly known as the 'Gillick competence', following the decision by the House of Lords that a child under 16 years old, would consent to medical treatment, if he or she could understand what was involved in such treatment and was capable of expressing his or her views and wishes. In this case, the health authority was taken to court by the mother of a child for providing contraceptive services without the mother's consent.

Although there is no set age at which children are considered mature enough, the older the child, the more their views are considered. For example, according to the Gillick principles, a child is entitled to choose his or her own religion, and where there is a dispute between the child and parents, the child's welfare will prevail against resolving the conflict (paramountcy principle); it is unlikely that the child's wishes would be agreed, for example if they wished to become members of a religious cult that demanded isolation from the parents or the world in general.

Parents have the right to administer reasonable physical punishment. Although this was considered to be incompatible with the Convention rights, the government carried out a consultation exercise, following which guidelines were issued to assist the courts in defining the concept of reasonable chastisement. Corporal punishment is prohibited in all the circumstances, including in education, in care or in foster homes.

Child protection

Local authorities have a statutory duty to investigate, where a child is suspected of suffering from significant harm, in order to decide what action should be taken to safeguard the child's welfare. This usually means inter-agency enquiries regarding the child's education, health, general welfare and any particular issues which may have caused a child come to the attention of the local authority. Sometimes, the child protection conference is convened to ascertain any needs that the child may have requiring local authority action. A decision will be made following the conference about whether the child should be put on the child protection register as a precautionary measure. Children on the child protection register usually live with their parents, who are supported by social services in the upbringing of their children. In some cases, however, the local authority may decide that the child is at risk of significant harm and should be removed from the parents. It is at this point that care proceedings are initiated through the courts. Children are usually represented by the children's guardian (guardian *ad litem*), who is an approved social worker and will represent the child in care proceedings.

Emergency protection orders

In crisis situations, where the child needs immediate protection, social services can acquire parental responsibility by applying to the courts. This can be done without notice to the parents, although the parents to have a right to apply to the court for the order to be discharged. Children can also be removed into police protection for a period of up to 72 hours, if the police have reasonable cause to believe that they would otherwise suffer a significant harm. The police are required to ascertain the child's own views and inform parents at the earliest opportunity, as well as notifying the local authority to ensure that the child is taken into care.

Care orders

Following an emergency protection order, the local authority, usually applies for a care order, allowing them to share parental responsibility. Under such orders, the child is usually removed from home and placed with foster carers or with other members of the family. Care orders can only be made where the court is satisfied that the child is suffering, or is like to suffer significant harm as a result of the way the parents are caring for the child, or because the child is beyond parental control and poses a risk to him or herself and others. The introduction of the Human Rights Act (in 1998) means that the courts are now required to ensure that decisions about care orders must also consider the rights of parents, under Article 6 of the Convention – the right to a fair hearing. Parents are entitled to be consulted at all stages of the decision-making process and should be entitled to legal representation. The local authority is required to produce a care plan, giving details of the action it intends to take in relation to the child's future, such as where the child will be placed, what long-term proposals should be made, and details about contact with the family. Children who are received into care are known as 'looked after children'. It is important to understand that a care order automatically comes to an end when the child reaches 18 years of age; however, the local authority has an obligation to advise and assist the child and carry out an assessment of the child's needs. They must also prepare our 'pathway plan' for the child and appoint an adviser to help the child moving to independent living. Local authorities must take reasonable steps to keep in touch with the child until he or she is aged 21.

Education supervision orders

If a child of compulsory school-age is not being properly educated, because of poor school attendance, for example, he or she can be placed under supervision of the local education authority. The aim of this is to encourage parents to fulfil their responsibilities towards the child and, therefore, it is important that there is cooperation between representatives of the local education authority, school and the parents.

Strengths of the Children Act 1989

1. The Act clearly acknowledges the rights of children and protects their welfare, it was based on the United Nations Convention on the Rights of the Child, which was formalised by international agreement in order to protect the rights of children.

2. It enables children to have their views heard in matters that affect them, and provides equal treatment to all children.

3. The Act is very clear that children have rights and parents have responsibilities; it is clear about the role of parents in caring for the well-being of their children.

4. The Act provides details of circumstances under which children can be taken into local authority care, including the role of the courts, the police and other professionals concerned with the well-being of children, and that intervention should only take place as a last resort, or to provide support for parents in their parenting role.

Weaknesses of the Children Act 1989

1. Young offenders are not offered the same protection as other children under the Children Act 1989; children can be remanded to secure accommodation and are not protected by Article 5 – the right to liberty – because children can be detained for educational supervision, which has a very broad interpretation and includes education offered in such accommodation. Children can be charged with a criminal offence at the age of 10, below this they are considered incapable of committing such criminal offences; however, this is much lower than most other countries and has been criticised by the United Nations Committee.

2. Court proceedings under the Act are not open to the public in order to protect the identity of any children involved. However, there have been complaints that this prevents accountability and the basis on which decisions are made are not always clear.

> **Consider this**

Charlotte is 12 years old and is a pupil at the local comprehensive school. She is a bright and able pupil. Three years ago her mother, Sally, was diagnosed with multiple sclerosis and now uses a wheelchair. Charlotte's father left the family home 18 months ago and has moved to a different part of the country to take up a new job; he has had little contact with Charlotte and her mother since then. Charlotte has to help her mother get up and dressed in the morning and assist her downstairs; she also goes home at lunchtime to make sure her mother has lunch and helps her upstairs to the toilet. Both Charlotte and her mother are reluctant to ask Social Services for help because they fear that they will be separated; however Charlotte has been returning late from lunch and missing school. She is falling behind with her schoolwork and the school is concerned that their letters have not been answered. They have contacted the Educational Welfare Services.

Can you identify?

1. Which aspects of the Children Act might apply to Charlotte?

Go further – can you analyse, using theories of rights and responsibilities?

2. What rights Charlotte and her mother have under the law?

Go further – can you evaluate?

3. What needs Charlotte and her mother have and what actions could be taken to support them?

Children Act 2004

This Act has come into being, as a response to the Victoria Climbie Inquiry Report (2003) and the green paper *Every Child Matters* (2003), which proposed changes to policy and legislation in England, in order to maximise opportunities and minimise risks for all children and young people by focusing the services more effectively upon the needs of the children, young people and their families. One of the findings of the Victoria Climbie Inquiry was the failure of social services and other organisations involved in the care of this young child to work together effectively to protect her; in particular, information was not shared across services. The new arrangements under the Act will require much closer working between health, social services, education and child care organisations, including integrated planning, commissioning, joint funding and delivery of services for children and families.

Key points

* Children's Commissioner has been appointed to represent the views of children, in particular:

  * to seek views and identify the needs of children and young people

  * to look into any matter which relates to the interests and well-being of children and young people

  * to initiate inquiries on behalf of children and young people.

* In order to provide clear accountability for children's services, the Act will require local authorities in England to put in place a Director of Children's Services and a Lead Member for Children's Services in the governance arrangements.

* An information database is to be set up so that practitioners can more easily share information about children who are causing concern.

* The establishment of Local Safeguarding Children Boards to coordinate child protection procedures more effectively. These will replace the existing arrangements.

* Local authorities will be required to produce plans for children and young people.

* Children's services will be inspected and a new framework for integrated inspections will be put in place. Social services department will have their performance rated.

Part 1 of the Act, establishing a Commissioner, extends to the whole of the United Kingdom; Part 2, concerning the arrangements for the delivery of children's services and Local Safeguarding Children Boards, relates only to England. Part 3 concerns Wales, and Part 4 devolves functions to

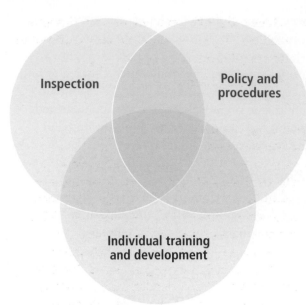

Inspection

Policy and procedures

Individual training and development

FIGURE 1.15 *The overlapping world of the individual and the legal and formal requirements in care environments*

Wales (The Welsh Assembly) that were previously carried out jointly across England and Wales. Other parts of the Act concern the application in Wales.

New legislation

With respect to laws that protect people from discrimination you should also be aware that new regulations now provide a legal right not to be discriminated against on the basis of sexual orientation and religious belief. These are the:

* Employment Equality (Sexual Orientation) Regulations 2003

* Employment Equality Regulations (Religion or Belief) Regulations 2003.

Northern Ireland

In Northern Ireland, health and social services operate jointly and services are managed through the Department of Health, Social Services and Public Safety. In order to meet the particular requirements of the population of Northern Ireland, some equality legislation has been amended; the implementation is monitored through the Equality Commission for Northern Ireland.

Equality (Disability, etc) (Northern Ireland) Order 2000 (EDO)

The Order extended the duties and powers of the Equality Commission Northern Ireland to include the requirement to:

* work towards the elimination of discrimination against disabled people

* promote the equalisation of opportunities for disabled people

* take steps to encourage good practice in the treatment of disabled people

* keep the Disability Discrimination Act 1995, and Part 2 of the EDO under review

* assist disabled people by offering information, advice and support in taking cases of discrimination forward

* provide information and advice to employers and service providers

* undertake formal investigations

* prepare statutory codes of practice, providing practical guidance on how to comply with the law

* arrange independent conciliation between service providers and disabled people in the area of access to goods, facilities and services.

Think it over...

Compare the powers and duties of the Equality Commission Northern Ireland with those of the Disability Rights Commission and identify any additional features.

Race Relations (Northern Ireland) Order 1997 (RRO)

Whilst this Order closely follows that of the Race Relations Act in the UK, it specifically outlawed discrimination against the Irish Traveller Community, which is identified as a racial group, against which racial discrimination is unlawful.

The Northern Ireland Act 1998

This Act places a statutory obligation and public authorities in Northern Ireland to carry out their functions relating to Northern Ireland with regard to the promotion of the equality of opportunity:

* between persons of different religious beliefs, political opinion, racial group, age, marital status or sexual orientation

* between men and women generally

* between people with the disability and people without

* between people with dependants and people without.

Public authorities must also promote good relations between persons of different religious belief, political opinion or racial group. This relates to the specific differences between the major communities within Northern Ireland.

The Employment Equality (Sexual Orientation) Regulations (NI) 2003

These regulations pre-empted the amendments to the Sex Discrimination Act 1975 in the UK by outlawing discrimination on grounds of sexual orientation in the areas of employment; vocational training, further and higher education.

The only explicitly stated exception in the regulations concerns employment for the purposes of organised religion. If the religious body or organisation does not wish to recruit people of the particular sexual orientation, they need to establish that this is in order to comply with that religious doctrine, or that the nature of the work and context in which it is carried out will cause conflict with significant number of followers with strongly held religious convictions.

Sex Discrimination (Northern Ireland) Order

The main differences here (the exceptions) concern:

* special treatment for women in connection with pregnancy and childbirth

* ministers of religion

* where the provision of goods, facilities and services may cause embarrassment/affront to decency/or physical contact.

In these areas, discriminatory treatment is allowed.

> **Key concept**
>
> *equality legislation* protects the right of all UK citizens to equal treatment. However, there is particular legislation to protect vulnerable people who cannot independently exercise their rights and these are of particular importance to workers in health, social care and childcare settings, as well as the organisations that provide such services. The law underpins philosophical ideas about equality that are a fundamental feature of the care services and which are reflected in the care values and principles.

Summary

As members of society we all have rights as well as responsibilities towards each other; this is a defining aspect of a civilised society. The purpose of the law is to uphold these rights and to allow individuals whose rights have been violated to seek redress.

While it is not possible for the law to prevent people from holding discriminatory views or expressing these, legislation can prevent individuals from acting upon these views and doing harm to others, either physically or emotionally. In the longer term, legislation can also help to promote a fairer society in which discriminatory attitudes and prejudices become socially unacceptable.

The main purpose of equality legislation is to promote equal treatment and to protect vulnerable people from those who would do them harm or take advantage of their inability to protect themselves. Care workers need to be aware of these laws in order to uphold them and to help to protect those they care for.

Section 3: Facilitation of access to services

Health, social care and child care service providers are required to ensure fair access to their services for all people. However, there are differences in the way the services are organised and delivered. It is important to recognise that not all services have 'open access'; individuals often have to be referred for consultation and treatment. There are three main types of referral as shown in Figure 1.16.

Physical barriers

It is extremely important that all buildings providing health, social care or childcare services are accessible to people with disabilities, including mobility problems and sensory difficulties, such a sight and hearing problems. Under the Disability Discrimination Act, all public services should be accessible. However, the level of accessibility tends to vary according to the focus of the services and the user groups for whom they are provided, as well as the limitations posed by financial constraints. For example, voluntary organisations that provide services may have relatively small budgets, which are only provided on a year-on-year basis, making long-term planning for capital projects such as altering premises very difficult. In contrast, statutory services (those which government funds) tend to have larger budgets and greater financial stability. Some examples of difficulties faced by particular types of provider are discussed below.

Hospitals

The historic development of hospital services means that many of them are housed in older buildings, which were often designed and built for a very different purpose, for example, those hospitals that were previously workhouses. Another problem faced by hospitals is that the range of services they now provide is much greater, and most hospitals have exceeded the capacity of their original buildings. This means that hospitals often do not have a consistent design or layout, with newer buildings being added over the years. In addition, modern medical technology requires much more equipment for both diagnosis and treatment; examples include Magnetic Resonance Imaging (MRI) scanners and mammography equipment, which require a lot of space. Most hospitals have made great efforts to make their buildings and

ACCESS TO SERVICES BY REFERRAL	
Self-referral	This is where individuals suspect that they have a health problem, or recognise that they need help with social problems. Individuals with health problems, access services through their GP, and anyone can make an appointment with the GP. It is also possible to self-refer to social services, by speaking to someone on the telephone, usually the duty social worker.
Professional referral	This is where individuals already have contact with health professionals, such as health visitors or midwives. If the professional suspects that there is an underlying health problem, the individual can be referred directly to the GP, social workers or the psychiatric services, for example. GPs also refer to specialists such as hospital consultants for treatments, following initial diagnosis.
Third-party referral	This is where a non-professional person such as a relative, friend or neighbour contacts the services on someone else's behalf. This may be because the person is unable to access the services for him or herself, for example in the case of an elderly housebound relative. In other cases, it may be because there are suspicions of child abuse or domestic violence. Sometimes the police will refer an individual to help for social services, following an incident, for example where there are suspected mental health problems. In such situations, the Mental Health

FIGURE 1.16 *Main types of referral*

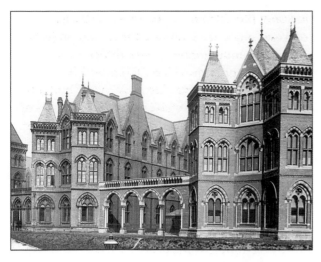

FIGURE 1.17 *A Victorian workhouse/hospital*

services physically accessible to people with mobility problems. However, people with sensory difficulties may be less well-served. Blind people may have particular difficulties negotiating the physical environment in hospital, particularly where there has been additional building work and new buildings have been added. Where hospitals are brand-new, most of the accessibility problems have been overcome at the design stage, and although there is a programme of the new building underway in the NHS, it will be some time before all hospital buildings are fully accessible and usable by disabled people.

Health centres and GP surgeries

These buildings house primary care services and are used as the first port of call for anybody who wishes to access health care. If these buildings are physically inaccessible, access to basic forms of healthcare such as diagnosis becomes difficult and sometimes impossible. Many health centres are now housed in purpose-built buildings, which have been designed in order to ensure they are accessible to people with disabilities. However, some small outlying clinics are still housed in unsuitable premises. Although health centres often incorporate GP surgeries, some GPs still run what is known as the 'single-handed practice'. GPs offer their services to the NHS under contract, and are therefore not employees of the NHS in the same way that other professionals are. This means that when GPs manage their own surgery as a single-handed practice in the same way that people may run their own business, they will need their own premises. The Family Health Services Authority, which manages the GP contracts on behalf of the NHS has been helping such GPs to upgrade their premises in order to meet the requirements of the Disability Discrimination Act, as well as helping them move into purpose built premises, which may house other facilities.

Voluntary organisations

Many voluntary organisations are registered charities, which have very different governance and management arrangements than statutory services. Much of their income may be derived from charitable donations, for example, and there are often rules about how such money may be spent. Perhaps only a certain percentage of the income is allowed for administration, because as much as possible of the money raised is intended to go to the specific cause for which the charity provides. There are likely to be limited funds for capital building work. Voluntary and charitable organisations may be housed in older buildings or listed buildings which are difficult to make accessible.

Think it over...

Take a trip to your local health centre or hospital, starting from your home.

1. Imagine being a wheelchair user, what difficulties might you face in getting to the health centre or hospital?

2. When you get there, make a note of the facilities to enable access for people with disabilities; for example, can wheelchair users access the main entrance?

3. What facilities are there for people with hearing or sight difficulties?

4. Are their facilities for people with young children, for example, a play area or somewhere to leave a pram safely?

5. What sort of seating arrangements are there?

6. Compare your findings with others in your group. Discuss what improvements might be made to enable easier access. You might wish to rate your findings on a scale of 1 to 10, with one being fully accessible.

Psychological barriers

The extent to which people are likely to face psychological difficulties in accessing health services, depends on their attitude towards their own health and illness. For example, the Department of Health carried out research into men's health as part of a campaign to reduce the suicide rate in young men (Inequalities in Health, 1998; www.doh.gov.uk/ih) and found that:

* men are less likely to see a doctor and therefore the extent of their health problems, particularly mental health difficulties, is hidden
* doctors are less likely to diagnose men with mental health problems than a woman.

The Men's Health Forum, a registered charity (founded in 2001), found that young men were reluctant to use any kind of service and displayed stereotypical male attitudes towards help seeking. Services showed little understanding of young men or have to work with them effectively. The chair of the Men's Health Forum, Iain Banks, stated that:

'If you compare the major killers, such as heart disease and lung cancer, men easily come out best, from the undertaker's point of view'.

This illustrates that for many men illness is seen as weakness and incompatible with what it means to be male in our society, where maleness is associated with strength. These attitudes are formed as a result of gender socialisation.

People understand their health in different ways. For example, some individuals seek their body is a machine, which is liable to break down; this view is particularly common amongst men, and has resulted in various initiatives aimed at helping men take more responsibility for their health by providing information to dispel fear and myths about health and illness. One example is a men's health book, which has been put together in a similar format to a car manual, using humour and factual information to inform men about how their body works, the warning signs and symptoms of illness, and when to see a doctor. Women often have much more contact with health services as a result of pregnancy and childbirth. However, stereotypical attitudes amongst some male doctors can sometimes prevent women from accessing services. For example, women may feel that their concerns are minimised by a patronising attitude, which also undermines their self-esteem and prevents them from asking questions.

SCENARIO

Brenda is a 52-year-old woman who has recently attended for a routine mammography examination (breast screening). When the result arrives, the letter informs her that no cancer has been detected; however, the test shows some minor abnormalities.

Brenda is concerned, and wishes to find out more about the condition, such as the effects that the menopause may have on it. She makes an appointment to see her GP.

Brenda's young GP is very brisk during the consultation. He asks her to undress and examines her saying, 'You don't need a chaperone for this, do you? You look like a woman who can take care of herself and it will only take a minute'.

When the examination is finished, and as Brenda is getting dressed, the doctor tells her that her condition is not clinically significant. Brenda tries to express her concerns and explains that she has been experiencing a prickly sensation in her breast, which is extremely uncomfortable. The doctor repeats that her condition is not clinically significant, and shows her to the door.

1. **How do you think Brenda might feel, following this consultation?**
2. **Do you think this will influence any future decisions to consult the doctor with breast problems?**

Some individuals feel that their health is a matter of willpower and determination, dependent on choosing a healthy lifestyle. For these people, ill-health is also seen as weakness, primarily a lack of willpower. Such people may feel guilty if they become ill, or experience denial, attributing symptoms of ill-health to other things such as tiredness or stress. Attitudes to health and illness behaviour are shaped through socialisation, and many people lack knowledge and understanding of how their bodies work. Other people may feel that they have no control over whether they become ill or not; illness is seen as a matter of fate and they are not worried about long-term risks to health, often because of more pressing and immediate problems, such as financial hardship. For such people, the link between lifestyle choices and ill-health is denied or minimised because it may not be borne out by their own life experience, and they are resistant to health promotion and health education campaigns.

Some illnesses have a degree of stigma attached to them, particularly cancer, which is seen as life-threatening, and mental ill-health. Fear of confirming such illnesses, and the implications for individuals and their families may prevent people from accessing services, feeling they may be unable to cope with such serious illnesses. People with mental health difficulties may not recognise that they have a problem until there is a crisis.

Financial barriers

Although health and social services are free at the point of use, there are sometimes charges attached to certain types of treatment. For example, people need to pay for dental treatment, even though it is subsidised by the NHS. Many dentists only take private fee-paying patients, and access to NHS dentists varies considerably across the country. Access to dental treatment may be particularly difficult for elderly people with mobility problems, who find it difficult to visit the dentist's surgery. When older people have problems with their teeth, it affects their ability to eat, which can lead to long-term health problems as a result of chronic malnutrition.

In other cases, particularly in rural areas, the cost of travelling may be very high. Similarly, for people on low incomes, who are not eligible for free prescriptions, the cost of treatment may be considered to be too high. This may deter them from going to seek treatment in the first place, or prevent them from taking medication, and is a particular risk for people with complex conditions that require several different types of medication, or people with chronic conditions. Some conditions are exempt from prescription charges, and there is financial assistance for some people with chronic, and long-term conditions such as diabetes.

Childcare services, such as day nurseries or childminders, and residential care services for older people are usually run by private organisations, which charge for their services. For many people, these services are too expensive and beyond their means; however, the government does provide some assistance in the form of tax credits, particularly for working families requiring childcare.

It is important that individuals have access to information about the type of financial help that is available for health, social and childcare services. Leaflets are available through the Post Office, additional help is available through the Department of Health website and Citizens Advice Bureau or welfare rights organisations can also provide information. In terms of childcare services, the government proposes to set up Children's Centres in all areas which will provide information and access to local children's services.

Geographical barriers

Services are not distributed evenly throughout the country, and this is particularly true of health services and childcare services. Although most areas have some provision, the number of GPs, for example, varies enormously across regions. There are more than twice as many GPs in Oxford than there are in Salford, for although GPs provide NHS services, they are not employed directly by the NHS and, therefore, are free to choose where they practice. Similarly, children's services are provided by private organisations and individuals and are therefore likely to be located in more affluent areas, where both parents work.

People living in rural areas often have trouble accessing services because of the geographical location; this is particularly the case, where they need to rely on public transport. Public transport tends to be more easily available, with more frequent services in areas with high-density populations. For example, it may not be considered cost-effective for companies to provide bus services, where there is likely to only be one or two passengers during the day. For low income families, the cost of public transport may be a barrier, whilst elderly people or those with mobility problems, who may not be able to use public transport, may need to make different travel arrangements, perhaps making use of taxi services. This will also add to the cost of travel.

Working people often have difficulty in accessing GP services, for example, because appointments are usually only made available during working hours. This means that people need to take time off work to visit their GP and may need to take annual leave, or may not be paid for time off work to attend appointments. It can also be difficult for women with small children to attend for appointments, as childcare arrangements may need to be made.

Where appointments are made centrally, as in the case of screening services, or outpatient appointments, people may be sent pre-arranged appointments, which may not be convenient.

Geographical aspects need to be taken into consideration when plans for services are made, and service providers should be aware of local bus services and other facilities such as 'Dial and Ride' or other voluntary services for people with mobility problems when planning new facilities. For those who can travel to hospital by car, parking is often difficult and limited. Many hospitals now charge for parking to prevent the public parking on hospital car parks when they are not using the services, so this can also add to the expense of accessing health care. It can be a particular problem if there are delays within the system and people are waiting to be seen for longer than planned.

Cultural and language barriers

Accessing services for people whose first language is not English can be a particular problem. In areas with high ethnic minority populations, information needs to be provided in more than one language. However, where several languages are spoken, it can be difficult for service providers to target the appropriate language. A good example of accessible information would be an invitation for breast screening, which contains information in English, together with the location and map, public transport information, and on the reverse the same information in eight different languages, as well as what to do if the individual is unable to keep the appointment. On health and social service premises, signs and directions are often only provided in English and receptionists and others who are sources of help and assistance may only be able to speak English. Many organisations now provide translation services; however, these often need to be arranged in advance, which can cause a problem for drop-in services and emergency provision. Some service providers allow family members who speak English to translate. It may be inappropriate in many cases, however, for an adult to be accompanied by children, particularly if sensitive or embarrassing issues need to be discussed. It can also be distressing for children and young people if they think that their parent is ill. Medical terms are often difficult to translate, causing problems with understanding, and this is why it is important to have specially trained translators available for people whose first language is not English.

Individuals from some cultures that have particularly strict gender roles may feel very uncomfortable in being seen or treated by health professionals of the opposite sex. It is therefore important that both male and female professionals are available to provide the required service. Other cultural issues include information about diet and nutrition. Unless a health professional is fully aware of the cultural and dietary requirements of a particular group, it may not be possible for the service user to make appropriate changes. Some services are particularly difficult for some cultures to access, such as family planning and sexual health services, because of religious beliefs relating to sex and sexuality. These issues can cause psychological as well as cultural barriers, and it is important for health and social care professionals to understand them and think about ways of providing culturally sensitive services.

Consider this

Narinder is a 36-year-old mother of two who speaks little English. She has recently discovered a lump in her breast; however, she has told no one. Narinder lives in a block of flats in an inner-city council estate with her husband and mother-in-law. Her husband is a bus driver and works irregular hours.

Using theory, can you identify?

1. What are the barriers to access facing Narinder?

Go further – can you analyse theories?

2. Why Narinder has not told anyone about her problems?

Go further – can you evaluate?

3. The ways in which an accessible, sensitive and culturally appropriate service could be provided for Narinder?

Ways of facilitating access

There are several ways in which service providers can facilitate access for all of their service users. These include:

* adapting premises
* raising awareness and changing attitudes
* promoting self-advocacy
* identifying additional funding
* joint planning and funding for integrated services and effective care.

Summary

The barriers to services are related both to an individual's ability and to their motivation to access services. In order to overcome these barriers, action needs to be taken by government to ensure fair distribution of services; by service providers to ensure they have appropriate facilities that everyone can use and by providing widely available information to tell about the services available in their local area, so raising awareness.

Section 4: Care values

'Service users rights are rooted in the history of social Care, healthcare and social work; in theories and philosophies underpinning the practices of the welfare state.'

(Tossell and Webb, 1994)

All health and social care workers have a 'duty of care'; this means that workers in the sector have clear responsibilities to the users of their services, and are personally and professionally accountable for the service they deliver. This responsibility and accountability includes both service users, their relatives and carers and is defined within professional guidelines and legal frameworks. Where it can be proven that such a duty of care was not exercised, professionals can be disciplined and may be legally liable for acts or omissions that cause harm to those in their care, whether these were caused by themselves or by someone under their supervision.

Recent occupational standards for National Vocational Qualifications (NVQs) in care emphasised the three principles of promoting equality and diversity, promoting individual rights and beliefs and maintaining confidentiality. Proposed 2005 standards do not define principles as such, but do include these broad values within training standards.

Promoting equality and diversity

In order to promote equality and diversity within health and care services, the following key principle must be followed by all workers:

∗ everyone must be treated fairly and impartially when receiving care services; this is their right.

Promoting individual rights and beliefs

Health and social care workers often work with vulnerable people, who may not be in a position to exercise their rights independently. The following principles are intended to protect the rights of vulnerable service users and should be followed by all workers in health and social care:

∗ all people have a right to be consulted and involved in decisions that affect them

∗ people have a right to express their views and beliefs, including the right to refuse care or treatment

∗ these rights are protected by law (see the section on equality legislation on page 15).

It is important to recognise, however, that health and social care workers also need to protect individuals, and in some cases this may mean restricting their rights and freedoms. The situations in which individual rights may be restricted include:

∗ *when individuals are at risk of harming themselves*, for example, people with mental health problems, people in a disturbed emotional state, and people considering suicide or self-harm, such as cutting or substance abuse

∗ *when the individual poses a risk to others*, for example, people demonstrating challenging behaviour, violent or disturbed individuals who are threatening other people

∗ *when the individual is at risk from others*, for example, children or vulnerable adults, who may be at risk of abuse, including emotional and psychological abuse or bullying, physical abuse, sexual abuse and neglect

∗ *when the individual is intending to break the law*, or has broken the law, for example, theft of property, fraud, substance abuse.

However, it is not always easy for care workers to achieve a balance between promoting individual rights and providing appropriate physical, emotional and social care for individuals.

Ellen is a resident in Church House care home for older people. She is a quiet person who spends a lot of time in her room. She occasionally speaks to one or two of the other residents but has no close friends. Recently Ellen has been refusing to have a bath. She will not let anyone help her and she will not do it herself. She has told the staff that she believes she will catch cold if she has a bath. Ellen's personal hygiene is now causing the other residents to avoid her and the staff find it unpleasant to carry out personal care with Ellen.

Using concepts within the care values can you identify?
1. Ellen's rights?
2. The rights of the other residents?
3. The rights of the staff?

Go further – can you analyse using theories of equality?
4. How the staff could manage this situation to ensure equal treatment.

Go further – can you evaluate using a range of theory?
5. What the likely outcomes for Ellen's health and well-being will be if this behaviour continues?

Maintaining confidentiality

Health and care workers are responsible for personal and private information about service users, including details of their personal lives, families, care and treatment. It is crucial that they keep this information private, and exercise tact and diplomacy when they are asked questions by others about the people in their care. This is called maintaining confidentiality, and it is crucial to developing trust between service users and the people who are caring for them. If the service users do not believe that the person asking the questions will keep the information confidential, they are not likely to be honest in their answers, and this could compromise their care and treatment. This is particularly important in sensitive situations, for example where domestic violence is suspected; however, it is important in all health and care situations. Confidentiality extends to all aspects of the service users' lives, including where they live. Maintaining confidentiality also demonstrates respect for service users, helping to promote trust, and helps them to feel valued and to maintain their self-esteem. It is important that clients are involved in discussions about confidentiality, and that those caring for them know what information they would prefer to be kept confidential. It is also important to let service users know in what situations practitioners are obliged to share information. For example, practitioners must be very careful not to promise to keep secrets and must make it clear to service users that they are acting on behalf of their organisation, and that any information given to them may need to be shared with others, in order to provide proper care for the individual. In such situations, it is important to reassure service users that only the information necessary for their care will be shared, and that any decisions will be discussed with them. Some service users may not want their families to know details of their medical condition, or their financial details.

Confidentiality is a basic human right, protected by law, through the Data Protection Act 1988, and the Freedom of Information Act 2000. Service users have a right to see records held about them, and it is important that practitioners write down clearly and concisely what they are told, and what they have observed without including their personal opinions or observations in the records. Health and care records are important documents that can be used in a court of law, for example, if service users have been unfairly treated or abused, whilst in the care of professionals, or the quality of care is being questioned.

Maintaining confidentiality does not mean that information about service users should never be shared. Services are often delivered by more than one professional and more than one organisation, and for effective continuous care, it is crucial that information is shared on a 'need to know' basis. This means that only information that is relevant to the care of the service user is passed on to others, usually other professionals. This is particularly important in relation to child

FIGURE 1.18 *Law, standards and policies influence practice*

protection, and the protection of vulnerable adults, who may not be in a position to speak for themselves. Please see Unit 2 for further discussion of confidentiality.

Principles and values for childcare workers

It is important to realise that the principles and values discussed above, relate to health and social care; the principles and values identified by the Early Years National Training Organisation for current NVQ qualifications are slightly different. These are set out below.

Principles:

The Underlying Principles of Early Years National Vocational Qualifications.
These principles draw on both the UN Convention on the Rights of the Child and the Children Act 1989, and also take into account the delivery of the School Curriculum and Assessment Authority (SCM) 'Desirable Outcomes for Children's Learning'. They are based on the premise that the earliest years of children's lives are a unique stage of human development, and that quality early years provision benefits the wider society and it is an investment for the future.

1. **The welfare of the child**
   The welfare of the child is paramount [the most important thing]. All early years workers must give precedence [attend to first] the rights and well-being of the children they work with. Children should be listened to, and their opinions and concerns treated seriously. Management of children's behaviour should emphasise positive expectations for that behaviour, and responses to unwanted behaviour should be suited to the child's stage of development. A child must never be slapped, smacked, shaken or humiliated.

2. **Keeping children safe**
   Work practice should help prevent accidents to children and adults, and should protect their health. Emergency procedures of the work setting, including record keeping, must be adhered to. Every early years worker has a responsibility to contribute to the protection of children from abuse, according to her/his work role.

3. **Working in partnership with parents/ families**
   Parents and families occupy a central position in their children's lives, and early years workers must never try to take over that role inappropriately. Parents and families should be listened to as expert on their own child. Information about children's development and progress should be shared openly with parents. Respect must be shown for families' traditions and child care practices, and every effort made to comply with parent's wishes for their children.

4. **Children's learning and development**
   Children learn more and faster in their earliest years than at any other times in life. Development and learning in these earliest years lay the foundations for their abilities, characteristics and skills in later life. Learning begins at birth. The care and education of children are interwoven.

Children should be offered a range of experiences and activities which support all aspects of their development: social; physical; intellectual; communication; emotional. The choice of experiences and activities (the 'curriculum') should depend on accurate assessment of the stage of development reached by a child, following observation and discussion with families. Early years workers have varying responsibilities concerning the planning and implementation of the curriculum, according to their work role, but all contributions to such planning and implementation should set high expectations for children and build on their achievements and interests. Child – initiated play and activities should be valued and recognised, as well as the adult planned curriculum. Written records should be kept of children's progress, and these records should be shared with parents.

5. Equality of opportunity

Each child should be offered equality of access to opportunities to learn and develop, and so worked towards her/his potential. Each child is a unique individual; early years workers must respect this individuality; children should not be treated 'all the same'. In order to meet a child's needs, it is necessary to treat each child ' with equal concern': some children need more and/or different support in order to have equality of opportunity. It is essential to avoid stereotyping children on the basis of gender, racial origins, cultural or social background (including religion, language, class and family pattern), or disability: such stereotypes might act as barriers to equality of access to opportunity. Early years workers should demonstrate their valuing of children's racial and other personal characteristics in order to help them develop self-esteem.

These principles of equality of access to opportunity, and avoidance of stereotyping must also be applied to interactions with adult family members, colleagues and other professionals.

6. Anti-discrimination

Early years workers must not discriminate against any child, family or group in society on the grounds of gender, racial origins, cultural or social background (including religion, language, class and family pattern), disability or sexuality. They must acknowledge and address any personal beliefs or opinions which prevent them respecting the value systems of other people, and comply with legislation and the policies of their work setting relating to discrimination. Children learn prejudice from their earliest years, and must be provided with accurate information to help them avoid prejudice. Expressions of prejudice by children or adults should be challenged, and support offered to those children or adults who are the objects of prejudice and discrimination. Early years workers have a powerful role to play in ensuring greater harmony amongst various groups in our society for future generations.

7. Celebrating diversity

Britain is a multi-racial, multi-cultural society. The contributions made to this society by a variety of cultural groups should be viewed in a positive light, and information about varying traditions, customs and festivals should be presented as a source of pleasure and enjoyment to all children including those in areas where there are few members of minority ethnic groups. Children should be helped to develop a sense of their identity within their racial, cultural and social groups, as well as having the opportunity to learn about culture that is different from their own. No one culture should be represented as superior to any other: pride in one's own cultural and social background does not require condemnation of that of other people.

8. Confidentiality

Information about children and families must never be shared with others without the permission of the family, except in the interest of protecting children. Early years workers must adhere to the policy of their work setting concerning confidential information, including passing information to colleagues. Information about other workers must also be handled in a confidential manner.

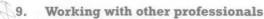

9. Working with other professionals

Advice and support should be sought from other professionals in the best interests of children and families, and information shared with them, subject to the principle of confidentiality. Respect should be shown for the roles of other professionals.

10. The reflective practitioner

Early years workers should use any opportunity they are offered, or which arises, to reflect on their practice and principles, and make use of the conclusions from such reflection in developing and extending their practice. Seeking advice and support to help resolve queries or problems should be seen as a form of strength and professionalism. Opportunities for in-service training/continuous professional development should be used to the maximum.

✳ DID YOU KNOW?

Under the new 2005 National Occupational Standards for Children's Care, Learning and Development, these values are expressed as follows:

* ✳ The needs, rights and views of the child are at the centre of all practice and provision
* ✳ Individuality, difference and diversity are valued and celebrated
* ✳ Equality of opportunity and anti-discriminatory practice are actively promoted
* ✳ Children's health and well-being are actively promoted
* ✳ Children's personal and physical safety is safe-guarded, whilst allowing for risk and challenge as appropriate to the capabilities of the child
* ✳ Self-esteem, resilience and a positive self-image are recognised as essential to every child's development
* ✳ Confidentiality and agreements about confidential information are respected as appropriate unless a child's protection and well-being are at stake
* ✳ Professional knowledge, skills and values are shared appropriately in order to enrich the experience of children more widely
* ✳ Best practice requires reflection and a continuous search for improvement

---

Consider this

Aaron is a 6-year-old boy whose family is in crisis and is currently being supported by a social worker. Aaron's father is an alcoholic with a violent temper when under the influence of alcohol. His mother is on anti-depressants and is a suspected victim of domestic violence. Both Aaron and his 2-year-old sister are on the child protection register as being 'at risk'.

Using the concepts of the paramountcy principle

Can you identify which of these people need to know that Aaron is on the child protection register?

His class teacher	His head teacher
The school nurse	The health visitor
The dinner lady	The caretaker
The family's neighbours	The GP

Go further – can you analyse using theory?

In the interests of confidentiality, which of the above need to know about:

Aaron's father's drink problem?
Aaron's mother being on anti-depressants?

Go further – can you evaluate using a range of theory?

Can you evaluate the impact of any breaches of confidentiality on:

Aaron	Aaron's mother
The social worker	Aaron's father?

As well as the care values defined within National Occupational Standards it is important to know that there is now a code of practice for social care workers and employers of social care workers published by the General Social Care Council (GSCC). This code of practice defines the principles that must guide working within health and social care. Further details of this code can be found in the next section of this unit.

Safe working

Safe working is concerned with the protection of the public, and this includes both workers and service users. There are two main groups of laws which concern people working in health, care and childcare services:

* laws that protect individuals at work and in employment
* laws that protect service users and vulnerable people.

In order to implement laws effectively, an organisation will need to have policies and procedures in place to raise awareness and explain what workers need to do in particular circumstances.

Laws protecting individuals at work

This is the equality legislation as described on page 15. In order to comply with the law, employers need to have policies and practices in place that enable the law to be implemented within the workplace and ensure that they do not discriminate against either their workers, or the people who use their services.

Organisations need to have an Equal Opportunities Policy, which should be based on the codes of practice produced by the Equal Opportunities Commission relating to equal pay and sex discrimination, and the code of practice produced by the Commission for Racial Equality. This will ensure that organisations do not inadvertently discriminate against individuals or groups. An Equal Opportunities Policy needs to be tailored to the specific requirements of any organisation and developed by the organisation itself, in consultation with recognised trade unions or representative bodies. It should cover the aspects outlined below.

A statement of policy

This should clearly describe the commitment of the organisation to the promotion of equality of opportunity, for example:

'It is our aim to provide employment equality to all. In particular, Cherry Trees Day Nursery is committed to promoting equal treatment irrespective of; age, sex, marital status, disability, sexual orientation, race, religion or ethnicity . We are opposed to all forms of unfair and unlawful discrimination, and will ensure that all workers and applicants for jobs, whether full-time or part-time, will be treated fairly and equitably in selection for employment, promotion, training or any other benefits. All opportunities will be on the basis of aptitude and ability, and it is our aim to ensure that all workers are able to develop their full potential, in order to benefit themselves and ensure efficiency within the organisation. We are committed to:

* preventing direct or indirect discrimination or victimisation
* promoting equal opportunities for all
* promoting harmonious working environments in which our staff are treated with dignity and respect and in which no form of intimidation harassment or bullying will be tolerated
* fulfilling all legal obligations under the relevant legislation and associated codes of practice
* ensuring that our policy is monitored and action taken to redress any imbalances, including taking positive or affirmative action, and setting targets and timescales for achievement.'

Implementation

The policy should clearly state the responsibility of senior management in relation to implementing the policy, including details of specific responsibilities for each tier of management. This section of policy should clearly state how it will be communicated to all workers, for example, through induction training, management training, team briefings, information on noticeboards, and staff handbooks. Training in non-discriminatory assessment and interview skills is particularly important for staff who are involved in the recruitment and selection of workers. Details of special measures to recruit members of underrepresented groups should also be outlined in the policy, and particulars about the information systems that will be used to assist the effective implementation of the policy should be provided to staff.

Monitoring and review

This section of the policy should say how the implementation of an Equal Opportunities Policy will be monitored following implementation, including how frequently it will be reviewed, and in what way. For example, there should be a statement, similar to the following:

> 'Provision of equality of opportunity between all men and women will be monitored through the collection and analysis of statistical data on the sex, marital status, ethnic origin, disability and full or part-time status of workers and job applicants. Progress on the implementation of this policy will be reviewed annually in consultation with staff representatives, who will be part of a joint employer/employee working group.'

Complaints

The policy should clearly state how employees who feel that they have suffered from any form of discrimination can complain. Organisations should ensure that where there are regulations relating to the timescales for taking complaints to an industrial tribunal, their internal systems for managing complaints do not cause undue delay. Employees are entitled to pursue internal complaints at the same time as taking action under any relevant legislation (tribunal procedures).

Harassment and bullying

The protection from the Harassment Act 1997 makes it a criminal offence to harass another person. It is also possible to sue an employer if you claim that harassment or bullying has taken place at work. Because of this, most employers are likely to have a policy to prevent harassment or bullying in order to protect staff from this form of abuse.

Codes of practice and their function

Health, social care and childcare services are strictly regulated; this means that people who work in the services need to have the right training and qualifications. It also means that organisations providing health, care or childcare services have to meet certain standards, and the care or treatment that is provided must be both effective and of a high standard.

In order to operate effectively, organisations offering health, social care and childcare services have a range of policies and procedures that are used to implement the standards and regulations set by government, as well as legislation relating to health and safety for example.

Historical codes of good practice provided by the regulatory bodies for health and social care have now been consolidated into a regulatory framework, in order to ensure a consistently high standard of care is being delivered across the UK. The Care Standards Act of 2000 established the framework for regulating the care sector and the organisations that are responsible for carrying out these regulatory duties. Because government responsibilities have been devolved to the four countries of Great Britain, different organisations have the responsibility for regulation in each of four countries.

The regulatory framework consists of:

* the professional councils that regulate practitioners and agree codes of professional practice
* the regulation and inspection bodies that regulate providers of health, care and early years services
* the national standards that set out minimum levels of care and evidence-based practice against which the organisation is measured.

The professional councils

The professional councils are responsible for the registration and regulation of practitioners, the individuals who provide direct care in health, social care or childcare settings.

Regulation of social care practitioners is the responsibility of the General Social Care Council (England), the Northern Ireland Social Care Council, the Care Council for Wales, and the Scottish Social Services Council. These organisations have produced a code of practice identifying the standards of professional conduct for both social care workers and employers, including what qualifications and training they require.

Some details of the GSCC code of practice are set out opposite:

The GSCC code of practice for social care workers

An outline summary

The Social Care Register was launched in April 2003; everyone working in social care will have to register, and abide by the code of practice. The register is being developed in stages, starting with the registration of qualified social workers, followed by social work students, residential childcare workers and care home managers. When applying to register, individuals will have their qualifications, health and character checked, including an enhanced check by the Criminal Records Bureau. Once this is completed satisfactorily, individuals will have a license to practice. Registers will have to renew their registration on a three-yearly basis, which will be subject to proof of continuing professional development.

In health, the Nursing and Midwifery Council (NMC) is the regulatory body for nursing, which replaced the United Kingdom Central Council (UKCC) in April 2002, and manages the registration and regulation of qualified nurses, midwives and health visitors.

Healthcare workers such as nurses follow a code of professional conduct published by the Nursing and Midwifery Council. The code has similar principles to the GSCC code for social care. Full details of the code can be found at www.nmc-uk.org but a summary of the key principles is listed below:

In caring for patients and clients, you must:

* respect each service user as an individual

* obtain consent before you give any treatment or care

* protect confidential information

* cooperate with others in the team

* maintain your professional knowledge and competence

* be trustworthy

* act to identify and minimise risk to patients and clients.

Other regulatory bodies for health professionals include the General Medical Council (GMC), which regulates doctors, and the Health Professions Council (HPC), which replaced the Council for Professions Supplementary to Medicine (CPSM). The HPC regulates around 13 professions including dieticians, speech therapists, chiropodists/podiatrists, orthoptists, operating department practitioners, paramedics, radiographers and physiotherapists among others. These regulatory bodies, as well as holding registers of qualified practitioners, are also responsible for maintaining professional standards and investigating any complaints against professionals.

Regulation and inspection bodies

It is important to recognise that all services provided for health, care and childcare are regulated and inspected against the standards set out by the government. The regulatory bodies monitor the standard of services provided for groups of patients and clients by the wide range of organisations that deliver health, care and childcare services, for example, the NHS, local authority social services, independent healthcare providers, voluntary and charitable organisations such as the National Society for the Prevention of Cruelty to Children (NSPCC) and providers of childcare services such as childminders and nurseries. The bodies responsible for this are outlined below.

The Commission for Social Care Inspection (CSCI)

This Commission, which was formed in April 2004, brings together the work previously undertaken by the Social Services Inspectorate and includes the social care functions of the National Care Standards Commission (NCSC). The Commission works on a local and national level, and in each local council area the CSCI carries out the following functions:

* registers private and voluntary care services to ensure they meet the national standards (see below)

* inspects, assesses and reviews all care services in a particular area, including private and

voluntary care services and local council social services departments

* provides the local council with details of the number and quality of private and voluntary care services in their local area
* deals with complaints about service providers
* reviews complaints about council social services departments.

The Healthcare Commission (Commission for Healthcare Audit and Inspection – CHAI)

This Commission undertakes all of the work previously carried out by the Commission for Health Improvement (CHI), the Mental Health Act Commission (MHAC) and the Audit Commission, as well as the independent healthcare work previously carried out by the National Care Standards Commission. It also monitors value for money in the NHS. The aims of the Commission are to:

* encourage improvement in the quality and effectiveness of care
* ensure that services are provided, economically and effectively
* inspect the management, provision and quality of healthcare services, including how effectively public resources are being used
* carry out investigations into serious service failures and report serious concerns about the quality of public services to the Secretary of State
* publish annual performance ratings for all NHS organisations (star rating)
* carry out an independent review function for NHS complaints
* collaborate with the Commission for Social Care Inspection (CSCI).

The government is currently planning to merge the Healthcare Commission and the Commission for Social Care Inspection to reflect the increasing collaboration between the health and social care sectors; it is anticipated that a new body will be in place by 2008.

Ofsted (Office for Standards in Education)

There are two main integrated aspects to pre-school childcare; the first is the provision of physical, social and emotional care for children and the second is promoting children's learning and development.

Unlike health and social care, which has separate bodies for registration and inspection, there is currently no register of childcare practitioners, and Ofsted is responsible for both inspection and regulation of pre-school provision such as childminders and nurseries, ensuring that individuals have appropriate qualifications and have been subjected to Criminal Records Bureau checks, for example.

Ofsted inspect childcare provision to ensure that providers are meeting the:

* Early Learning Goals, set by the Qualifications and Curriculum Authority, which identifies what children should be able to do and understand in the pre-school years, i.e. the expected learning and development
* National Standards for Under Eight's Day Care and Childminding, which are a set of outcomes introduced by the Department for Education and Skills, identifying the levels of provision needed for the effective physical, social and emotional care of children, such as ratios of staff to children. Local authorities are responsible for ensuring that the childcare provision in their area meets the required standards, against which they are inspected by Ofsted
* Ofsted is also responsible for inspecting:
  * all state and independent schools
  * local education authorities
  * teacher training institutions
  * youth work
  * further education colleges
  * 14–19 education and training in partnership with the Adult Learning Inspectorate.

It is expected that the children's social care function of the CSCI (those services provided by social services departments for children in need) will merge with Ofsted to create a single children's services inspectorate with a new inspection framework in the near future.

National Minimum Standards

The Care Standards Act 2000 identified National Minimum Standards for a range of care services, which all service providers must meet. The standards form the baseline against which services are inspected and registered. For example, if a residential home for older people fails to comply with the minimum standards, it could lose its registration and be forced to cease operating. There are minimum standards covering the following areas:

* care homes for older people
* care homes with adult placements
* care homes for adults aged 18–65
* adult placement schemes (foster-type care for adults with particular needs)
* domiciliary care (care in a person's own home)
* nurses' agencies
* children's homes
* adoption
* residential family centres
* fostering services
* boarding schools
* residential special schools
* accommodation of students under 18 by Further Education Colleges.

National minimum standards apply to issues such as staffing levels, qualifications and training of staff and standards relating to the care and treatment of the particular service-user group. For example, the National Minimum Standards for the Care of Older People has sections on:

* choice of home; including how the service user's needs are assessed, trial visits and contracts
* health and personal care standards; including privacy and dignity, dying and death, health care provision, medication and a service user

plan, which states the individual's preferences and personal details

* daily life and social activities: including meals and mealtimes, social contact and activities, community contact, autonomy and choice
* complaints and protection: including policies such as how to complain and service users' rights to complain
* environment: such as the type of premises and space requirements, shared facilities, washing and toilet facilities, adaptations and equipment, heating and lighting facilities, hygiene and infection control.

It is through the National Minimum Standards that the values and principles of care are delivered.

National Service Frameworks

The National Service Frameworks (NSF) apply to health care services. They describe the standards of treatment for particular conditions or service-user groups: they are based on evidence from research and are currently in development. Completed frameworks at the present time include those for:

* diabetes
* coronary heart disease
* cancer
* renal services
* mental health
* older people's services
* children, young people and maternity services.

It is important to recognise that the NSF for Children, Young People and Maternity Services are the standards for children's health and social services combined, and the framework also covers the interface with education to reflect the proposed integration of these services for children in all local authority areas over the next 10 years.

Organisational policies

Organisational policies are the mechanism through which legislation is delivered and implemented. Examples of policies that organisations are likely to include are outlined below.

Child protection policy

Such a policy enables organisations and individuals concerned with the care and welfare of children to fulfill their responsibilities under the Children Act 1989 and subsequent amendments. The policy will give details of reporting mechanisms, lines of accountability and procedures to be followed in cases of suspected child abuse. Each local authority area has a designated Area Child Protection Committee consisting of professional representatives, police and local authority representatives. Under new arrangements proposed, these will be superseded by Local Protecting Children Boards.

Bullying policy

This is often part of a protection from harassment policy that will also link with the organisation's equal opportunities policy in order to protect staff in the workplace and, as such, will provide details of how a complaint may be taken forward within an organisation. However, schools are also required to have anti-bullying policies, which detail the approach the school takes to manage bullying and protect children while at school.

Confidentiality

Whilst this is covered in the National Minimum Standards, it is still necessary to have a policy which explains what staff should do if they feel that confidentiality has been broken. Such a policy is also likely to state what protection the organisation offers to 'whistle blowers', i.e. those individuals who go public with information that may be confidential to an organisation – for example, systematic abuse within a care environment.

Summary

Care workers are members of the public and therefore have to obey the law, especially in relation to equality legislation to ensure that all service users are treated equally. In addition, the regulatory bodies and regulatory frameworks for health, social care and childcare services ensure that the services are delivered in a way that protects and promotes service users' rights, by inspecting the premises, policies and procedures that organisations have in place to implement the law. There are also regulations to ensure that care workers are appropriate people to undertake such responsibilities, and there are mechanisms in place to deal with care workers who have been found guilty of abusing their positions of trust. Service users' rights, health and well-being are protected by both national law and regulations relating to care premises, the way in which care is delivered and the people delivering it.

Useful websites

www.open2.net/childofourtime/2005/
www.crimereduction.gov.uk
www.mhac.org.uk
www.doh.gov.uk/ih

References

Oakley, A. (1974) *The Sociology of Housework* (Oxford: Martin Robertson) in Giddens, A. (2001) *Sociology* (4th edition) (Polity Press) p. 177
Tossell, D. and Webb, R. (1994) Inside the Caring Services (2nd edition) (Arnold Publishers)

Aaron is having an unhappy time at school and at home. His father is a violent alcoholic and his mother is on anti-depressant medication. Aaron and his sister have been placed on the child protection register.

Aaron often has to get himself ready for school and sometimes looks rather scruffy because he has no clean clothes. One of the boys in Aaron's class has found out about Aaron's home situation and has started teasing him and calling him names. Last week, this boy and his friends cornered Aaron in the school toilets and started calling his mother names, making Aaron angry. He lashed out at one of the boys, who ran into the corridor crying loudly and was asked by a passing teacher what had happened. The boy replied that Aaron had hit him and the teacher punished Aaron.

Using theory, can you identify?
The responsibilities of the school
The responsibilities of the family social worker

Go further – can you analyse issues using theory?
Two actions Aaron could take to help himself
Actions which those responsible for Aaron's health, safety and well-being could take to help Aaron resolve the situation in school

Go further – can you evaluate using theory?
Two ways in which anti-bullying strategies in school could prevent such a situation
Likely outcomes for the school if they fail to act

UNIT 1 ASSESSMENT

How you will be assessed

This unit is externally assessed. You will need to make sure you understand how care workers' attitudes and values affect service users and the key principles and features of each of the Equality Acts.

Test questions

1. Give two examples of primary socialisation.

2. Give three influences on secondary socialisation.

3. Explain the importance of the four basic needs of human beings.

4. Explain the link between an individual's identity, self-esteem (self-worth) and socialisation.

5. Describe three examples of discriminatory actions.

6. Describe five types of abuse.

7. Explain what is meant by direct and indirect discrimination.

8. What are the main duties and responsibilities of the Commission for Racial Equality?

9. What are the implications of the Human Rights Act on new laws proposed by Parliament?

10. Describe three strengths and three weaknesses of the Mental Health Act 1983.

11. Identify four of the seven key principles contained in the Children Act 1989.

12. Using examples, describe the five common barriers which can be experienced by different people when accessing services.

13. What are the key values of care?

14. Describe the three main aspects of the regulatory framework for care established by the Care Standards Act 2000.

15. Identify the key components of an organisation's equal opportunities policy.

16. Why is it important that care workers are trusted by service users?

17. Describe the purpose of the new Children Act 2004 and three key features of this.

18. Why is it important for childcare workers to work in partnership with parents? Explain what this means in practice.

19. Why is it important for childcare workers to offer a range of different experiences to children?

20. Why should childcare organisations have child protection policies? What information should such a policy contain?

Answers to these questions are provided on page 163.

UNIT 2

Communication in Care Settings

This unit covers the following sections:

2.1   Types of communication

2.2   Factors that support and inhibit communication

2.3   Communication skills

2.4   Theories relating to communication

2.5   Interaction with the service users

Introduction

This unit focuses on communication skills in detail. In doing so, it explores different types of communication, together with some of the factors that may support or inhibit communication. There is an emphasis throughout on the importance of using theory to analyse practice.

How you will be assessed

As part of your studies you are required to produce a range of evidence as set out in assessment objectives (AO), and a report as set out in the fourth objective (AO4). Your report should explore the effectiveness of your communication skills in an interaction with an individual service user, or care worker, or with a small group of service users or care workers; it should also include an analysis of your performance.

Section 1: Types of communication

Different types of communication used in care settings

There are many different ways in which people communicate with each other. These can include: oral communication, body language, signs and symbols, written and electronically transferred communication.

Oral communication

Tearesa Thompson (1986) writing about health work, argues that communication is important for two major reasons. Firstly, communication enables people to share information; but secondly, communication enables relationships between people. Thompson states that 'communication is the relationship' (1986). So speaking or signing is central to establishing relationships between people, and care workers need to have highly developed social skills, in order to work with the

FIGURE 2.1 *Communication enables people to share information*

wide range of emotional needs that service users will have. Face-to-face, oral (or mouth) communication involves using words and sentences (verbal communication) together with a range of body language messages (non-verbal communication). Section 3 of this unit explores these issues in detail.

Oral communication may be central to the kind of tasks listed in Figure 2.2.

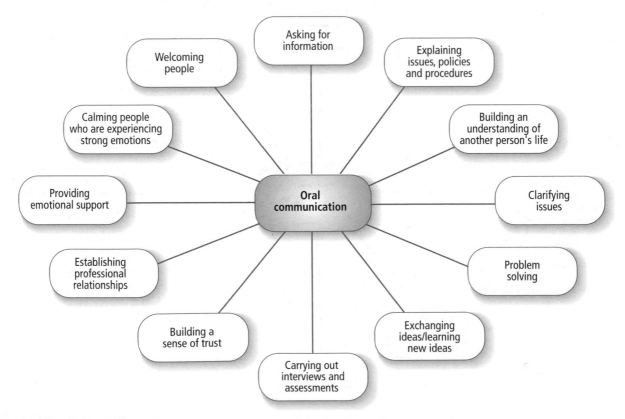

FIGURE 2.2 *Examples of tasks in which oral communication is key*

Written communication

There is an old saying in Chinese culture that 'the faintest ink is stronger than the strongest memory'. Written records are essential for communicating formal information that needs to be reviewed at a future date. When people remember conversations they have had, they will probably miss some details out, and also change some details. Written statements are much more permanent and if they are accurate when they are written they may be useful at a later date.

Some examples of important written documents are shown in Figure 2.3.

When an issue is recorded in writing it becomes formal. It is important that records of personal information are as factual and accurate as possible. You should describe only the facts or the events that happened, without giving your own interpretation or saying how you feel.

If written communication is inaccurate it could result in the following problems:

* serious delays in meeting people's needs
* inability to follow up enquiries
* making mistakes with arrangements for people's care
* missing meetings or important arrangements
* not providing a professional service for people
* inability to organise services for others properly
* other professional workers not having the right information to help them with decision-making.

Many organisations use printed forms to help staff to ask important questions and check that they have taken accurate information. Service users' personal records are likely to be written on forms that use headings. When writing information down it is a good idea to:

* check that the interviewee is giving you the information agrees with what you are writing
* check the spelling of names and repeat phone numbers back to interviewee in order to check that they are correct
* use a form or a prepared set of headings to

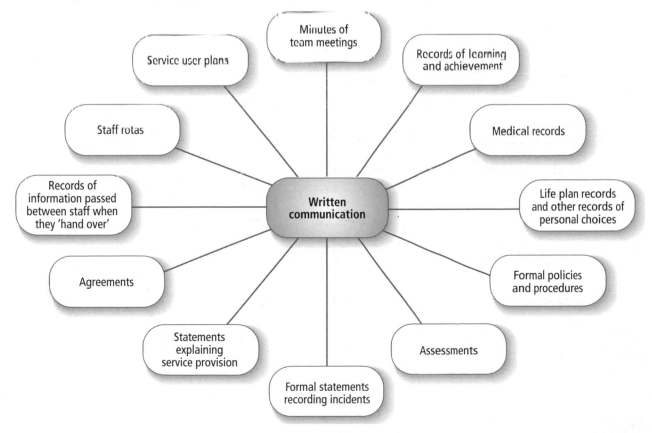

FIGURE 2.3 *Examples of important written communication*

help check that you are collecting the right information.

Computerised communication (Information and communication technology)

Nowadays, individuals can access a vast amount of information through the Internet. Email and text messages can reach people in a fraction of the time that paper-based written communication used to take. It is possible to network with a wide range of other professionals rapidly using electronically recorded messages. An important issue here is to consider the degree of formality involved. Some electronic communication, such as text messages between friends, can use short cuts to communicate. For example, everybody understands 'How R U?' But more complex informal systems of communication might confuse or exclude people in a work context.

Computerised records are very important in care work and should be treated with the same degree of formality as other written records. There will be a range of security measures designed to make sure the information stays confidential and is not lost or inappropriately altered. With electronic records it will be important to:

* keep a 'back-up copy' in case the system crashes

* use a password security check to ensure that only appropriate staff have access

* find out about the policy on the printing of details (similar to written records) so that hard copies do not get lost, or seen by others

* know the policy on who is authorised to update or change records. The recording system must prevent information being altered or lost by accident

* print out faxed documents in an appropriate confidential area and keep the documents in a safe system to prevent unauthorised people having access to confidential material.

Special methods

People who are Deaf may not use a spoken language system. The first (or main) language of many deaf people may be a signed language. People who are registered blind may use Braille, as opposed to English, in order to read information.

British Sign Language

The British Deaf Association states that British Sign Language (BSL) 'is the first or preferred language of nearly 70,000 Deaf people in the United Kingdom'. The British Deaf Association explains that BSL 'belongs to deaf people. It is not a communication system devised by hearing people. It is a real language which has evolved in the UK's Deaf community over hundreds of years.' The British Deaf Association campaign for the right of Deaf people to be educated in BSL and to access information and services through BSL, arguing that the Deaf community is a 'linguistic and cultural minority and is not measured in medical terms'.

Further details of BSL can be found at www.britishdeafassociation.org.uk. Details of signs and the finger spelling alphabet can be found at www.british-sign.co.uk and at www.royaldeaf.org.uk.

Makaton

Makaton is a system for developing language that uses speech, signs and symbols to help people with learning difficulties to communicate and to develop their language skills. People who communicate using Makaton may speak a word and perform a sign using hands and body language. There is a large range of symbols that may help people with learning difficulty to recognise an idea or to communicate with others. Further information on Makaton can be found at www.makaton.org.

Braille

Braille (a system of raised marks that can be felt with your fingers) provides a system of written communication, based on the sense of touch, for people who have limited vision. The communication system known as Braille was first published by Louis Braille, a blind 20-year-old, in 1829. The system is now widely adopted in the form of writing and reading and is used by people who cannot see written script.

Nowadays, computer software can translate written material into Braille, which can be printed out using special printers. Further details on Braille can be found at www.brailleplus.net.

Summary

There are many situations in care work, in which it is important to exchange information. Communication is also important because care work is about building, appropriate relationships and meeting social, emotional and intellectual needs, as well as the physical needs of service users. The quality of communication will establish the quality of relationships and the ability of carers to meet service users' needs.

Consider this

A 55-year-old man telephones a care home to request information about its services. The home has a clearly written booklet that explains details of the home's facilities and services. The man would like to make an appointment for himself and his 85-year-old father so that his father can decide whether the home would be suitable or not.

1 What ideas do you have that might help a care worker to clearly pass on information to these people?

2 Communication is also about relationships, what ideas do you have that would help a care worker to establish a caring relationship when meeting with these two people?

Section 2: Factors that support and inhibit communication

In order to work supportively it is important to understand and work within a system of care values. Care values include understanding the importance of diversity and cultural variation, maintaining confidentiality and promoting the rights of service users.

Care values

Skilled caring does not result from just knowing the right skills and techniques. A carer also needs to 'value' the service users that he or she works with. The 1998 National Vocational Qualifications (NVQs) in Care Standards identified key values to 'Foster equality and diversity of people', 'maintain the confidentiality of information' and 'Foster people's rights and responsibilities'. The proposed standards for 2005 have been designed differently but still identify values that include: the promotion of equality and diversity; the ability to challenge discrimination; and an understanding of the rights and responsibilities of people involved in care settings.

Key concept

care values are occupational standards and codes of practice that identify a framework of values and moral rights of service users. In 2002 the General Social Care Council (GSCC) published a '**code of practice**' for both employees and employers. A summary of the code of practice for employees is set out in Unit 1 together with other codes of practice that provide a basis for care values.

Other codes of practice

Healthcare workers such as nurses follow a code of professional conduct published by the Nursing and Midwifery Council (NMC). The code has similar principles to the GSCC code for social care. Full details of the code can be found at www.nmc-uk.org. A summary of the key principles are listed below.

In caring for patients and service users, you must:

* respect each service user as an individual
* obtain consent before you give any treatment or care
* protect confidential information
* cooperate with others in the team
* maintain your professional knowledge and competence
* be trustworthy
* act to identify and minimise risk to patients and service users.

The majority of early years services are inspected by Ofsted and do not involve the GSCC code of practice. Instead Early Years National Vocational Qualifications have a set of 'underlying principles'; see Figure 2.4 for an outline specification.

UNDERLYING PRINCIPLES OF EARLY YEARS NVQS	
1	the welfare of the child is the most important issue
2	children must be kept safe
3	workers must work in partnership with parents and families
4	children's learning and development are centrally important
5	the principle of equality of opportunity is critically important
6	anti-discriminatory practice is vital
7	care practice must 'celebrate diversity'
8	the principle of confidentiality must be followed
9	workers must work with other professionals in the best interests of children and families
10	early years workers must learn to reflect on their practice and principles

FIGURE 2.4 *Outline specification of underlying principles of Early Years NVQs*

Promoting equality and diversity – diversity in individuals

You are special and no one is exactly the same as you. But you will be more like some people and less like others. We try to make ourselves individual; but we are also influenced by the 'groups' that we belong to. Some general differences between people (aspects of diversity) are listed in Figure 2.5.

DIFFERENCES BETWEEN PEOPLE	
Age	People may think of others as being children, teenagers, young adults, middle-aged or old. Discrimination can creep in to our thinking if we see some age groups as being 'the best' or if we make assumptions about the abilities of different age groups.
Gender	People are classified as male or female. In the past, men often had more rights and were seen as more important than women. Assumptions about gender still create discrimination.
Race	People may understand themselves as being black or white, as European, African or Asian. Many people have specific national identities such as Polish, Nigerian, English or Welsh. Assumptions about racial characteristics lead to discrimination.
Class	People differ in their upbringing, the kind of work they do and the money they receive. People also differ in the lifestyles they lead and the views and values that go with different levels of income and spending habits. People may discriminate against others because of their class or lifestyle.
Religion	People grow up in different traditions of religion. For some people, spiritual beliefs are at the centre of their understanding of life. For others, religion influences the cultural traditions that they celebrate; for example, many Europeans celebrate Christmas even though they might not see themselves as practising Christians. Discrimination can take place when people assume that their customs or beliefs should apply to everyone else.
Sexuality	Many people see their sexual orientation as very important to understanding who they are. Gay and lesbian relationships are often discriminated against. Heterosexual people sometimes judge other relationships as 'wrong' or abnormal.
Ability	People may make assumptions about what is 'normal'. People with physical disabilities or learning disabilities may become labelled or stereotyped.
Health	People who develop illnesses or mental health problems may feel that they are valued less by other people and discriminated against.
Relationships	People choose many different lifestyles and emotional commitments, such as: marriage, having children, living in a large family, living a single lifestyle but having sexual partners, being single and not sexually active. People live within different family and friendship groups. Discrimination can happen if people think that one lifestyle is 'right' or best.
Politics	People can develop different views as to how a government should act, how welfare provision should be organised, and so on. Disagreement and debate are necessary; but it is important not to discriminate against people because of their views.

FIGURE 2.5 *Some aspects of diversity*

Understanding diversity

Our own culture and life experience may lead us to make assumptions about what is right or normal. When we meet people who are different from ourselves it can be easy to see them as 'not right' or 'not normal'. People see the world in different ways. Our way of thinking may seem unusual to others. Look at Figure 2.6. Which is the 'normal front of the cube'?

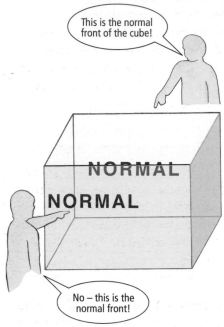

FIGURE 2.6 *Different individuals have different views*

If we were used to seeing the cube from only one direction we might be sure that our view is right. Our culture may lead us to think that some habits are more normal than others, but often there are many ways of looking at things. For instance, different cultures and different individuals have different views about what is right to eat or drink.

Think it over...

Do you think that it is appropriate for you to eat meat, insects, frogs, snakes? There is great diversity in what people believe is appropriate to eat. Culture, politics and religion play a role in influencing what people believe.

Skilled carers have to get to know the people that they work with in order to avoid making false assumptions. In getting to know an individual, carers will also need to understand the ways that class, race, age, gender and other social categories influence the person. A person's culture may include all social groups that he or she belongs to.

Knowledge of diverse characteristics

There are many different ethnic groups in the world, many different religions, cultural values, variations in gender role, and so on. Individuals

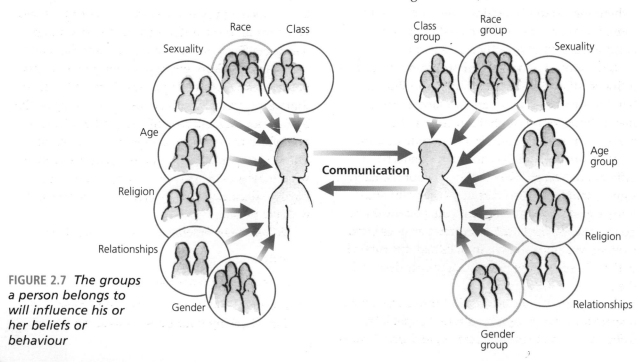

FIGURE 2.7 *The groups a person belongs to will influence his or her beliefs or behaviour*

may belong to the same ethnic group yet belong to different religions or class groups. Knowing someone's religion will not necessarily tell you all about his or her beliefs, or general culture.

You can pick up background knowledge on different ethnic and religious customs, but it is impossible to study and learn all the differences that can exist for individual service users. The best way to learn about diversity is to listen and communicate with people who lead very different lives.

Promoting equality and diversity in communication

It is important to be able to identify the different interpretations that words and body language have in different cultures. This is not a straightforward issue – words and signs can mean different things depending on their context. For example, the word 'wicked' can have different meanings. If older people were to use this phrase to describe their experience of World War II, it would mean 'horrific' or 'terrible'. In a TV comedy script written 15 years ago, the phrase would mean 'cool', i.e. something very desirable. In a religious context 'wicked' might relate to the concept of sin.

Making sense of spoken language requires knowledge of the context and intentions of the speaker. Understanding non-verbal communication involves exactly the same need to understand 'where the person is coming from', or, to put it more formally, what the circumstances and cultural context of the other person are.

Both spoken and non-verbal communication is influenced by culture. For example, in Britain the hand gesture with palm up and facing forward, means 'Stop, don't do that'. In Greece it can mean, 'You are dirt', and is a very rude gesture.

Why do the same physical movements have different meanings? One explanation for the hand signs is that the British version of the palm-and-fingers gesture means, 'I arrest you, you must not do it'; whereas the Greek interpretation goes back to medieval times when criminals had dirt rubbed in their faces to show how much people despised them.

Using care values means that carers must have respect for other people's culture. People learn different ways of communicating, and good carers will try to understand the different ways in which people use non-verbal messages. For instance, past research in the USA suggests that white and black Americans might have used different non-verbal signals when they listened. It suggests that some black Americans may tend not to look much at the speaker. This can be interpreted as a mark of respect; by looking away it demonstrates that you are really thinking hard about the message. Unfortunately, not all white people understood this cultural difference in non-verbal communication. Some individuals misunderstood and assumed that this non-verbal behaviour meant exactly the same as if a white person had looked away from the speaker. That is, it would mean the individual was not listening.

Key concept

cultural variation describes the different special systems of meanings across different cultures. Cultures that are different from our own interpret body language differently: communication is influenced by these cultural systems of meaning.

There is an almost infinite variety of meanings that can be given to any type of eye contact, facial expression, posture or gesture. Every culture develops its own special system of meanings. Carers have to understand and show respect and value for all these different systems of sending messages. But how can you ever learn them all?

No one can learn every possible system of non-verbal message, but it is possible to learn the ones that people you are with are using. You may do this by first noticing and remembering what others do and which non-verbal messages they are sending. The next step is to make an intelligent guess about what messages the person is trying to give you. Finally, check your understanding (your guesses) with the person.

Skilled interpersonal interaction involves:

* watching other people

* remembering what they do

* guessing what words and actions mean and then checking your guesses with the person

* never relying on your own guesses, because these might turn into assumptions

* understanding that assumptions can lead to discrimination.

Think it over...

Imagine that you are working with an older female service user. Whenever you start to speak to her she always looks at the floor and never makes eye contact. Why is this?

Your first thought is that she might be depressed. Having made such an assumption, you might not want to talk to this person. But instead, you could ask 'How do you feel today; would you like me to get you anything?' By checking out how she feels you could test your own understanding. The service user might say that she feels well and is quite happy, and then suggest something you could do for her. This would indicate that she cannot be depressed.

Why else would someone look at the floor rather than at you?

Using care values involves getting to understand people and not acting on unchecked assumptions. Non-verbal messages should never be relied on; they should always be checked.

Stereotyping

Sometimes people try to save mental energy and just make the assumption that groups of people are 'all the same'. Perhaps a younger person meets an 80-year-old, who has a problem with his or her memory, perhaps they have seen someone with a poor memory on TV – it is then easy to think that 'all old people are forgetful'. This would be a stereotype.

A stereotype is a fixed way of thinking. People may make assumptions based on stereotyped thinking. For example, a carer who works with older people might say 'I'll just go in and wash and dress this next one. I won't ask what she would like me to do because she's old. Old people don't remember, so it doesn't matter what I do'. Stereotyping is the opposite of valuing diversity.

Key concept

stereotyping is a fixed way of thinking involving generalisations and expectations about an issue or a group of people.

Maintaining confidentiality

Confidentiality is an important right for all service users. Confidentiality is important because:

* service users may not trust a carer if the carer does not keep information to him or herself

* service users may not feel valued or able to keep their self-esteem if their private details are shared with others.

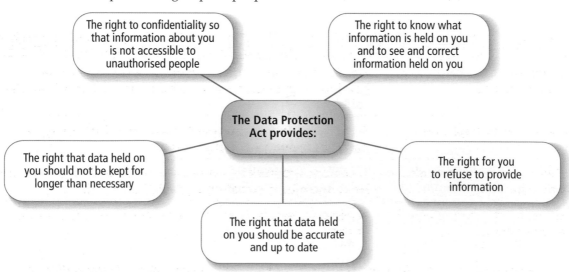

The right to confidentiality so that information about you is not accessible to unauthorised people

The right to know what information is held on you and to see and correct information held on you

The Data Protection Act provides:

The right that data held on you should not be kept for longer than necessary

The right for you to refuse to provide information

The right that data held on you should be accurate and up to date

FIGURE 2.8 *Some rights provided under the Data Protection Act 1998*

* service users' safety may be put at risk if details of their property and habits are shared publicly

* a professional service which maintains respect for individuals must keep private information confidential

* there are legal requirements to keep personal records confidential.

The Data Protection Act 1998

The 1998 Data Protection Act establishes rights to confidentiality covering both paper and electronic records. This Act provides people with a range of rights including those shown in Figure 2.8.

> **Key concept**
>
> *confidentiality* involves keeping information safe and only passing it on where there is a clear right and a clear need to do so. Confidentiality is an important moral and legal right, promoting the safety and security of service users and their property. The maintenance of confidentiality is vital, in order to keep a sense of trust.

Service users have a right to confidentiality but also have a responsibility in relation to the rights of others. Confidentiality often has to be kept within boundaries, or broken where the rights of others have to balance with the service user's rights. An example of keeping confidentiality within boundaries would be a situation in which a carer tells his or her manager about something learned in confidence. As the information is not made public it is still partly confidential. Some of the situations in which information may need to be passed to managers are shown in Figure 2.9.

Confidentiality and the need to know

Good care practice involves asking service users if we can let other people know things. It would be wrong to pass on even the date of a person's birthday without asking him or her first. Some people might not want others to celebrate their birthday. Jehovah's Witnesses, for example, believe that it is wrong to celebrate birthdays. Whatever we know about a service user should be kept private unless the person tells us that it is all right to share the information. The exception to this rule is that information can be passed on when others have a right and a need to know it.

Some examples of people who have a need to know about work with service users are:

* the manager (he or she may need to help make decisions, which affect the service user)

* colleagues (these people may be working with the same person)

* other professionals (these people may also be working with the service user and need to be kept up to date with information).

SITUATION	EXAMPLE
Where there is a significant risk of harm to a service user	An older person in the community refuses to put her heating on in winter; she may be at risk of harm from the cold
When a service user might be abused	A person who explains that his son takes his money; he might be being financially abused
Where there is a significant risk of harm to others	A person who lives in a very dirty house with mice and rats; he or she may be creating a public health risk
Where there is a risk to the carer's health or well-being	A person is very aggressive; he or she is placing the carer at risk

FIGURE 2.9 *Examples of situations in which carers may need to pass on confidential information to managers*

FIGURE 2.10 *Service users have a right to know that information about them is recorded accurately*

When information is passed to other professionals it should be passed on with the understanding that they keep it confidential. It is important to check that other people are authentic. If you answer the telephone and the person speaking claims to be a social worker or other professional, you should explain that you must phone back before giving any information; this enables you to be sure that you are talking to an authorised person within an organisation. If you meet a person you don't know, you should ask for proof of identity before passing any information on.

Relatives will often say that they have a right to know about service users. Sometimes it is possible to ask relatives to discuss issues directly with the service user rather than giving information yourself, as shown in the illustration opposite, for example.

All services now have to have policies and procedures on the confidentiality of recorded information.

If service user records are not managed in accordance with the Data Protection Act and NCSC regulations, service users might suffer a range of damaging consequences, which might include those shown in Figure 2.11.

Values and moral rights

The table opposite lists key (value base principles) that might also be considered to be service users'

SCENARIO

Ethel is 88 years old and receives home care. One day she says 'Keep this confidential, but I don't take my tablets [pain killers for arthritis and tablets for blood pressure]. I'm saving them so that I can take them all at once and finish my life if my pain gets worse.' Ethel manages to say this before you can tell her that some things cannot be kept confidential.

Do you have to keep this information confidential? Ethel has a right to confidentiality but she also has a responsibility not to involve other people in any harm she may do to herself. Ethel does not have a right to involve you. The information about the tablets should be shared with managers and Ethel's GP, who can discuss the matter with her.

Ethel's neighbour stops you as you are leaving one day. The neighbour asks, 'How is Ethel, is she taking her tablets?'

Can you tell the neighbour of your worries? Before giving any information to anyone, carers have to ask the question, 'Does this person have a need to know?' A need to know is different from wanting to know. Ethel's neighbour might just be nosy, and it would be wrong to break the confidentiality without an important reason. If the GP knows Ethel does not take her tablets, she may be able to save her health or even her life. But the neighbour should not be told.

moral rights, together with other rights that are specified within the GSCC code of practice.

Other factors that support or inhibit communication

Communication can be supported or inhibited by both practical and emotional factors. This is because communication depends on receiving the message – a practical or physical issue – and on correctly interpreting the message – an emotional issue. So even if information is seen or heard, it can still be misunderstood because of other issues.

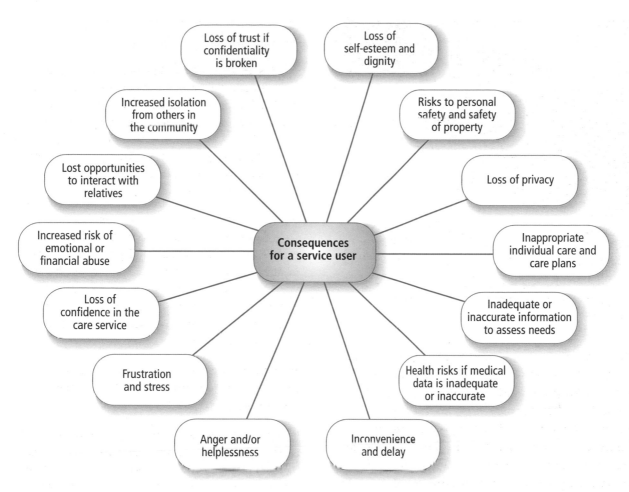

FIGURE 2.11 *Some of the consequences for service users if their records are not managed in accordance with current legislation and regulations*

Positioning

Positioning can create both physical and emotional barriers that inhibit communication. If a person cannot see you this may inhibit communication. On an emotional level, leaning over somebody and looking down at them can send a message of dominance and power. Historically, courtrooms were designed so that the judge sat much higher than the defendant and also looked down on everyone else. The ability to look down shows how powerful you are. In care work it is very important not to look down on the people you care for. It is important that your eyes are at the same level as the person that you are communicating with.

It is important to consider positioning when working with people who have a hearing difficulty. Many people with partial hearing use lip-reading and this enables them to understand

FIGURE 2.12 *A carer moves to the same eye level as a service user*

what other people are saying. It is therefore important that you position yourself so that the person can see your face clearly. In this situation, therefore, it does make sense for a person who lip-reads to say, 'I'm sorry I can't hear you, I need to put my glasses on.'

Positioning is very important in group communication. Seating patterns can have a major influence on how a group works. In discussion groups it is very important that everyone can see and hear one another. Non-verbal communication will be important, and if people cannot see everybody's faces, this may not be possible. Usually, chairs are placed in a circle to enable all those taking part in a discussion to receive non-verbal messages from everyone in the group.

Organising a group to sit in a circle may suggest that everyone is equal and that everyone is expected to communicate with everyone else. This freedom to communicate is also linked with creating a feeling of belonging: 'We can all share together – this is our group.' (See Figure 2.13a).

Other patterns of seating will send different messages. Teachers might sit in the middle of a half-circle. This sends the message, 'We are all equal and we can all communicate with each other, but the teacher is going to do most of the communicating.' (See Figure 2.13b).

At a formal lecture, people sit in rows. This sends the message, 'The lecturer will talk to you. You can ask questions but you should not talk to one another.' (See Figure 2.13c).

Some less formal seating arrangements can create blocks. Sometimes a desk or table acts as a block. For example, in Figure 2.13d, the two people on their own might be sending the message, 'We are not sure we want to be with this

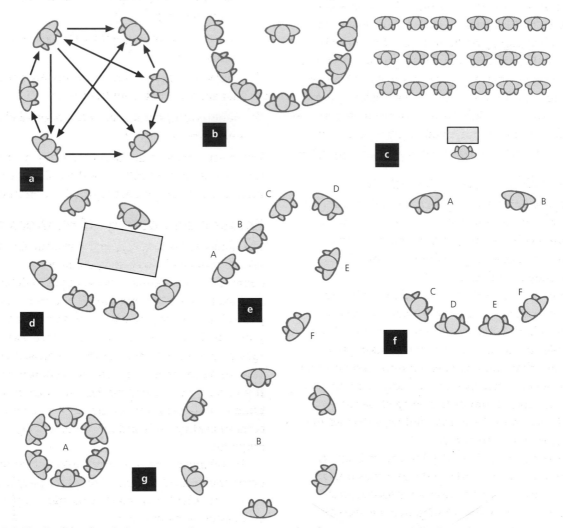

FIGURE 2.13 *Positioning is important in group communication*

group.' The table can make them feel separate: 'We'll join in only if we feel like it.'

Sometimes space can be used to create a gulf. In Figure 2.13e, person A cannot see person C properly; so the two of them are unable to exchange non-verbal messages. Person A sits 'square on' to person F. Perhaps A does not want to talk to C. Perhaps F and A do not trust each other. The layout of seats makes it look as though there could be tension or reluctance in this group.

Space can also signal social distance (see Figure 2.13f. A and B are keeping their distance from the rest of the group. There could be many reasons, but perhaps they are sending the message, 'We do not really belong with you four.'

Another consideration is whether a group of people is sitting close together or spaced apart. In Figure 2.13g, group A are huddled together, whereas group B are spaced further apart. There might be a number of reasons why people get closer or further apart in groups. For example, being close can signal that the environment is noisy and that the group has to get close to hear. It can suggest that the members like each other and are very interested in the discussion topic. Alternatively, it might be that group members feel unsafe and that being together gives each one more confidence that everyone will be supportive.

Proximity and personal space

The space between people can sometimes show how friendly or 'intimate' the conversation is. Different cultures have different assumptions about how close people should be (proximity) when they are talking.

In Britain, there are expectations or 'norms' as to how close you should be when you talk to others. When talking to strangers we may keep an arm's-length apart. The ritual of shaking hands indicates that you have been introduced and may come closer. When you are friendly with someone you may accept him or her being closer to you. Relatives and partners may not be restricted in how close they can come.

Personal space is a very important issue in care work. A care worker who assumes it is all right to enter a service user's personal space without asking or explaining, may be seen as being dominating or aggressive.

Another aspect of positioning is that of face to face. In many cultural contexts within the UK, standing or sitting eye to eye can send a message of being sincere, or it can mean formality, or it can mean confrontation and threat. A slight angle may create a more informal, relaxed and friendly feeling.

Emotion

Service users often have serious emotional needs; they are afraid or depressed because of the stresses they are experiencing. Sometimes service users may lack self-awareness or appear to be shy or aggressive. Listening involves learning about frightening and depressing situations. Carers sometimes avoid listening to avoid unpleasant emotional feelings. Emotion can create barriers because care workers:

* are tired – listening takes mental energy
* believe that they do not have sufficient time to communicate properly
* are emotionally stressed by the needs of service users
* react with negative emotions towards cultures that are different from their own
* make assumptions about others, or label or stereotype others.

When service users are depressed, angry or upset these emotions will influence their ability to understand what you are trying to communicate.

Emotion and quality of relationship

The ability to build a supportive relationship with service users will also greatly influence communication. People who trust you will be more inclined to share information. If you are attentive to people's needs they may respond to you with some gratitude. If you show respect to service users this may help to meet their self-esteem needs. If you are responsive to others they may be responsive to you. If you are good at listening then you may be able to build an understanding of the person you are communicating with and this, in time, may lead to empathy.

It will always be important to consider the emotional impact you have on other people and to try and adapt your communication to meet the emotional needs of others.

How do you know if another person sees you as being supportive? One of the key issues will be how the individual responds to you. If people treat you with respect perhaps it is because they perceive you as being respectful. If they try to please you perhaps it is because you meet their self-esteem needs.

Being assertive

Some people may seem shy and worried; they say little and avoid contact with people they do not know. Other people may want people to be afraid of them; they may try to dominate and control others. Fear and aggression are two of the basic emotions that we experience. It is easy to give in to our basic emotions and either become submissive or aggressive when we feel stressed. Assertion is an advanced skill that involves controlling the basic emotions involved in running away or fighting. Assertion involves a mental attitude of trying to negotiate, trying to solve problems rather than giving in to emotional impulses.

Key concept

assertion is different from both submission and aggression. Assertion involves being able to negotiate a solution to a problem.

Winning and losing

During an argument, people who are aggressive might demand that they are right and others are wrong. They will want to win while others lose. To be weak or submissive is the opposite of being aggressive. Submissive people accept that they will lose, get told off, or be put down. Assertive behaviour is different from both of these responses. In an argument an assertive person will try to reach a solution in which no one has to lose or be 'put down'. Assertion is a skill which facilitates 'win-win' situations – no one has to be the loser. For example, consider the situation illustrated in Figure 2.14 in which a service user is angry because of the carer's late arrival.

Assertive skills can help enable carers to cope

The aggressive response meets the needs of the carer and not the service user. The service user is kept vulnerable: 'I win you lose.'

The assertive response is aimed at meeting the needs of both the carer and the service user: 'We both win.'

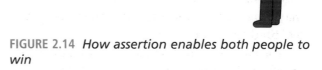

The submissive response meets the needs of the service user and not the carer. The service user may dominate the carer: 'You win I lose.'

FIGURE 2.14 *How assertion enables both people to win*

with difficult and challenging situations. To be assertive a person usually has to:

* understand the situation – including the facts, details and other people's perceptions
* be able to control personal emotions and stay calm
* be able to act assertively using the right non-verbal behaviour
* be able to act assertively using the right words and statements.

Some verbal and non-verbal behaviours involved in assertion are summarised in Figure 2.15.

Aggressive behaviour	Assertive behaviour	Submissive behaviour
Main emotion: anger	*Main emotion*: staying in control of own actions	*Main emotion*: fear
Wanting your own way	Negotiating with others	Letting others win
Making demands	Trying to solve problems	Agreeing with others
Not listening to others	Aiming for no one to lose	Not putting your views across
Putting other people down	Listening to others	Looking afraid
Trying to win	Showing respect for others	Speaking quietly or not speaking at all
Shouting or talking very loudly	Keeping a clear, calm voice	
Threatening non-verbal behaviour including: fixed eye contact, tense muscles, waving or folding hands and arms, looking angry	**Normal non-verbal behaviour** including: varied eye contact, relaxed face muscles, looking 'in control', keeping hands and arms at your side	**Submissive non-verbal behaviour** including: looking down, not looking at others, looking frightened, tense muscles

FIGURE 2.15 *Aggressive, assertive and submissive behaviours*

Environmental conditions

It is very hard to hear what someone is saying if there is a great deal of background noise. It is also very difficult to make sense of other people's facial expressions if you cannot see their face properly due to poor lighting. A group of people might not see each other comfortably in rooms that have awkward seating positions. People sometimes feel uncomfortable if they are trying to communicate with a person who is too close or at a distance. A room that is too hot, or stuffy or cold may inhibit communication, if it makes people feel tired or stressed.

The environment also plays an important role in influencing the effectiveness of aids for communication. For instance, hearing aids will amplify background noise as well as the voice of the speaker. A noisy environment may therefore make the situation more difficult and unpleasant for someone who is using a hearing aid than for someone who does not use one. Good lighting will be critical for those who lip-read to support their understanding of speech, whereas the quality of lighting may not be quite as important for someone with good hearing.

Special situations and systems

Many service users will have specific communication needs. It may be important that service users employ an interpreter if they use a different language such as BSL. Some carers learn to use communication systems such as Makaton, in order to help them communicate with service users.

Hayman (1998) notes the following points for communicating with people with hearing impairments:

* make sure the person can see you clearly
* face both the light and the person at all times
* include the person in your conversation
* do not obscure your mouth
* speak clearly and slowly. Repeat if necessary, but you may need to rephrase your words
* do not shout into a person's ear or hearing aid
* minimise background noise
* use your eyes, facial expressions and hand gestures, where appropriate.

If people have limited vision it may be important that carers use language to describe issues that a sighted person might take for granted, such as non-verbal communication or the context of certain comments. Touch may be an important aspect of communication. Some registered blind people can work out what you look like if they touch your face (to build an understanding of your features).

It is always important to choose the right style of language when communicating with people from different language communities.

The content of communication

Unless you find yourself communicating in an emergency situation, most communication will involve some 'small talk' or relationship-building conversation at the beginning of an interaction. It is usually important to feel at ease and to put other people at ease during an interaction. When a lengthy conversation or interaction ends, it is usually important to leave on a positive emotional note; in most conversations this involves further 'small talk' or personal discussion that is not connected with the business of the conversation.

Some interactions are purely about social, emotional and relationship-building work.

When people meet together in family groups, or when friends meet in clubs, the purpose of communication may be to build emotional bonds or relationships. The whole content of the communication may be 'small talk' because it is the act of being together that is important, not the content of the communication.

Think it over...

Think about some instances when you have chatted to friends or relatives. If somebody had asked you 15 minutes later what you talked about, could you have remembered? Might you have said, 'I don't know we just talked – but it was enjoyable'?

Some communication is just about relationship building, but other communication is task-focused. When there is some business to resolve or a decision to be made, this is likely to form the 'serious' or task-focused content of communication. Task-focused communication should take place in-between social small talk if you are behaving in an unhurried and supportive way. Task-focused communication is likely to involve asking for information, giving information and using skills such as asking questions, and clarifying other people's answers.

Sometimes the content of communication will focus on major emotional issues. Service users might share their worries or feelings of anger or grief with you. When the content of communication focuses on issues that have great emotional significance for a service user it would be important to use advanced listening skills. Issues about self-esteem, trust and empathy will be very important when the content of communication focuses on emotional needs.

Some conversations are predictable. If you are going out with friends, for example, you might expect conversation to be mainly about relationship building. If you are attending a formal meeting with an agenda, on the other hand, then there will almost certainly be task-focused content to people's conversation. If you were working as a counsellor you might expect communication to address emotional issues. But sometimes in care settings, a service user might start with small talk or even task-focused discussion that then leads on to major emotional content. For example, an older service user might start a conversation by complimenting you on your appearance and then ask for your advice on some shopping that he or she wants, before reminiscing about the loss of a partner. You might need to change your style of response as the content of the conversation changes. It is not always possible to predict the content of an interaction in advance.

Summary

The foundation for conveying to others that you are a supportive care worker is to believe in, and work from, a set of values. It is vitally important that you value diversity and can identify the influence of cultural context on communication.

If you do not respect service users' rights, including their right to confidentiality, they are likely to feel threatened by your behaviour.

It is also important that you can identify the role of the following factors in influencing communication:

* emotion
* the importance of positioning
* environmental conditions
* special communication needs.

In order to earn extra pocket money, Zoe, who has never had any professional training, does some babysitting during the day with 10-month-old Mark. Zoe likes children but is 'addicted' to day-time TV 'soaps'. Zoe plays with Mark for a little while, but as soon as her favourite programme begins, she straps Mark into his pushchair in the hope that he will go to sleep if she ignores him.

Zana is a professional early years worker. Zana is focused on the need to work within a professional value system. When Mark makes sounds Zana will respond to him by speaking in a high-pitched tone, designed to attract his interest. Zana spends time smiling at Mark and talking to him to build a relationship with him.

Zana sees the purpose of her work as meeting Mark's needs, which include emotional and intellectual developmental needs. Mark has a right to appropriate communication and to be valued as an individual.

Using theory – can you identify?
Why Zoe does not understand the importance of responding to Mark and not ignoring him.

Using theory – can you explain?
Why Zana is a much better carer. Can you analyse how using care values might make her more responsive to Mark?

Using theory – can you evaluate?
Why it is important that care workers are sensitive to the rights of service users.

Section 3: Communication skills

Formal and informal communication in care

Speaking is about much more than just communicating information between people. For a start, many people may speak with different degrees of formality or informality. The degree of formality or informality is called the language 'register'.

For example, suppose you went into a hospital reception. You might expect the person on duty to greet you with a formal response such as, 'Good morning, how can I help you?' An informal greeting (typically used by white males in the South-east of England) might be 'Hello mate what's up then?' or 'How's it going?' It is possible that some people might prefer the informal greeting; this could put you at ease and make you feel that the receptionist is like you. But in many situations, the informal greeting might result in people feeling that they are not being respected.

The degree of formality or informality establishes a context. At a hospital reception you are unlikely to want to spend time making friends and chatting things over with the receptionist. You may be seeking urgent help. Your expectations of the situation might be that you want to be taken seriously and put in touch with professional services as soon as possible. You might see the situation as a very formal encounter.

If you are treated informally, you may interpret this as not being treated seriously, or in other words 'not being respected'.

Speech communities

Another issue is that informal speech is very likely to identify a specific speech community. Different localities, ethnic groups, professions and work cultures all have their own special words, phrases and speech patterns. An elderly middle-class woman is very unlikely to start a conversation with the words 'Hello mate'. Some service users may feel threatened or excluded by the kind of language they encounter. However, just using formal language will not solve this problem. The technical terminology used by social care workers may also create barriers for people who are not part of that 'speech community'.

Think it over...

Consider the following conversation.

Service user: I come about getting some help around the house, you know, 'cause it's getting 'ard' nowadays, what with me back an' everything.

Service worker: Well you need to speak to the Community Domiciliary Support Liaison Officer, who can arrange an assessment in accordance with our statutory obligations.

1. The two statements above use different levels of formality, but they also represent speech from different 'speech communities'. Can you work out what each person is saying?

2. How do you think the service user will feel given such a response? Will the service user feel respected and valued?

Professional relationships

People who are good at communication and assertive skills are likely to be good at building social relationships. Professional relationships may be regarded as different from ordinary social relationships and friendships because:

* professionals must work within a framework of values

* professional work always involves a duty of care for the welfare of service users (see Section 1.2 on rights)

* professional relationships involve establishing appropriate boundaries.

A boundary is a line that must not be crossed. In care work the metaphor of a boundary means that there are limits to the degree of emotional involvement and commitment within a relationship. Although professionals care about what happens to service users they do not form an emotional bond in the way that parents and children do.

Tone of voice

Tone involves the way our voice resonates as we speak. It is not just what we say, but the way that we say it. If we talk quickly in a loud voice with a fixed voice tone, people may perceive that we are angry. In most UK-contexts, a calm, slow voice with varying tone may send a message of being friendly. A sharp tone may be associated with angry or complaining behaviour. A flat tone might be associated with exhaustion or depression. A faint tone might be associated with submissive behaviour.

Pace of speech

Bostrom (1997) states that announcers (such as radio or TV presenters) speak at a rate of between 100 and 125 words per minute; this pace of speech might represent the ideal for explaining information. A great deal of speech is used to express emotional reaction rather than simply explaining issues to an audience. A faster pace of speech might indicate that the speaker is excited, anxious, agitated, nervous, angry or seeking to impress or dominate the listener. Alternatively, a fast pace of speech might simply mean that the speaker is in a hurry. Exactly what a fast pace of speech means can only be worked out by interpreting other non-verbal body language and the cultural context and situation of the speaker. Individuals who wave their arms, wide-eyed and smiling, talking rapidly about exam results might be interpreted as being excited at the news of having done well.

A slow pace of speech can indicate sadness or depression. Slow speech may sometimes be associated with impairment of thought processes, or might indicate tiredness or boredom. Slow emphasised speech might be used to convey dominance or hostility. Sometimes slow speech can indicate attraction, love and affection between individuals who know each other. Once again, this aspect of communication can only be interpreted once the non-verbal, social, cultural and practical context of the conversation have been understood.

In formal communication work – for example, if you were meeting people at an information desk or hospital reception – it might be important to maintain a normal pace of speech. This is because your work might focus on the formal exchange of information. Informal situations often involve a need to communicate emotions: for example, talking to a service user you know well. In this situation you might want to speak faster or slower to communicate your emotions clearly.

Eye contact

We can guess the feelings and thoughts that another person has by looking at their eyes. One poet called the eye 'the window of the soul'. We can sometimes understand the thoughts and feelings of another person by eye-to-eye contact. Our eyes get wider when we are excited, attracted to, or interested in someone else. A fixed stare may send the message that someone is angry. In European culture, looking away is often interpreted as being bored or not interested.

Body language

When we meet and talk with people, we will usually use two language systems: a verbal or spoken language and non-verbal or body language. Effective communication in care work requires care workers to be able to analyse their own and other people's non-verbal behaviour. Our body sends messages to other people – sometimes unconsciously. Some of the most important body areas that send messages are shown in Figure 2.16.

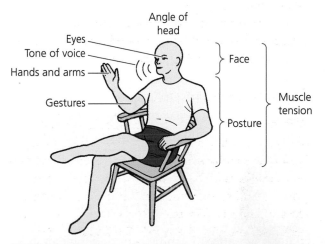

FIGURE 2.16 *Areas of the body that we use in communication*

body language is the way we use our bodies to communicate messages to other people. People communicate using words and also by using body language.

Facial expression represents a very important component of body language. The face can send very complex messages and we can read them easily – even in diagrammatic form.

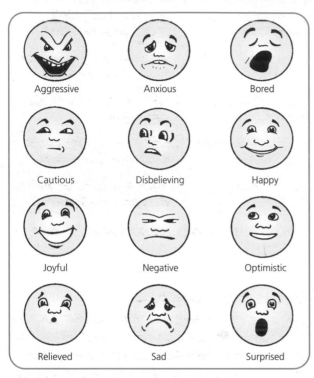

FIGURE 2.17 *The face expresses emotion*

Our face often indicates our emotional state. When individuals are sad they may signal this emotion with eyes that look down; there may be tension in their face and their mouth will be closed. Their shoulder muscles are likely to be relaxed but their face and neck may show tension. A happy person will have 'wide eyes' that make contact with you and a smiling face. When people are excited they may move their arms and hands to signal their excitement.

The way we sit or stand can send messages. Body language includes the posture that a person takes. Sitting with crossed arms can mean 'I'm not taking any notice'. Leaning can send the message that you are relaxed or bored. Leaning forward

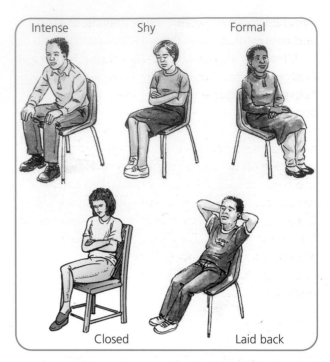

FIGURE 2.18 *Body postures that send out messages*

can show interest. See Figure 2.18 for illustrations of body postures and the messages they send.

Body language includes the movement of the body. The way we walk, move our head, sit, cross our legs and so on, send messages about whether we are tired, happy, sad or bored.

Muscle tension represents another aspect of body language. The tension in our feet, hands and fingers can tell others how relaxed or how tense we are. When we are very tense our shoulders might stiffen, our face muscles might tighten and we might sit or stand rigidly. Our mouths might be firmly closed and our lips and jaws tightly

FIGURE 2.19 *Gestures are important in communicating effectively*

clenched. A tense person might breathe quickly and become hot.

Our body also sends messages through gestures. Gestures are hand and arm movements that can help us to understand what a person is saying. Some gestures carry a meaning of their own.

The way in which we touch or avoid touching another person communicates important messages. Touching another person can send messages of care, affection, power over them, or sexual interest. The social setting and other body language usually help people to understand what touch might mean. Carers should not make assumptions about touch. Even holding someone's hand might be seen as trying to dominate them!

Clarifying

A central skill of all caring work is the ability to understand the thoughts and feelings of other people. An explanation of how to use the **communication cycle** to build an understanding is given in the next section. You may build an understanding of another person's thoughts by clarifying what he or she may have said. One way to seek clarification is to paraphrase or put what you think a person has said into your own words. Another way is to use open questions, probes or prompts in order to help build your understanding.

Some questions, which do not really encourage people to talk, or to clarify what they think, are called closed questions. For example, 'How old are you?' is a 'closed' question because there is only one, right, simple answer the person can give: 'I'm 84', and so on. Similarly, 'Do you like butter?' and 'Are you feeling well today?' are closed questions, as the person can only reply 'yes' or 'no.' Closed questions do not lead on to discussion.

Open questions are 'open' for discussion. Instead of giving a yes or no answer, the person is encouraged to think and discuss his or her thoughts and feelings. A question such as 'How do you feel about the food here?' means that the other person has to think about the food and then discuss it.

Open questions help to keep the conversation going. Sometimes closed questions can block a conversation and cause it to stop.

In some formal conversations it can be important to clarify a defined issue by asking direct closed questions; but the best way to ask closed questions is to ask open questions beforehand. There is an old saying that if you really want to find out what someone else thinks then, 'Every closed question should start life as an open one'. See Figure 2.20 for some examples of open and closed questions.

CLOSED QUESTION	OPEN QUESTION
Do you like your teacher?	What do you think about your teacher?
Is the food good in here?	What would you say the food is like here?
Do you like rock music?	What kind of music do you enjoy?
Do you sometimes feel lonely?	How do you feel about living on your own?
Do you enjoy drawing?	What are your favourite activities in school?

FIGURE 2.20 *Open and closed questions – some examples*

Probes and prompts

A probe is a very short question, such as 'Can you tell me more?' This kind of short question usually follows on from an answer that the other person has given. Probes are used to 'dig deeper' into the person's answer; they probe or investigate what the other person just said.

Prompts are short questions or words, which you offer to the other person in order to prompt them to answer. Questions such as 'So was it enjoyable or not?' or 'Would you do it again?' might prompt people to keep talking and clarify their thoughts. Sometimes a prompt might just be a suggested answer; for example, 'More than 50?' might be a prompt if you had just asked how many service users a carer worked with in a year and he or she seemed uncertain.

Probes and prompts are both useful techniques to help achieve a clearer understanding of another person's thoughts.

Some ideas that might help to clarify issues in a conversation include:

* use short periods of silence to prompt the other person to talk

* paraphrase or reflect back what the other person has said so that they will confirm that you have understood him or her

* ask open questions

* use probes and prompts to follow-up your questions.

Summarising

Summarising means to sum-up what has been said. It is a very important technique within group discussion, as creating a summary of what has been said may help to keep the group focused on their work. Summarising is also an important skill used in formal conversations, where information is to be written down; and it is important that people involved in the conversation agree about what is to be written. The ability to summarise requires a good memory and the ability to extract the important points in a conversation. Summarising is different from paraphrasing in that it results in a **synopsis** of a range of material rather than seeking to clarify a point.

Paraphrasing

Paraphrasing means to express the same meaning in other words. If you can use your own words to reflect back what another person has said then you are paraphrasing that individual's speech. It is very important to reflect back what another person has said, because this demonstrates that you have listened and built an understanding of their views. Paraphrasing is an important part of listening (see next section).

Empathising

Key concept

empathy has been defined by Gerard Egan (1986) as 'the ability to enter into and understand the world of another person and communicate this understanding to him or her.'

At a deep level, empathy comes about within a relationship where one person has a deep understanding that involves both intellectual and emotional understanding of another person. Person-centred counsellors try to develop this deep level of empathy as a way of working, or indeed, a 'way of being' when they work with people.

Egan (1986) argues that the term 'empathy' can also be used to identify a communication skill – the skill of communicating an accurate understanding of the feelings and thoughts of another person. As a communication skill, empathy might involve a more superficial or short-term relationship than might be expected in professional counselling. Empathy as communication still involves the ability to understand the world of another person and the feelings that he or she has.

Empathising with another person is a skill based on **active listening**. Empathy may grow out of the ability to understand the thoughts and feelings of another person. But empathy is not a behavioural skill that can be defined in terms of a series of non-verbal and verbal components. Empathising identifies a caring attitude, where an individual person can see beyond his or her own assumptions about the world; and can imagine the thought and feelings of someone who is quite different. Many people have difficulty imagining the experiences of other people. The ability to empathise is the ability to see beyond assumptions that you have grown up with. Burnard and Morrison (1997) state 'caring and communicating are inseparably linked. You cannot hope to communicate effectively if you do not care about the person on the receiving end. You only have to study some of the 'professional communicators' whom we find in shops and offices to establish this point. The use of the term empathy might be used to identify the complex emotional and intellectual skill that lies at the heart of a genuine caring attitude.

Minimising communication barriers

Communication can become blocked if individual differences are not understood. There are three main ways that communication becomes blocked, as shown in Figure 2.21.

Examples of the first kind of block, where people do not receive the communication, include

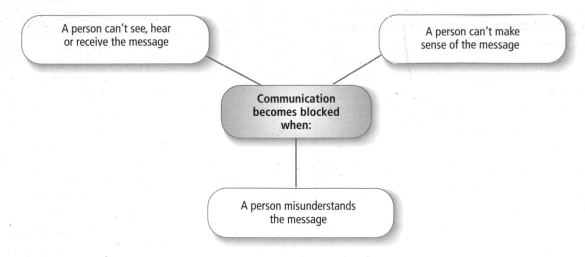

FIGURE 2.21 *Ways in which communication is blocked*

visual disabilities, hearing disabilities, environmental problems such as poor lighting and noisy environments, and speaking from too far away. See Figure 2.22.

> ### Key concept
>
> *barriers* that may block understanding need to be identified in order for effective communication to take place. Barriers can exist at a physical and sensory level, at the level of making sense of a message and at a cultural and social context level where the meaning of a message may be misunderstood.

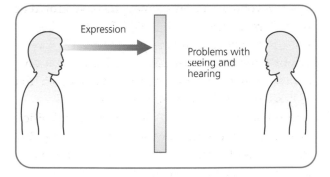

FIGURE 2.22 *Problems such as noise and poor light can create communication barriers*

Examples of situations in which people may not be able to make sense of the message include:

* the use of different languages, including signed languages

* the use of different terms in language, such as jargon (technical language), slang (different people using different terms), or dialect (people using different sounds to say the same words)

* physical and intellectual disabilities, such as dysphasia (difficulties with language expression or understanding), aphasia (an absence of language ability), being ill, or suffering memory loss or learning difficulty.

Reasons for misunderstanding a message include:

* cultural influences – cultures that are different from our own interpret non-verbal and verbal messages and humour, in different ways

* assumptions about people – race, gender, disability and other groupings

* labelling or stereotyping of others

* social context – statements and behaviour that are understood by friends and family may not be understood by strangers

* emotional barriers – a worker's own emotional needs may stop him or her wanting to know about others

* time pressures – mean that staff may withdraw from wanting to know about others

* emotional differences – these can sometimes be interpreted as personality clashes, or personality differences. Very angry, or very happy, or very shy people may misinterpret communication from others.

MINIMISING BARRIERS TO COMMUNICATION	
Visual disability	✳ Use language to describe things. ✳ Assist people to touch things (e.g. touch your face to recognise you). ✳ Explain details that sighted people might take for granted. ✳ Check what people can see (many registered blind people can see shapes, or tell light from dark). ✳ Explore technological aids such as information technology that can expand visual images. ✳ Check glasses, other aids and equipment.
Hearing disability	✳ Do not shout, keep to normal clear speech and make sure your face is visible for people who can lip-read. ✳ Show pictures, or write messages. ✳ Learn to sign (for people who use signed languages). ✳ Ask for help from, or employ a communicator or interpreter for signed languages. ✳ Check that technological aids, such as hearing aids, are working.
Environmental constraints	✳ Check and improve lighting. ✳ Reduce noise. ✳ Move to a quieter or better-lit room. ✳ Move to smaller groups to see and hear more easily. ✳ Check seating arrangements.
Language differences	✳ Communicate using pictures, diagrams and non-verbal signs. ✳ Use translators or interpreters. ✳ Be careful not to make assumptions or stereotype. ✳ Increase your knowledge of jargon, slang and dialects. ✳ Re-word your messages – find different ways of saying things appropriate to the service user's 'speech community'. ✳ Check your level of formality; speak in short, clear sentences if appropriate.
Intellectual disabilities	✳ Increase your knowledge of disabilities. ✳ Use pictures and signs as well as clear, simple speech. ✳ Be calm and patient. ✳ Set up group meetings where people can share interests, experiences or reminiscences. ✳ Check that people do not become isolated. ✳ Use advocates – independent people who can spend time building an understanding of the needs of specific individuals to assist with communication work.
Preventing misunderstandings based on cultural differences	✳ Try to increase your knowledge of cultures and speech communities that are different from your own. ✳ Watch out for differing cultural interpretations. ✳ Avoid making assumptions about, or discriminating against, people who are different from yourself ✳ Use active listening techniques to check that your understanding is correct. ✳ Stay calm and try to create a calm atmosphere. ✳ Be sensitive to different social settings and the form of communication that would be most appropriate in different contexts. ✳ Check your work with advocates who will try to represent the best interests of the people that you are working with.

FIGURE 2.23 *How to minimise barriers to communication*

In order to minimise communication barriers it will be important to learn as much as possible about others. People may have 'preferred forms of interaction'. This may include a reliance on non-verbal messages, sign language, lip-reading, use of description, slang phrases, choice of room or location for a conversation, and so on. Everyone has communication needs of some kind.

Figure 2.23 lists some ideas for minimising barriers to communication.

Valuing people as individuals

The psychologist Abraham Maslow (1970) explained human needs in terms of five levels. Barriers to communication might block human need as shown in Figure 2.24.

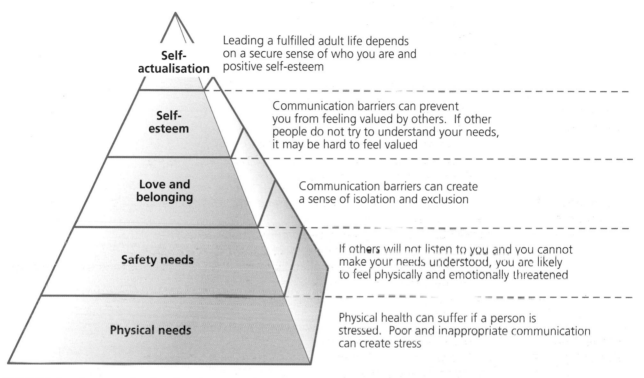

FIGURE 2.24 *Communication barriers can damage a person's quality of life (Maslow, 1970)*

Summary

This section has explored a range of skills that include:

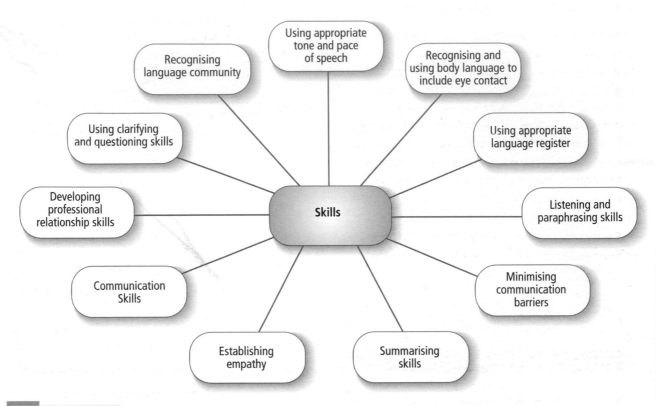

Skills:
- Using appropriate tone and pace of speech
- Recognising language community
- Recognising and using body language to include eye contact
- Using clarifying and questioning skills
- Using appropriate language register
- Developing professional relationship skills
- Listening and paraphrasing skills
- Communication Skills
- Minimising communication barriers
- Establishing empathy
- Summarising skills

Consider this

Chloe works at a day nursery. Parents sometimes make an appointment to see the nursery and to talk to the staff in order to decide whether the nursery would be appropriate for their children. Chloe expects to meet some parents in order to show them around the nursery and talk about the work they do. These parents do not live locally, and are from different ethnic and age groups to Chloe. Both parents have well-paid professional jobs.

Using theory – can you identify?
1. What communication skills Chloe is likely to need in order to provide an appropriate welcome and to clearly explain the work of the nursery.

2. What barriers to communication Chloe should be prepared for as she takes the parents around the nursery.

Using theory – can you analyse?
How could Chloe know whether she was communicating clearly and effectively with the parents. How could Chloe know if she was successful at providing a warm and friendly welcome.

Can you evaluate – using a range of theory?
Chloe feels confident that she was highly skilled at holding the conversation with the parents. As she remembers how the conversation went, she can check what she did using the range of theory in this section. Can you imagine how you could use a range of concepts in order to judge the value of a conversation you have had.

Section 4: Theories relating to communication

The structure of interaction

When we talk to people we have to start the conversation off. Usually we start with a greeting or ask how someone is. Conversations have a beginning, a middle and an end. We have to create the right kind of atmosphere for a conversation at the beginning. We might need to help someone relax. We might need to show that we are friendly and relaxed. We then have the conversation. When we end the conversation we usually say something like 'See you soon'. When we end a conversation we have to leave the other person with the right feelings about what we have said. Figure 2.25 illustrates this structure.

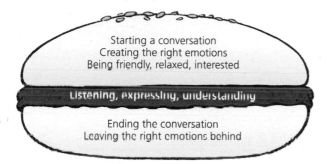

FIGURE 2.25 *The conversation sandwich: beginning, middle and end*

Listening skills and the communication cycle

When we communicate with other people we become involved in a process of expressing our own thoughts and interpreting the other person's understanding of what we are communicating. This process should usually involve the steps set out in figure 2.26.

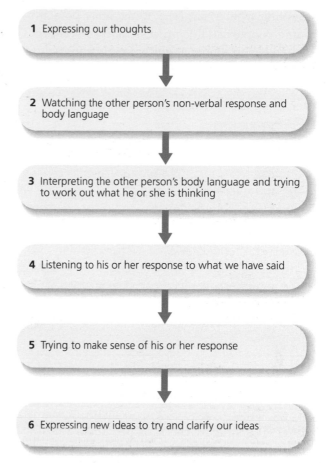

1 Expressing our thoughts

2 Watching the other person's non-verbal response and body language

3 Interpreting the other person's body language and trying to work out what he or she is thinking

4 Listening to his or her response to what we have said

5 Trying to make sense of his or her response

6 Expressing new ideas to try and clarify our ideas

FIGURE 2.27 *The process of expression and interpretation*

Communication needs to be a two-way process whereby each person attempts to understand the viewpoint of the other. The **communication cycle** requires professionals (at least) to have advanced listening skills and the ability to check their understanding of others' responses. See Figure 2.26.

Listening is not the same as hearing the sounds people make when they talk. Listening involves hearing another person's words, then thinking about what they mean, and then

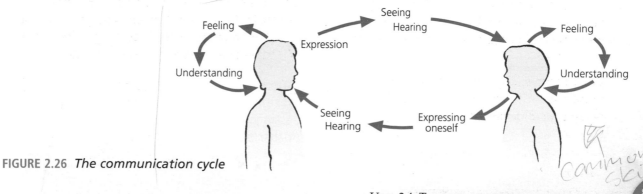

FIGURE 2.26 *The communication cycle*

thinking what to say back to the other person. Some people call this process **'active listening'**. As well as thinking carefully in remembering what someone has said, good listeners will also make sure their non-verbal communication demonstrates interest in the other person.

Key concept

active listening involves more than hearing, it also involves using the communication cycle and the ability to demonstrate what you have understood when you listen to another person.

Gerard Egan (1986) states that 'the goal of listening is understanding'. Active listening involves more than hearing, it also involves using the communication cycle and being able to demonstrate what you have understood when you listen to another person.

It is usually easier to understand people who are similar to ourselves. We can learn about different people by checking our understanding of what we have heard.

Checking our understanding involves hearing what the other person says and asking the other person questions. Another way to check our understanding is to put what a person has just said into our own words and to say this back to them. This technique is called paraphrasing; this enables us to find out whether or not we understood what another person said.

When we listen to complicated details of other people's lives, we often begin to form mental pictures based on what they are telling us. Listening skills involve checking these mental pictures to make sure that we understand correctly. It can be very difficult to remember

Skilled active listening involves:

1. Looking interested and ready to listen
2. Hearing what is said
3. Remembering what is said
4. Checking understanding with the other person

things accurately if we don't check how our ideas are developing.

Good listening involves thinking about what we hear while we are listening and checking our understanding as the conversation goes along. Sometimes this idea of checking our understanding is called 'reflection' because we reflect on the other person's ideas.

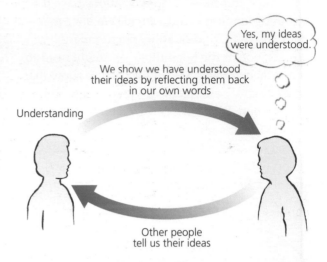

FIGURE 2.28 *Reflection is an important part of understanding*

SOLER principles

Egan (1986) argues that there are some basic **'micro skills'** that can help to create a sense of involvement or caring presence when working with another person. Egan defines these skills, as explained in Figure 2.29.

Think it over...

Egan's five SOLER principles were based on his experience of North American culture.

How far do you believe each of these five principles works within different cultural contexts within the UK? You could experiment by videoing a conversation between two students using the SOLER principles and videoing a conversation that did not use all of the SOLER principles. Students could then rate each conversation in order to find out how important the principles are within their cultural assumptions about interpreting non-verbal behaviour.

SOLER	
KEY IDEA	**EXPLANATION**
S: Face squarely	Egan states: 'In North American culture, facing another person squarely is often considered a basic posture of involvement... What is important is that the bodily orientation you adopt conveys the message that you are involved with the client. If, for any reason, facing a person squarely is too threatening, then an angled position may be called for. The point is the quality of your attention.' The key issue is that you have to face other people in a way that shows that you feel involved.
O: Keep an open posture	Egan says: 'In North American culture an open posture is generally seen as non defensive.' Crossed arms or legs might send a message that you do not feel involved with the person you're talking to. An open posture involves not crossing arms or legs (see Figure 2.18).
L: lean	Egan states: 'In North American culture a slight inclination towards a person is often interpreted as saying, I'm with you; I'm interested in you and what you have to say.' A degree of movement may help to convey interest in another person.
E: Use good eye contact	Egan argues that: 'Maintaining a good eye contact with a client is another way of saying I'm with you.' Steady but varied eye contact is associated with deep conversation within a North American cultural context.
R: Be relaxed	Egan argues that it is important not to fidget, and important to feel comfortable and relaxed with your own non-verbal behaviour.

FIGURE 2.29 *Skills that can help to create a sense of involvement or caring presence (Egan, 1986)*

Egan proposes the principles given in Figure 2.29 as guidelines to help with learning how to look like a caring person. He emphasised the importance of cultural context and that the SOLER rules should not be used rigidly. Egan states: 'These 'rules' should be followed cautiously. People differ both individually and culturally in the ways in which they show attentiveness.' The important issue is that your non-verbal behaviour comes across to another person as meaning that you are interested and involved with them.

Group structures

In everyday language, 'group' can mean a collection or set of things, so any collection of people could be counted as a group. For example, a group of people might be waiting to cross the road. They are a group in the everyday sense of the word but not in the special sense of 'group' that is often used in care work.

Think it over...

Can you remember back to the time you first joined the student group that you are doing this course with? How does it feel if you have to mix with new people? Did you feel stressed in any way if you had to work with people you had not met before?

What sort of experience is involved in communicating with new people and what does it feel like as people within a group get to know one another?

Use your memory of your own experience to interpret some of the theory below.

Working with a group is usually taken to imply that the individuals identify themselves as belonging to a group. Groups have a sense of belonging that gives the members a 'group feeling'. This could be described as a group identity.

Social scientists sometimes use the term '**primary group**' and '**secondary group**'. The term 'secondary group' is used when people simply have something in common with each other.

Primary groups usually share the following features:

* people know each other
* there is a 'feeling of belonging' shared by people in the group
* people have a common purpose or reason for coming together
* people share a set of beliefs or norms.

How do people get to know each other and develop a sense of belonging, common purpose and norms? Some researchers claim that there is a pattern to the way the communication develops in group formation.

Theories of group formation

Tuckman's sequential theory

The way in which people come together in a group can be understood as involving stages. Tuckman (1965) analysed around 50 studies on group development and concluded that groups generally go through a process of development that can be identified as four stages: Forming, Storming, Norming and Performing. In 1977 Tuckman and Jensen identified a fifth stage of Adjourning in order to describe the process of ending a group. Tuckman's stage (sequence) theory is one of the best known and most quoted theories. Johnson and Johnson (1997) state, 'Of all the sequential stage theories Tuckman's emphasis on forming, storming, norming, performing, and adjourning still seems the most useful and creates the most interest.'

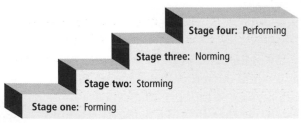

FIGURE 2.30 *Tuckman's four stages of group formation*

An outline explanation of group formation is given in Figure 2.31.

GROUP FORMATION	
Stage 1: Forming	When people first get together there is likely to be an introductory stage. People may be unsure about why they are attending a meeting. The purpose of the group may not be clear. People may have little commitment to the group and there may be no clear value system. Stereotyping and prejudice may be expressed.
Stage 2: Storming	There may be 'power struggles' within the group. Different individuals may contest each other for leadership of the group. There may be arguments about how the group should work, who should do tasks, and so on. Groups can fail at this stage and individuals can decide to drop out because they do not feel comfortable with other people in the group. Teams might split into sub-groups who refuse to communicate with each other if they become stuck in the storming stage.
Stage 3: Norming	At this stage group members develop a set of common beliefs and values. People are likely to begin to trust each other and develop clear roles. Norms are shared expectations which group members have of each other. Norms enable people to work together as a group.
Stage 4: Performing	Because people share the same values and norms the group can perform tasks effectively. People may feel that they are comfortable and belong in the group. There may be a sense of high **morale**.
Stage 5: Adjourning	The group has to conclude their activities and find an acceptable way for group members to part. The group has to complete and end the existence of the group's identity.

FIGURE 2.31 *An outline explanation of group formation (Tuckman, 1965 and 1977)*

Key concept

group norms For a group to perform effectively, group members will need to share a common system of beliefs, values or norms relevant to the purpose of the group. It may be very important to identify the extent to which a group does share a common set of beliefs and norms when observing a group or planning to run an activity.

Non-sequential theories

When people get together to create a group – such as a new student group – they may recognise Tuckman's stages described above. However, it may not always be the case that the stages are clear cut. If you were to join a group of carers or nurses working in health or social care you might not be aware of any stages. Some groups of people do not all come together at the same time. Some theorists identify general processes within a group rather than focusing on stage theories of group formation.

Bales (1970) put forward a theory of 'task and maintenance' activity within the group. Primary groups need to have a purpose; a student group, for example, might have the purpose of achieving their qualification. A group of nurses might have the purpose of providing quality health care. But working together with other people is a social activity. People cannot just concentrate on the work as if they were machines; they need to feel that they belong and that other people in the group respect them. Sometimes tensions need to be relieved with humour. Bales argued that there needs to be a balance between the practical work of achieving a task and the social needs of group members. Bales suggested that observers could understand and analyse what was happening in a group by using an **interaction analysis** of an individual member's behaviour. Such an analysis might enable the observer to understand how a group was moving between the focus on task activity and a focus on social activity. An interaction analysis involves classifying the way people behave using defined categories. Bales' categories are outlined in Figure 2.32.

PROCESSES WITHIN A GROUP	
Group task	✳ Gives suggestion (including taking the lead) ✳ Gives opinion (including feelings and wishes) ✳ Gives information (including clarifying and confirming) ✳ Asks for information ✳ Asks for opinion ✳ Asks for suggestion
Group maintenance (called 'Social-emotional area' by Bales)	✳ Seems friendly ✳ Dramatises ✳ Agrees ✳ Disagrees ✳ Shows tension ✳ Seems unfriendly

FIGURE 2.32 *Bales' 'task and maintenance' categories*

Think it over...

In a group of five or six people, take four matchsticks each and agree on a topic for group discussion. Next, agree the following rules for the discussion.

✳ Only one person may speak at a time.

✳ Whenever that person speaks, he or she must place a matchstick on the floor.

✳ When people run out of matchsticks they cannot say anything.

✳ No one may say anything unless others have finished.

✳ Non-verbal communication is allowed.

✳ People should not speak for more than one minute.

This exercise should emphasise the importance of group maintenance activity. The 'match stick game' can make people very focused on the task to the exclusion of much of the social maintenance activity. So being in the group might make you feel awkward or tense.

	1	2	3	4	5	6	7	8	9	10
Group task										
Starting discussion										
Giving information										
Asking for information										
Clarifying discussion										
Summarising discussion										
Group maintenance										
Humour										
Expressing group feelings										
Including others										
Being supportive										

FIGURE 2.33 *Grid to categorise the task and maintenance behaviours occurring in groups*

Using categories can be a useful way of gaining an insight into how an individual is influencing the work and the emotional maintenance or feeling involved in group communication. It is possible to design a grid that can be used 'minute by minute' to try to categorise the task and maintenance behaviours occurring in groups. An example is suggested in Figure 2.33.

Burnard's group dynamics

Burnard (1996) identifies the importance of Tuckman's theory of stages to explain group formation, but then points out the importance of identifying some of the processes that can happen as groups work together. A summary of the categories that Burnard identifies is set out in Figure 2.34.

Thompson's theory of defensive versus supportive communication

Thompson (1986) identified a range of issues that may result in people feeling that they are being attacked or being supported. These issues may be equally important in one-to-one communication, as in group settings. The value in exploring this theory is that it provides another way of monitoring the effect we may be having on others when we try to communicate. See Figure 2.35.

> **Think it over...**
>
> Do you ever watch 'reality TV', i.e. programmes in which a group of people are observed over a period of time? The people who are observed usually have to work with one another in order to perform certain tasks. Next time you watch such a programme, see if you can spot any of the group dynamics listed in Figure 2.34.

GROUP DYNAMIC	EXPLANATION
Pairing	Sometimes two people will choose to work together and ignore other members of the group. Sometimes people conduct a discussion with just one other person and other people are left out. These behaviours can disrupt a group and may create problems for group cohesion (feeling of belonging).
Scapegoating	A 'scapegoat' is someone who is 'picked-on' or 'attacked' by other people. When people feel threatened or unhappy they may 'take it out' on someone who appears to be an appropriate target. Again, this behaviour will disrupt group cohesion and will need to be challenged.
Projecting	Projecting occurs when a person places his or her own feelings on to the whole group. To quote Burnard's example, a person who is feeling anxious might say 'this is a very tense group' even though everyone else is relaxed. Another kind of projection occurs when the group projects their emotions onto an issue. Burnard describes an example of this as 'having a group moan' whereby the group describes how awful its problems are, but the issues are emotional rather than real.
Forming a 'league of gentlemen'	This term is used to describe a sub-group of 'hostile and often sarcastic' people 'whose aim is to make life in the group difficult'. It is important to understand this term as a metaphor; both men and women can form sub-groups that seek to wreck group cohesion and they are unlikely to be 'gentle'. Burnard points out that it is important to deal with such a sub-group as soon as possible.
Wrecking	This is when an individual person attempts to sabotage the group. Sometimes when people feel that they are being forced to attend a meeting they may 'take their emotions out' on the group.
Taking flight	When people's emotions create threat and stress, group members and sometimes the whole group try to avoid the issues. People may become silent or try to avoid the topic of discussion.
Shutting down	When individuals feel frightened they may become silent and withdraw.
Rescuing	Rescuing is where one or more members of the group always protects an individual. This can mean that the rescued individual does not need to take responsibility for his or her work within the group. Although 'rescuing' sounds caring, constant protection can disrupt group cohesion.
Introducing a hidden agenda	Groups usually have tasks to achieve as Bales identified. Many formal groups literally have a written agenda that defines the tasks of the meeting. A 'hidden agenda' may arise because of other issues of concern. For instance, people may have rivalries or emotional needs. This hidden agenda may strongly influence what happens in the group, although it may not be understandable to an observer.

FIGURE 2.34 *A summary of Burnard's categories*

ISSUE	EXPLANATION
Evaluation versus description	Thompson points out the importance of not making judgmental or evaluative comments about other people. If we simply stick to descriptive information then we are less likely to make other people feel that they are being attacked.
Control versus problem orientation	It is important not to manipulate and control other people if we wish to be supportive. Thompson recommends taking a problem-solving approach to encourage discussion amongst equals.
Strategy versus spontaneity	Sometimes people have prepared things that they wish to say. They use communication in order to make a speech. Thompson points out that when people follow their own strategy like this, then they are less likely to listen and use an appropriate communication cycle. Responding to other people and being spontaneous is a more supportive way of communicating.
Certainty versus provisionalism	Some people come across as being rigid and fixed in their ideas. These people are certain that they are right about issues. This kind of certainty will create defensiveness in other people. In order to be supportive it is important to appear open to other people's ideas. Thompson calls this openness 'provisionalism'.
Superiority and neutrality versus empathy	People who are fixed and rigid, often come across as being superior. Neutrality means a lack of concern for others. Thompson stressed the importance of empathy and trying to understand others as a key component of being supportive.

FIGURE 2.35 *Thompson's theory of defensive versus supportive communication*

Think it over...

One idea for studying group behaviour is to use the fish bowl method of observation.

The people in the middle are being watched; they probably feel like goldfish in a bowl. They will need to trust you if the observation is going to work. They discuss something important, while those outside only listen and watch. What will you monitor? You might like to watch things such as:

* non-verbal messages, such as eye contact

* task behaviour – keeping people focused on the discussion

* maintenance behaviour – maintaining an appropriate emotional atmosphere in the group

* supportive behaviour.

After five minutes or so of listening and watching, the group should stop and people should share their ideas about what happened. Did the people in the group remember what the people outside reported? After discussing the exercise, the group on the inside of the goldfish bowl should change places with the observers.

Summary

This section has covered the following theories:

THEORY	DESCRIPTION
The structure of interaction	Interaction involves the stages of introduction, main content and winding down (beginning, middle and end)
The communication cycle	Communication involves reflection on the meaning of messages. You need to communicate that you have understood the content of another person's communication
Egan's theory of SOLER (1986)	A specific theory of non-verbal behaviour to communicate supportiveness
Group dynamics	Theories that explain people's behaviour within groups: Burnard (1996), Thompson (1986), Bales (1970) were explored
Group formation theories	Theories that explain how groups go through stages: Tuckman (1965) was described.

Consider this

Imagine you witnessed the following conversation taking place among a group of six early years workers.

Group member 1: I think it's our job to encourage the children to become as independent as possible; that's why I encourage them to play with the apparatus.

Group member 2: [angry tone] Well that's all right but safety comes first. I don't like to see too many children using the equipment at the same time. There will be an accident you know.

Group member 1: Children know what they can cope with; they will be all right.

Group member 2: So you think you know everything do you?

Group member 1: No, all I'm saying is that we can trust children more. It is important not to be over-controlling.

Group member 2: I think you want to put them at risk.

Group member 1: What do other people think?

Response of other four members: long silence then one person says: 'don't know'.

There is not enough information here to be certain of what is happening, but there is enough information to guess at the basic assumptions that might be informing the group's behaviour. Interpret this interaction in terms of group dynamic theory. If this group is just getting together, what stage might they be at? Use any of the theories in this section.

Using theory – can you identify?
The basic assumptions associated with Bion's theory that might be operating in this group.

Using theory – can you analyse?
Some possible explanations for what is going on, using a range of theory on group dynamics.

Using theory – can you evaluate?
Can you explain a range of different interpretations of what is happening in this group? Can you use different theories of group formation and group dynamics in order to suggest a range of explanations? What is your preferred explanation, and why?

Section 5: Interaction with the service user

A systematic approach

Thompson (1996) emphasises the importance of 'being systematic' as an important skill in care work. Thompson summarises systematic practice as knowing:

1. What are you trying to achieve?
2. How are you going to achieve it?
3. How will you know when you have achieved it?

Thompson argues that vague, unfocused care work can result in poor quality care and also in stress for the care worker. Some benefits of planned, systematic work based on Thompson's analysis are shown in Figure 2.36.

For these reasons it is important to be able to imagine how you will communicate with service users before you start your work. It will be important to use your imagination in order to explain what you are hoping to achieve, what skills you will use and how you will be able to recognise whether or not you have been successful.

Applying Thompson's systematic practice:

1. In terms of studying your own interaction you might, for example, have the aim of establishing a degree of trust, with a service user.
2. You would not be able to plan a mechanical strategy to produce trust. Trust is an emotional feeling that might grow and develop within a caring relationship. But you could list some of the skills that you would be using in your communication work that would contribute to the development of a caring relationship.
3. You would have to have an understanding of relationships and trust in order to be able to explain the degree to which you have established a trusting relationship. You should use theory during the planning stage of your work in order to identify how you would know if you have achieved a trusting relationship.

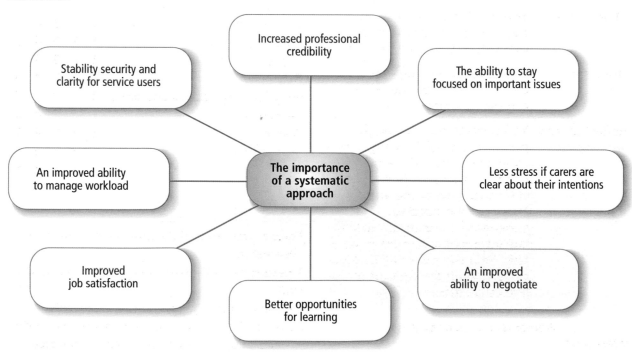

FIGURE 2.36 *Some benefits of planned, systematic work, based on Thompson's analysis (1996)*

Evaluating the effectiveness of an interaction

Planning

Your report must include records of your plans for interaction. The work that you plan may be simple. It could be that you plan just to talk to somebody about their likes and dislikes on a menu. It will be important to keep notes of how you prepared for your communication work. You will probably need to discuss your plans with a tutor and work out the aims and objectives you have for the practical work. It is vital that you do discuss your plans with a tutor, and/or with someone in the care setting before you undertake any practical communication work.

Detailed plans

Your plans should include the elements identified in Figure 2 .37.

PLANS FOR INTERACTION	
Introduction	You need to plan how you will start the interaction, or in other words what your introduction will involve
Main content	You need to think through the kind of content that the interaction is likely to involve.
Discussion	You need to be prepared to discuss issues that may arise during your interaction.
Reflection and winding up	You need to think through possible ways of finishing your interaction that will result in a positive emotional feeling at the conclusion of the work. You may also need to summarise issues at the end of the interaction in order to do this. Your summary will involve reflecting on the content of the interaction.

FIGURE 2.37 *Elements of a plan for your interaction*

Aims

Any communication work you do should aim to improve the quality of life for the people you are communicating with. Whatever happens, your communication work must not exploit others or make them more vulnerable. Following Thompson's (1996) advice it will be important to be systematic and to produce statements of your aims before you undertake any practical work. These statements should be checked with a tutor before the work is undertaken.

Your aims should also clarify whether the purpose of the interaction involved giving information, asking for information or exchanging ideas and opinions, perhaps as part of your supportive relationship-building work.

Skills

In order to evaluate your skills it will be important to identify the skills that you used during your communication work. The grid below might provide one way of starting to identify the quality of your verbal and non-verbal skills.

Communication rating scale:
How good were different aspects of non-verbal communication?

Eye contact	1 2 3 4 5
Facial expression	1 2 3 4 5
Angle of head	1 2 3 4 5
Tone of voice	1 2 3 4 5
Body language: hands and arms	1 2 3 4 5
Gestures	1 2 3 4 5
Posture	1 2 3 4 5
Muscle tension	1 2 3 4 5
Touch	1 2 3 4 5
Proximity	1 2 3 4 5

How to rate behaviour:
Place a circle around the number that fits your observation.
1 means: very effective and appropriate use of a skill.
2 means: some appropriate use of the skill.
3 means: the skill was not demonstrated or it does not seem appropriate to comment on the area.
4 means: some slightly ineffective or inappropriate behaviour in relation to the area.

5 means: very inappropriate or ineffective behaviour in relation to the area.

How good were verbal communication and listening skills?

Appropriate language: Speech community and register	1	2	3	4	5
Encouraging others to talk	1	2	3	4	5
Listening skill: Reflecting back what others have said	1	2	3	4	5
Clarifying: use of appropriate questions	1	2	3	4	5
Clarifying: use of prompts	1	2	3	4	5
Summarising	1	2	3	4	5
Paraphrasing	1	2	3	4	5
Pace of conversation	1	2	3	4	5
Tone of voice	1	2	3	4	5
Empathising	1	2	3	4	5

How to rate:

Place a circle around the number that fits your observation. Use the same rating as for non-verbal communication above.

This grid may help you to analyse and provide examples of your communication skills. In order to achieve the highest marks your report will need to go beyond a description of skills and you will need to provide comparisons and contrasts between different interactions. You will also need to explain some of the theory of that helps you to understand what is happening as you interact with others.

The barriers to communication grid

Barriers

In the environment

Lighting	1	2	3	4	5
Noise levels	1	2	3	4	5
Physical barriers to communication	1	2	3	4	5

Language differences

Appropriate use of language: (terminology and level of formality)	1	2	3	4	5
Your skills with different languages	1	2	3	4	5
Your skills with non-verbal communication	1	2	3	4	5
Availability of interpreters	1	2	3	4	5

Avoidance of assumptions/valuing diversity	1	2	3	4	5

Emotional barriers

Stress levels and tiredness	1	2	3	4	5
Being stressed by the emotional needs of others	1	2	3	4	5

Cultural barriers

Inappropriate assumptions made about others	1	2	3	4	5
Labelling or stereotyping present	1	2	3	4	5

Interpersonal skills

Degree of supportive non-verbal behaviour	1	2	3	4	5
Degree of supportive verbal behaviour	1	2	3	4	5
Appropriate use of listening skills	1	2	3	4	5
Appropriate maintenance of confidentiality	1	2	3	4	5

Rating Scale:

1 means: Good – there are no barriers.
2 means: Quite good – few barriers.
3 means: Not possible to decide or not applicable.
4 means: Poor – barriers identified.
5 means: Very poor – major barriers to communication.

Once you have identified potential barriers you need to research other people's perception of these issues. You might discuss your analysis of your interaction with a tutor or colleague. If possible, it would be ideal to discuss your work with a member of staff in the care setting where your interactions took place.

The views of service users are very important, and it might be possible for you to ask service users about issues such as the clarity of what you said, and whether or not there were any environmental barriers. It will be important to plan any questioning work carefully and to check your plans with a tutor before undertaking any research.

In order to achieve the highest marks you will need to take the initiative in obtaining feedback from others. You should analyse why people have responded in the way that they have. You will need to gain information from different sources and to provide an analysis of the issues you have identified.

Evaluation of your report

You must provide an evaluation of how well your interactions went and draw conclusions from the evidence you were able to gather. To achieve the highest marks you will need to evidence an in-depth evaluation of your own performance, identifying realistic and informed recommendations for improvement.

To achieve a good mark you will need to be able to show that you have fully understood what took place during your interactions and what impact you had on others. You will need to be able to give reasons for any conclusions you make and these conclusions will need to be supported with evidence.

Perspectives – getting feedback

You must evaluate the effectiveness of your interaction from the perspective of the service user, your own perspective, and the perspective of your assessor and/or your peers.

FIGURE 2.38 *Use three different perspectives to evaluate the effectiveness of your work*

Your own perspective

You should have been clear about your perspective before you started the work. Your aims might have involved clearly communicating information and will almost certainly have involved some aspect of relationship work – Thompson (1986). Issues to do with supportiveness, establishing a relationship, self

disclosure and empathy may be important issues to consider from your own perspective.

The service user's perspective

The service user's perspective will be much harder to discover. You will have observed the response(s) to your communication. You will have observed any non-verbal behaviour, and you will probably have some idea whether the service user appeared to be comfortable, or whether he or she enjoyed interacting with you. Your observations will provide very important evidence, and you should record the non-verbal feedback you received from service users in order to help you evaluate your interaction.

The other main way you can get information and evidence is to ask service users what they experienced. Asking people what they thought of a conversation is not straightforward. People can be easily embarrassed when asked to give feedback and often avoid giving a detailed analysis by saying things like, 'Oh it was very good!' The quality of the information you obtain will be influenced by the quality of the questions that you ask. You must also be careful not to ask questions in a way that might make service users feel that they are being manipulated or exploited. For these reasons, it is important that you should check your plans for any questions with a tutor before you ask for feedback.

Your assessor's perspective

Other students can often give useful feedback on your work, so you may receive peer assessment or feedback to help you develop your skills. Assessors will have a range of questions that may include:

* Were your aims appropriate?

* Did you work within an appropriate value system for care work?

* How far did you succeed in meeting your aims?

* Did you establish an appropriate professional, supportive and/or empathetic relationship with the person or people you worked with?

* Did you communicate clearly? Were you aware of factors that may enhance, inhibit, or create barriers to communication?

∗ How effectively did you use theory in order to analyse what happened?

Try to guess what your assessor will be looking for, or better still, ask for this information directly.

The structure of an evaluation – why evaluation is important

Interpreting and explaining your interaction with others will not be a simple task. People have complex feelings and thoughts and each person is unique. Because people are different from one another, care work involves constant learning. If people were not complicated – if they were all the same – then it would only be necessary to learn a few simple rules and procedures in order to work effectively. It is the diversity and complexity of service users that makes the work interesting, as well as complicated to evaluate. Evaluation involves applying theory to practice.

Emotions and working with people

The great thing about working with people is that they are all so different and each person provides a new learning situation. Not evaluating your own performance saves emotional energy, but it can lead to a feeling that care work is boring. Emotions connected with boredom can make us want to give up and withdraw. Evaluation is important because it can help us to avoid thinking of service users as 'all the same' and the emotional feeling of boredom that can go with this.

Working with people creates emotional feelings. Working with interesting, attractive or kind people may make us feel good. But many service users will be worried or even depressed or upset; as such, they may not always be rewarding to work with. Our first emotional reaction may be to want to avoid them. When we have to work with a difficult child it is only natural to feel 'I don't want to. I'd rather do something else.'

If we are to work in a professional way then we have to be sure that we don't follow the emotional urge to withdraw, but instead we have to find ways of coping. Thinking a situation through can help us to solve problems. When

people have a problem to solve they sometimes go through a process like the one shown in Figure 2.39.

A theory of reflection and problem solving

Evaluation is sometimes understood as a process of actively **reflecting** on and developing our thoughts. Simply having experiences or simply reading about theories will not be enough on their own to develop the personal knowledge needed to guide skilled care work.

Kurt Lewin (as explained in Kolb, 1984) originally developed a theory of practical learning that could be used to improve problem-solving skills. Lewin's model argued that learning started with the concrete, practical experience that a carer might have, such as undertaking communication work. If workers carefully thought about their experiences they would be able to form ideas and generalisations that might help them to explain their experiences. The next step of the process would be to test the new ideas out in practice. Experimenting with new ideas would lead to new experiences.

David Kolb (1984) adapted Lewin's approach to problem solving and argued that effective learning depended on a '**learning cycle**' or a four-stage process, which might be summarised as in Figure 2.39.

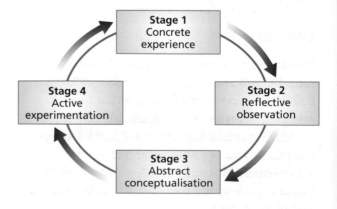

FIGURE 2.39 *Kolb's learning cycle: a four-stage process (1984)*

An example of this learning process might work something like the study opposite:

SCENARIO

Imagine that you are working with a man with learning difficulty. It is the first time you have met him and you offer him a drink at lunchtime. You place a glass of orange squash in front of him. He immediately pushes the glass away and communicates with a facial expression that you assume means he is angry.

Within Kolb's four-stage learning cycle you have had a concrete experience.

STAGE 1

Stage 1 of the learning cycle about the individual needs of this service user is that he has rejected your provision of orange squash and communicated that he is angry. But why has he reacted this way?

STAGE 2

Stage 2 involves thinking through some possible reasons for the person's reaction. Perhaps he does not like orange squash? Perhaps he does not like the way you put it in front of him? Perhaps he does not like to take a drink with his meal? Could it be an issue to do with status? For example, could a cold drink symbolise being treated as a child for this individual? Does he see adult status as defined by having a hot drink? Reflection on the non-verbal behaviour of the service user may provide a range of starting points for interpreting his actions.

STAGE 3

Stage 3 involves trying to make sense of our reflections. What do we know about different cultural interpretations of non-verbal behaviour? What are the chances that the way we positioned ourselves when we placed the drink in front of the person have been construed as an attempt to control or dominate him? We did not intend to send this message, but the service user may have interpreted our behaviour as being unpleasant. The more we know about communication the more in-depth we can analyse the service user's reaction. We need to think through the most likely explanation for the service user's behaviour using everything we know about people.

STAGE 4

Stage 4 involves 'experimenting' or checking out ideas and assumptions that we may have made. The worker might attempt to modify his or her non-verbal behaviour to look supportive; the worker might show the service user a china cup and saucer to indicate the question, 'Is this what you would like?' If the service user responded with a positive non-verbal response then the worker would have been around the four stages of the cycle and would have solved the problem in a way which valued the individuality and diversity of the person he or she is working with.

Learning from experience

In real-life, workers might expect to have to go round this 'learning cycle' a number of times before they may correctly understand and interpret a service user's needs. (See Figure 2.40).

The important thing is to not just let things happen to you, but to think about your experiences and learn from them. It is easy to forget experiences if we don't think about them and discuss them.

Think about the reactions you get from service users. Try to imagine how they see you. What does a person's non-verbal behaviour toward you mean? What do service users say to you? How effective is your communication at meeting

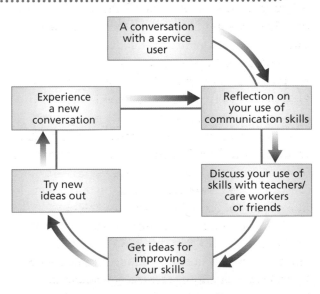

FIGURE 2.40 *The learning cycle in practice*

EVALUATION OF EFFECTIVENESS OF INTERACTION	
Reflection	Your evaluation should explain how you have thought things through and talked things through with other people, in order to reflect and develop your own understanding of the quality of your skills. Reflection is the second stage in Kolb's theory (1984).
Analysis	You must use theory to analyse the quality of your interaction. This is the third stage of the cycle identified by Kolb. Being able to explain issues using theory enables us to develop a deeper understanding of our experience.
Conclusions	You need to sum up what you have learned from reflection and from analysing your experience using theory. Your conclusions will emphasise the key things that you have learned.
Realistic improvements	The fourth stage in Kolb's theory is to be able to think of new ideas. Your reflection, analysis and conclusions should lead you to be able to suggest new ideas for developing and improving your interaction with service users. You could use Kolb's 'learning cycle' as a theory to explain how you intend to learn and develop your interaction skills.

FIGURE 2.41 *The four parts of an evaluation*

people's needs, including needs to belong and needs for self-esteem?

It is very difficult to check our own thoughts alone. A good way to check assumptions is to discuss practice with tutors or workplace supervisors. Skilled care workers may be able to help us question assumptions in our thinking and see new possibilities. If we get new ideas then they can be tried out in practice to see if they are right.

Summary

＊ It is important to be systematic and to plan and check your work before you undertake any practical interaction with service users.

＊ You must evaluate the effectiveness of your interactions from the perspective of the service user, your own perspective, and the perspective of assessors.

＊ Evaluation is an important skill because it can help us to make sense of our feelings, help us to avoid fixed thinking and develop a problem-solving attitude.

＊ The 'Kolb learning cycle' provides a theory for explaining the importance of reflection, analysis and ideas for improvement

＊ Your evaluation must include an explanation of your reflection, analysis, conclusions and realistic improvements.

Consider this

Caitlin undertook some conversational work with a 92-year-old woman. Caitlin reported that she spent over an hour listening and asking questions about the woman's past. Caitlin said 'I don't know where the time went. I guess I lost track of time. I was so interested.' The service user said she was very pleased to have a chance to talk about her life and that she thoroughly enjoyed talking to Caitlin.

Caitlin's aims included that of establishing a good relationship – perhaps involving empathy, using the communication cycle effectively and also being well organised.

Using theory – can you identify?
Any evidence that Caitlin may have established a good working relationship in this interaction.

Anything that might suggest effective use of the communication cycle.

Can you analyse – issues using theory?
Why might the conversation have become so enjoyable for both the people involved.

Can you evaluate – using theory?
If you were providing assessment feedback to Caitlin how would you balance the significance of losing track of time? Caitlin spent longer than she intended to in conversation, but she did establish a good relationship and perhaps a degree of empathy. How would you judge the relative importance of these issues.

UNIT 2 ASSESSMENT

How you will be assessed

You must produce evidence for the four assessment objectives shown below. Your report must evidence the following.

ASSESSMENT OBJECTIVE	DETAILS
AO1 An understanding of the different types of communication used in care settings and of the factors that support and inhibit communication, giving examples.	In order to achieve the highest marks you will need to show a comprehensive in-depth understanding of different kinds of communication and of the range of factors that support or inhibit communication.
AO2 An explanation of how care workers use four different communication skills in the care setting to value service users, giving examples.	In order to achieve the highest marks you will need to produce an in-depth analysis of how care workers apply different communication skills. You will need to provide examples of how care workers use skills in order to value others as individuals. Although you must clearly identify four skills it may be appropriate to discuss theories such as Thompson's theory of supportiveness (1986) when analysing skills.
AO3 Relevant research and analysis of two theories that provide guidance about the effects of communication on service users and/or care workers	In order to achieve the highest marks you should undertake research, using a range of sources, such as interviewing care workers, observing communication in care settings, reading, and researching information on Internet. Your analysis must provide guidance about the way in which two theories inform understanding of communication with service users.
AO4 The production of records to show the effectiveness of your communication skills in an interaction with an individual service user/care worker or a small group of service users/care workers, evaluating your own performance and making recommendations for improvements.	To achieve the highest marks your report must provide an in-depth evaluation of your own performance, making realistic and informed recommendations improvement.

(See Section 2.5 for more ideas on producing these records.)

References

Altman, I and Taylor, D. A. (1973) *Social Penetration: The Development of Interpersonal Relationships* (New York: Holt, Rinehart & Winston)

Bales, R. (1970) *Personality and Interpersonal Behaviour* (New York: Holt, Rinehart & Winston)

Benson, J. F. (2001) *Working more creatively with groups* 2nd edition (London & New York: Routledge)

Bion, W. R. (1961) *Experiences in Groups and Other Papers* (London: Tavistock Publications)

Bostrom, R. N. (1997) *The process of listening* in Hargie, O.D.W. (ed.) *The Handbook of Communication Skills* (2nd edition) (London and New York: Routledge)

Burnard, P. (1996) *Acquiring Interpersonal Skills* (2nd edition) (London: Chapman & Hall)

Burnard, P. and Morrison, P. (1997) *Caring and Communicating: Interpersonal Relationships in Nursing* (Basingstoke and London: Palgrave)

Egan, G. (1986) *The Skilled Helper* (Monterey, California: Brooks/Cole Publishing Company)

Garland, J., Jones, H. and Kolodny, K. (1965) *A model for stages in the development of social work groups*, in Bernstein, S. (ed) *Explorations in Group work* (London: Bookstall)

Hargie, C.T.C. and Tourish, D. (1997) *Relational Communication* in Hargie, O.D.W. (ed.) *The Handbook of Communication Skills* (2nd edition) (London and New York: Routledge)

Hayman, M. (1998) A *Protocol for People with Hearing Impairment* Nursing Times, October 28, Volume 94, No. 43.

Johnson D. and Johnson F. (1997) *Joining together: group theory and group skills* (6th edition) (Boston: Allyn & Bacon)

Kolb, D. (1984) *Experiential Learning: Experience as the Source of Learning and Development* (New Jersey: Prentice Hall)

Maslow, A. H. (1970) *Motivation and Personality* (2nd edition) (New York: Harper & Row)

Morgan, H. and Thomas, K. (1996) *A Psychodynamic Perspective on Group Process* in: Wetherell, M. (ed. *Identities, Groups and Social Issues* (London: Sage & Open University)

Morrison, P. and Burnard, P. (1997) *Caring and Communicating* (Basingstoke and London: Macmillan Press Ltd)

Pease, A. (1997) *Body Language* (London: Sheldon Press)

Schutz, W. (1979) *Profound Simplicity* (London: Turnstone Books)

Thompson, N. (1996) *People Skills* (Basingstoke and London: Macmillan)

Thompson, N. (2001) *Anti-Discriminatory Practice* 2nd edition (Basingstoke and London: Macmillan)

Thompson, T., L. (1986) *Communication for Health Professionals* (New York: Harper & Row)

Tuckman, B. (1965) *Development Sequence in Small Groups,* in Psychological Bulletin, Vol 63, No 6.

Tuckman, B. and Jensen, M. (1977) 'Stages of Small Group Development Revisited', *Group and Organisational Studies*, vol. 2, pp 419–27

Useful websites

www.britishdeafassociation.org.uk
More about British Sign Language (BSL) can be found at this website

www.british-sign.co.uk
Details of a sign and the finger spelling alphabet are outlined on this website

www.royaldeaf.org.uk
More information on special methods and alternative language methods are described here

www.makaton.org
Makaton is a language system that uses speech, signs and symbols

www.brailleplus.net
Braille is a communication system of raised marks that can be felt with the fingers and interpreted; it is used by people who cannot see print.

UNIT
3

Promoting Good Health

This unit covers the following sections:

3.1 Concepts and models of health and well-being

3.2 Preventative measures and job-roles

3.3 Factors affecting health and well-being

3.4 Health promotion

Introduction

This unit investigates the range of lifestyle choices and societal factors which influence health and well-being. You will investigate the ways in which ill health can be prevented in care settings and the health-promotion methods that are used by health-and-social care practitioners. This unit has links with Unit 1: 'Promoting Quality Care'; Unit 7: 'Health as a Lifestyle Choice'; Unit 8: 'Complementary Therapies'; Unit 10: 'Care Practice and Provision'; and Unit 14: 'Mental Health Issues'.

In this unit you will learn about differing views and models of health and how these influence health-promotion activity, and key government policy initiatives to promote health. This unit also looks at health education, health protection and health promotion, and key people in the local community involved in health promotion. The range of factors affecting health and well-being including people's attitudes, lifestyle choices, social factors, environment, income and disability are discussed, along with varying approaches to health promotion and how to go about planning and carrying out a campaign.

The background to this unit is best summed up by the following passages from the recent government white paper *Choosing Health – Making Healthy Choices Easier* (DOH, 2004):

'There have been big improvements in health and life expectancy over the last century. On the most basic measure, people are living longer than ever before.

Boys born in 2004 can expect to live to the age of 76, compared with a life expectancy of 45 in 1900, and girls to 80, compared with 50 in 1900. A child born today is likely to live $9\frac{1}{2}$ years longer than a child born when the NHS was established in 1948.

Future progress on this dramatic scale cannot be taken for granted. England faces new challenges to ensure that as a society we continue to benefit from longer and healthier lives. Whilst the threat of childhood death from illness is falling and the big infectious killer diseases of the last century have been eradicated or largely controlled, the relative proportion of deaths from cancers, coronary heart disease (CHD) and stroke has risen. They now account for around two-thirds of all deaths. Cancer, stroke and heart disease not only kill, but are also major causes of ill health, preventing people from living their lives to the full and causing avoidable disability, pain and anxiety. And there are some worrying pointers for our future health:

* Smoking remains the single biggest preventable cause of ill health and there are still over 10 million smokers in the country.

* As many as one in 10 sexually active young women may be infected with chlamydia, which can cause infertility.

* Surveys carried out since 1974 show an increase in the mental health problems experienced by young people.

* Suicide remains the commonest cause of death in men under 35.

* Around one-third of all attendances to hospital Accident and Emergency departments are estimated to be alcohol related.'

Therefore, the government recognised that whilst we now live longer, and the major causes of premature death of the last century are largely under control, the same cannot be said for today's main killers. It is how we tackle these diseases of the modern day that is explored in this unit.

Section 1: Concepts and models of health and well-being

In this section you will explore the factors that can affect a person's health; the various concepts of health and ill health, which are used to try and understand how health is created and maintained; and the types of policy and strategy that governments have adopted to address these factors. The starting point is to consider what is important for your own health using this activity below:

Think it over...

	1	2	3
What does being healthy mean to you? In Column 1, tick any statements which seem to you to be important aspects of your health. In Column 2, tick the six statements which are the most important aspects of being healthy to you. In Column 3, rank these six in order of importance – put '1' by the most important, '2' by the next most important , and so on, down to '6'.			
1. Enjoying being with my family and friends			
2. Living to be a ripe old age			
3. Feeling happy most of the time			
4. Being able to run when I need to (e.g. for a bus) without getting out of breath			
5. Having a job			
6. Taking part in lots of sport			
7. Being able to get down to making decisions			
8. Hardly ever taking tablets or medicines			
9. Being the ideal weight for my height			
10. Feeling at peace with myself			
11. Never smoking			
12. Having clear skin, bright eyes and shiny hair			
13. Never suffering from anything more serious than a mild cold, flu or stomach upset			
14. Not getting things confused or out of proportion – assessing situations realistically			
15. Being able to adapt easily to changes in my life such as moving house, or changing jobs			
16. Feeling glad to be alive			
17. Drinking moderate amounts of alcohol or none at all			
18. Enjoying my work without much stress or strain			
19. Having all the parts of my body in good working order			
20. Getting on well with other people most of the time			
21. Eating the 'right' foods			
22. Enjoying some form of relaxation/recreation			
23. Hardly ever going to the doctor			

When you have finished the exercise ask yourself...

1. Was this what I expected to find?
2. Which of the lay perspectives from box 1 can I see in my own answers?
3. How might the outcome vary if I was were to complete this when I was 20 or 40 years older?
4. How might the responses from someone with a physical disability have differed from mine?
5. How might the responses from someone living on benefits have differed from mine?

Defining health

You may have found some surprising results from the activity on page 105: you will understand your responses better if you consider what a broad meaning the term 'health' has. It is derived from the Old English term *Hael* meaning 'whole', suggesting that health deals with the whole person, the entirety of their well-being. This brings together a range of facets of health, which together contribute to a person being healthy – as you will have discovered for yourself in carrying out the first activity in this unit.

A brief overview of facets of health is given in Figure 3.1.

FACET	DESCRIPTION
Physical health	the mechanical ability of the body
Mental Health	the ability to think clearly and coherently, strongly allied to emotional health
Emotional health	the ability to recognise emotions and express them appropriately. The ability to cope with potentially damaging aspects of emotional health, e.g. stress, depression, anxiety and tension
Social health	the ability to make and maintain relationships with others
Spiritual health	concerns personal creeds, principled behaviour, achieving peace of mind or religious beliefs and practices
Societal health	concerns wider societal impact on our own individual health, e.g. the impact of racism on people from a minority ethnic culture, the impact on women of living in a patriarchal society, and the impact of living under political oppression

FIGURE 3.1 *Facets of health*

In society today, 'health' is a term used most usually to express two aspects of well-being. It is used:

* as a negative expression, where health is viewed as the absence of disease or illness

* positively to express a state of well-being, perhaps most widely known through the 1948 World Health Organisation (WHO) definition shown below.

✻ DID YOU KNOW?

Definitions of 'health' include:

✻ 'A state of complete physical, psychological and social well-being and not merely the absence of disease and infirmity'
World Health Organisation, 1948

✻ 'A satisfactory adjustment of the individual to the environment'
Royal College of General Practitioners, 1972

✻ 'By health I mean the power to live a full adult, living, breathing life in close contact with what I love. I want to be all I am capable of becoming'

Katherine Mansfield

✻ 'The extent to which an individual or group is able on the one hand, to realise aspirations and satisfy needs and on the other hand, to change or cope with the environment. Health is therefore seen as a resource for everyday life, not the objective of living: it is a positive concept emphasising social and personal resources as well as physical capabilities'
World Health Organisation, 1984

Think it over...

If you examine the alternative definitions of health given above, can you identify which reflect either the positive or the negative use of the word health?

Defining health in terms of illness and disease

Illness, disease and ill health are terms often used interchangeably when in reality they have very different meanings. Disease is derived from the Middle English term *desaise* meaning discomfort, whilst illness is used to identify that a condition exists that causes a person harm or pain. Today, to be 'ill' usually requires the patient's condition to be classified according to current medical knowledge and practice: for example, by displaying a specific list of symptoms or by scientific testing. It is this focus on the scientific nature of diagnosis of illness, which emphasises the importance of the biomedical model in modern-day health care.

Illness is a subjective state, where the person may experience a range of symptoms but tests may not be able to identify a cause. For example, this can often be the case with **myalgic encephalopathy** (ME) where patients can experience a range of symptoms associated with the syndrome but medical testing may not be able to confirm the condition or identify a cause for the symptoms.

Disease and illness do not have to coexist. For example, a person may be diagnosed with a condition through routine screening prior to exhibiting any symptoms. This illustrates the reasoning behind screening programmes, i.e. to ensure that disease can be identified early enough to treat successfully. Therefore, the person may be defined as having the disease (for example, breast or cervical cancer) but not feel ill.

Personal responsibility and health

To the general public to be healthy is usually associated with not being ill: this is a negative perspective, one which is best summarised as not knowing what you had till you lost it. However, the way in which we view our health determines how we take responsibility for it. Stainton and Rogers (from Katz and Perberdy, 1997) summarise a variety of lay perspectives (held by members of the public) which illustrate that the ways in which people view their health will inevitably be reflected in their expression of taking responsibility for their own health. See Figure 3.2.

Therefore, people's notion of what being healthy means varies widely and is shaped by their experiences, knowledge, values and expectations, as well as what others expect of them. These differing attitudes to health influence their behaviour. For instance, a person who believes in the robust individualism model might well choose to smoke and take regular exercise, because these are both satisfying and that individual believes in the right to choose. This, however, would be a difficult position for someone who subscribes to the health promotion account or the will power model, both of which emphasise personal responsibility to maintain

---

✳ DID YOU KNOW?

* ✳ Myalgic encephalopathy (ME)
* ✳ Chronic fatigue syndrome (CFS)
* ✳ Post-viral fatigue syndrome (PVFS)
* ✳ Chronic fatigue immune dysfunction syndrome (CFIDS)

are all names for conditions of uncertain causes affecting many thousands of people. All types of people at all ages are affected. Common symptoms include severe and debilitating fatigue, painful muscles and joints, disordered sleep, gastric disturbances, and poor memory and concentration. In many cases, onset is linked to a viral infection. Other triggers may include an operation or an accident, although some people experience a slow onset.

In some the effects may be minimal, but in a large number, lives are changed drastically. For instance: in the young, schooling and higher education can be severely disrupted; in the working population, employment becomes impossible for many; for all, social life and family life become restricted and, in some cases, severely strained. People may be housebound or confined to bed for months or years.

Recovery is variable and unpredictable. Some people may recover completely, although it may take a number of months or years; in the majority, recovery is only partial and typically follows a slow course of variable improvement and relapse; a significant minority remain severely affected and may require a great deal of practical and social support.

WAYS IN WHICH PEOPLE VIEW THEIR HEALTH	
Body as machine	This has strong links to the medical model of health in that it sees illness as a matter of biological fact and scientific medicine as the natural type of treatment for any illness.
Inequality of access	This perspective is rooted in a reliance on modern medicine to cure illness but is less accepting than 'body as machine' because of awareness that there are great inequalities of access to treatment.
Health promotion account	This model emphasises the importance of a healthy lifestyle and personal responsibility: for example, if you are overweight it is simply a matter of your own choice of diet and lack of exercise that has led to this.
God's power	In this model health is viewed as part of spirituality, i.e. a feature of righteous living and spiritual wholeness. This might be seen as abstinence from alcohol consumption because it is an impure substance, which is not only unholy but also can lead to immoral activity.
Body under siege	This view perceives the world to be a sea of challenges to their health, be they communicable diseases such as colds and flu, or stress at work, and so on.
Cultural critique of medicine	This view sees science and the medical model on which healthcare is based as oppressive to certain groups (e.g. can take away their rights to self determination), e.g. the way health care manages pregnancy can be seen as an example of oppressive practice against women for the natural process of birth is routinely medicalised by health services
Robust individualism	A view best summarised as 'It's my life and I will do with it as I choose'.
Will power	This model considers that we all have a moral responsibility to remain healthy. This relies on strong will power to manage our health: for example, to eat the right things, take regular exercise and drink moderately.

FIGURE 3.2 *Lay perspectives of health*

health. In this situation that person's decision would appear to be contradictory. Therefore, it illustrates how our own attitudes to health define how we view our personal responsibilities for maintaining our own health.

The biomedical model of health

Central to our modern-day understanding of health is the biomedical model, which since the beginning of the 19th century has come to dominate all other models of health in the Western world. Its history lies in the developing understanding of how the various parts of the body might work together to ensure good health. Figure 3.4 summarises this scientific view of health and body functioning.

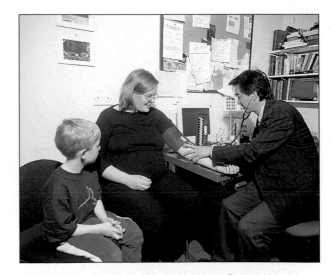

FIGURE 3.3 *A general practitioner focuses on cure rather than prevention*

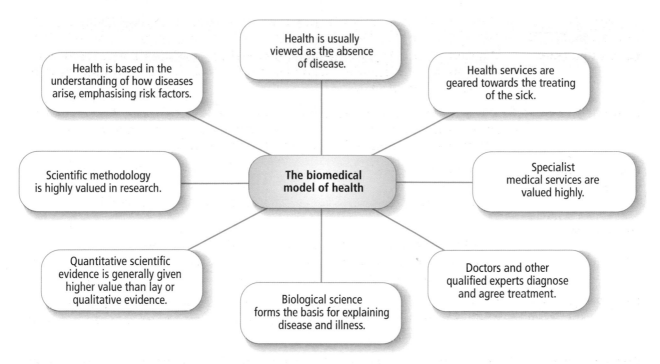

FIGURE 3.4 *Characteristics of the biomedical model of health*

This is the model of health most frequently used by members of the health care professions. In particular, it is the foundation of most medical science and therefore is central to the practice of medicine. As a result, it is the cure that doctors focus upon, their approach being founded in an impression of what is normal and what is abnormal in terms of bodily function. It is most effective with short-term or acute illness, where a cause is identified and the relevant treatment administered. The biomedical model is at its least

Think it over...

1. A diagnosis of ME is based on a collection of symptoms rather than a diagnostic test.

2. Looking at the type of symptoms outlined in this unit, what tensions might there be for a person with ME when they first visit their doctor with the symptoms?

3. Why might a doctor find it difficult to help a person with this condition?

4. As part of learning how to manage their condition, people with ME often learn a great deal about their condition. How might this challenge the usual doctor–patient relationship?

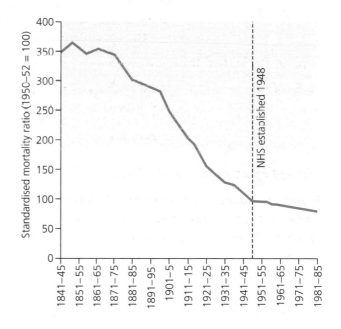

FIGURE 3.5 *Mortality rates (UK) 1841–1985*

effective with chronic illnesses, i.e. those which persist over longer periods of time and are managed rather than cured: examples include ME or Parkinson's disease, terminal care of the dying, and other aspects of health care (such as maternity care where the patient is not actually ill).

Think it over...

Look at the graph of Mortality rates (Figure 3.5).

1. What period saw the greatest decline in mortality?

2. Where does the introduction of the NHS fit in this time scale?

3. What impact has the introduction of the NHS had on mortality rates?

A social model of health

Although the biomedical model has contributed greatly to the increase in life expectancy during the 20th century, it is public health measures based on the social model of health that have contributed most to the decline in mortality.

A social model of health emphasises that in order to improve health it is necessary to address the origins of ill health, i.e. the social conditions that make ill health more prevalent in some groups than others. Its underlying philosophy is that the health differences between individuals and social groups are the result of a complex mixture of behavioural, structural, material and cultural factors, which together impact on health. The social model has strong links to the lay models of health because it recognises that people often have firmly held views about their own health, which are sometimes at odds with those of professionals. For example, the need to address damp conditions in housing and its link to childhood asthma might be prioritised by people

FIGURE 3.6 *Landfill sites cause public health concerns*

living in those conditions, as opposed to the need to tackle parental smoking amongst those living in the same houses, as prioritised by health practitioners.

Think it over...

1. How have the environmental challenges facing humans changed in the last 100 years?

2. What local measures are you aware of that are being taken to improve the environment where you live?

3. What three things would you suggest as changes which would greatly improve the health of your local neighbourhood?

Health policy linked to national targets

Examples of health-promoting activity at the national level include:

* legislation such as the factory acts of the 19th century, which limited the hours that children, women and men could work

* public health legislation, which required towns to take steps to improve sanitary conditions

* the Clean Air Acts of the 1950s, which reduced city 'smogs' (pollution-laden fogs) considerably

* the Water (Fluoridation) Act of 1985, which enabled health authorities to ask water companies to add fluoride to drinking water to cut dental decay.

However, legislative action at the national level is strongly linked to political and ideological factors and evidence for a particular course of action. For example, it is widely accepted that tobacco kills more people than all the 'soft and hard drugs' that are often the cause of many media crusades. However, it can still be bought freely over the counter, the government generating enough revenue in the process to more than equal the expenditure on health care for people with smoking-related health conditions. Manufacturers spend millions of pounds advertising the product, particularly to recruit new young smokers. And yet there remains considerable reluctance to legislate against tobacco. In the 2004 public health white paper *Choosing Health*, the government of the day shied away from introducing a total ban on smoking in public areas, choosing instead to adopt a partial ban with some pubs and clubs being able to continue to allow smoking on the premises: this measure was heavily criticised by health campaigning groups like ASH (Action on Smoking and Health) and doctors' representatives.

It was a concern over the public reception for this sort of measure that probably contributed to the reluctance to act. However, the public clearly supports government action in a range of fields, as is stated in the white paper (2004): 'The response to consultation suggests that government is expected (by the public) and trusted to act on inequalities and on wider issues that impact on society... Whilst people want to make their own health decisions they do expect the government to help by creating the right environment.'

National health strategy

This country's first ever health strategy (as opposed to health services) was published by the government in 1992 (with specific similar policy documents for both Wales and Scotland). Its stated aim was to ensure that 'action is taken whether through the NHS or otherwise, to improve and protect health'. It initiated action at three levels:

* through the Department of Health, which was given the lead role (viewed as a mistake by many as the department's role was in ill-health care)

* through some opportunities for the State but mainly focusing on the role of the individual

* and, for the first time, through a range of national health targets.

Independent inquiry into inequalities in health

In July 1997 Donald Acheson was invited by the Secretary of State for Health to review and summarise inequalities in health in England and to identify priority areas for the development of policies to reduce them. This followed in the wake of two renowned previous reports in this field: the report of Douglas Black in 1977 and the updated version from 1987. Both these reports suffered a degree of suppression at the time of their release because of their bleak picture of the widening health inequality in a developed country at the turn of the century, and the implications for the government of the day.

Acheson concluded his report (1998) with a list of 39 recommendations for addressing health inequality, 'judged on the scale of their potential impact on health inequalities and the weight of evidence'. The three areas identified as crucial to this process are:

* all policies likely to have an impact on health should be evaluated in terms of their impact on health inequality

* a high priority should be given to the health of families with children

* further steps should be taken to reduce income inequalities and improve the living standards of poor households.

Think it over...

Imagine you are the estates officer for a local Primary Care Trust. You are about to build a new health centre in the middle of the most deprived estate in your district. On paper this seems like an excellent opportunity to improve the health of this community. But what things might change for the better and the worse as a result of the health centre being built?

The 1992 health strategy was followed up in 1997 by the government publication *Saving Lives – Our Healthier Nation*. The revised strategy made clear links to the Acheson report, proposing to tackle the root causes of ill health: including air pollution, unemployment, low wages, crime and disorder and poor housing. It focused on prevention of the main killers: cancer, coronary heart disease and stroke, accidents and mental illness. It also included a wide range of service providers such as local councils, the NHS, and local voluntary bodies and businesses. Included within the strategy were specific health targets in key disease areas.

The main targets of the 1997 health strategy are:

Cancer	To reduce the death rate in under 75s by at least 20 per cent
Coronary heart disease and stroke	To reduce the death rate in under 75s by at least 40 per cent
Accidents	To reduce the death rate by at least 20 per cent and serious injury by at least 10 per cent
Mental illness	To reduce the death rate from suicide and undetermined injury by at least 20 per cent

The NHS plan (2000)

The NHS Plan (2000) is a government policy paper that outlines the modernisation of the NHS. It includes a stated intention to tackle the health inequalities that divide Britain and sets out national targets for tackling health inequalities with the relevant supporting investment such as:

* a £500 million expansion of 'Sure Start' projects

* a new Children's Fund for supporting services for children in the 5–13 age bracket: to improve educational achievement, reduce crime and improve attendance at schools, for example

* a more effective welfare foods programme with increased support for breast feeding

* a 15 per cent cut in teenage conception

* the number of smokers to be cut by at least 15 million by 2010

* every child in nursery and infant school aged 4–6 years to be entitled to a free piece of fruit each school day.

Health inequalities

In February 2001 the government announced two national health inequalities targets, one relating to infant mortality and the other to life expectancy. They complemented a range of other targets that had been set with an inequalities focus, in the areas of smoking and teenage pregnancy. The targets were:

* 'Starting with children under one year, by 2010 to reduce by at least 10 per cent the gap in mortality between manual groups and the population as a whole...

* Starting with health authorities, by 2010 to reduce by at least 10 per cent the gap between the quintile (fifth or 20 per cent) of areas with

* DID YOU KNOW?

Children's centres

The Children's Centre programme is based on the concept that providing integrated education, care, family support and health services are key factors for helping children and their parents to escape the poverty trap. Children's centres bring an integrated approach to service delivery in areas where it is most needed, as it is targeted into the top 20 per cent of deprived wards in the country. They will provide the following services to children under 5 years of age and their families:

* early education integrated with full day care, including early identification of and provision for children with special educational needs and disabilities

* parental outreach, e.g. to parents with additional needs

* family support, including support for parents with special needs

* health services, e.g. health visitors, mental health services

* a base for childminders, and a hub within the community for providers of childcare services

* effective links with Jobcentre Plus, local training providers and further and higher education institutions

* effective links with children's information services, neighbourhood nurseries, out of school clubs and extended schools

* management and workforce training for the services operating into the centre.

the lowest life expectancy at birth and the population as a whole.'

This announcement was followed up in 2003 by *A Programme for Action* (DOH) which set out plans to tackle health inequalities over the following three years. It established the foundations required to achieve the national targets. The different dimensions of health inequalities were set out in the document across four themes:

* *supporting families, mothers and children* – reflecting the high priority given to them in the Acheson report (1998)

* *engaging communities and individuals* – strengthening capacity to tackle local problems

* *preventing illness and providing effective treatment and care* – by tobacco policies, improving primary care and tackling the 'big killers' of coronary heart disease (CHD) and cancer

* *addressing the underlying determinants of health* – emphasising the need for concerted action across government at national and local level up to and beyond the 2010 target date.

'Choosing Health' (2004)

The public health white paper *Choosing health: making healthy choices easier* was published by the government in November 2004. It recognised that interest in health was increasing and recommended a new approach to public health that reflected the rapidly changing and increasingly technological society we live in. The document reviewed health and health inequalities and acknowledged the strong role for government in promoting social justice and tackling the wider causes of ill health and inequality, as well as recognising the need to support and empower individuals to make changes in their own lives:

The strategy set out in the document had three underpinning principles, outlined below.

1. Informed choice: although with two important qualifications –

    * protect children

    * do not allow one person's choice to adversely affect another, e.g. passive smoking

2. Personalisation: support tailored to the needs of individuals

3. Working together: real progress depends on effective partnerships across communities.

Its main priorities were to:

* reduce the number of people who smoke

* reduce obesity and improve diet and nutrition

* increase exercise

* encourage and support sensible drinking

* improve sexual health

* improve mental health.

The public health paper set out the areas for action shown in Figure 3.8.

FIGURE 3.7 *Walking to school is a health-promoting activity*

Think it over...

Look at the difference between the types of actions in the most recent public health white paper, *Choosing Health* (2004), and *Our Healthier Nation* (OHN, 1997). The former is built around programmes of work as opposed to disease reduction targets.

* Which types of targets are more meaningful for the public and why?

* Both documents include actions that may take many years to produce improvements in health. Do you think it likely that the same government will be in power at the end of the ten-year time span set for achieving the targets?

* How does this influence campaigning at election times when the health agenda tends to focus on ill health services?

Children and young people	* *Personal health plans* for children – to develop their own health goals with help from their parents or carers, school staff and health professionals. * Healthy Start – a new scheme to provide disadvantaged pregnant women and mothers of young children with vouchers for fresh food and vegetables, milk and infant formula. * Support and information for young people – e.g. a new magazine, *FIT,* to get health information across to young men aged 16 to 30 years. * School travel – all schools in England should have active travel plans by 2010. * Food in schools – all 4–6-year-olds in LEA maintained schools in England will be eligible for free fruit or vegetables.
Communities leading for health	* *Communities for Health* – to promote action on locally chosen priorities for health across the local voluntary sector, the NHS, local authorities, business and industry. * Local authorities to work with the national transport charity Sustrans – to build over 7,000 miles of new cycle lanes and tracks. * National and local organisations invited to develop their role as corporate citizens – by making their own pledges on improving health to their workforce and local community. * All government departments and the NHS (subject to limited exceptions) – be smoke-free by 2006.
Health as a way of life	* Everyone who wants to will have the opportunity to use a Personal Health Kit to develop his or her own personal health guide. * A personal health resource where NHS health trainers help people to make healthy choices and stick to them.
Health-promoting NHS	* All NHS staff will be trained to deliver key health messages effectively as part of their day-to-day work with patients. * A national screening programme for chlamydia will cover all areas of England. * Guidance and training to ensure all health professionals are able to identify alcohol problems early.
Work and health	* The NHS will become a model employer. * New initiatives to challenge discrimination and improve access to work for people with mental illness.

FIGURE 3.8 *Areas for action set out in* Choosing Health *(2004)*

Local health strategy

The 1997 white paper *The New NHS – Modern and Dependable* created a responsibility for Primary Care Trusts to draw up a local health strategy and targets in a document called the *Health Improvement Programme* (HImP). These documents had to:

* give a clear description of how the national aims, priorities, targets and contracts can be tackled locally

* set out a range of locally determined targets

* show the action proposed is based on evidence of what is known to work

* show that measures of local progress will be used

* indicate which local organisations have been involved in compiling it

* ensure the plan is easy to understand and accessible

* be a vehicle for shaping future NHS strategy.

HImPs have now, largely, been subsumed within the community strategy, a partnership document which is drawn up through the district's Local Strategic Partnership (LSP). An LSP is a single body that:

* brings together, at a local level, the different parts of the public sector as well as the private, business, community and voluntary sectors so that different initiatives and services support each other and work together

* is a non-statutory, non-executive organisation

* operates at a level which enables strategic decisions to be taken and is close enough to individual neighbourhoods to allow actions to be determined at community level

* should be aligned with local authority boundaries.

The role of the LSP is to:

* prepare and implement a community strategy for the area, identify and deliver the most important things which need to be done, keep track of progress, and keep it up to date

* bring together local plans, partnerships and initiatives to provide a forum through which mainstream public service providers (local authorities, the police, health services, central government agencies, and so on) work effectively together to meet local needs and priorities

* develop and deliver a local neighbourhood renewal strategy to secure more jobs, better education, improved health, reduced crime, and better housing, closing the gap between deprived neighbourhoods and the rest, and contributing to the national targets to tackle deprivation.

From the list of responsibilities it is possible to see that the planning led by LSPs will be at the centre of improving local health and well-being; therefore, in most districts the HImP has been incorporated within the community strategy or no longer exists in any identifiable form. The community strategy is a local plan 'to improve the economic, social and environmental well-being of each area and its inhabitants, and contribute to the achievement of sustainable development in the UK' (*The New NHS – Modern and Dependable*, 1997).

It is the role of the Primary Care Trust to contribute to the process of drawing up a community strategy, informing the planners about local health patterns and to lead on planning local health services through the Local Development Plan (LDP), which is a five-year business plan for developing local health services drawn up by the PCTs.

Summary

* Health can be defined in many ways and has several aspects to it including physical, emotional, psychological, and so on

* Health can be defined both positively and negatively in terms of illness and disease

* People have their own perspectives on health, which influence their health behaviours

* The two dominant models of health are the biomedical model (on which modern medicine is based) and the social model

* Government has a major part to play in promoting health, as illustrated through the many policy initiatives such as *The Health of the Nation (1992)* through to the most recent, *Choosing Health (2004)*

* Local health strategy is defined in the health improvement plan (HImP) or increasingly in the community strategy.

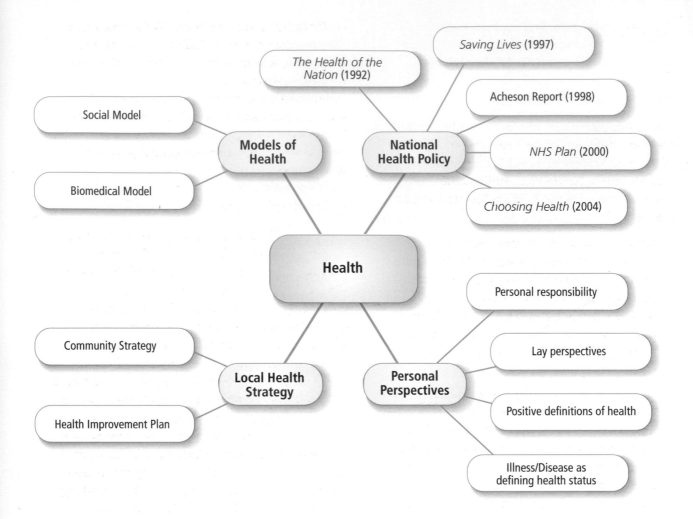

Consider this

1 Imagine you are a senior civil servant tasked by the Secretary of State for Health to draw up a discussion paper that will form the basis of a tobacco-control strategy for the country:

2 As a starting point you will need to review local action plans to see what is happening within local health districts. What actions are mentioned in your local community strategy or Primary Care Trust health plan?

3 You are approached by many pressure groups, some of which base their suggestions on a medical model of health. What types of actions might they be suggesting?

4 Other groups base their suggestions on a societal view of health. What actions might they be suggesting the government adopt?

5 One of your suggested actions is a campaign to alert people to the dangers of smoking. Pick three of the lay models of health and describe how you would tailor the message to meet the specific needs of people with that perspective.

6 Previous government action like that through taxation measures, for example, has been criticised for compounding health inequalities by encouraging wealthier groups to quit smoking with little impact on lower socio-economic groups. What steps could you suggest to counter the risk of adding to existing health inequalities?

Section 2: Preventive measures and job roles

Measures and models

Just as there are many models of health, so too there are many models of health promotion. One of the most widely accepted is that suggested by Tannahil (from Naidoo and Willis, 2000), who describes three overlapping and related areas of activity:

* **Health Education** – communication to improve health and prevent ill health by improving people's knowledge on health, and changing their attitudes to aspects of their health. The possibilities for health education to make a difference can be seen in the decline in smoking rates over the latter years of the last century.

* **Health Protection** – population measures to safeguard health, for example through legislation, financial or social means. This might include legislation to govern health and safety at work or food hygiene, and using taxation policy to reduce smoking levels or car use, by raising the price of cigarettes or petrol.

* **Prevention** – reducing or avoiding the risks of diseases and ill health primarily through medical 'interventions'.

There are several approaches and levels for health promotion activity to take place: these are dealt with in more detail in the next section.

Tannahil's model emphasises the breadth of activities that can be included in the term health promotion, and the way the various spheres of activity interconnect.

Figure 3.8 illustrates the wide variety of activities that can be classed as health promoting, from those which operate at an individual level to those which depend upon national government action.

Health education

This is usually defined as the process of giving information and advice and of facilitating the development of knowledge and skills in order to change behaviour. Health educators include a wide range of professions including teachers, social workers, practice nurses, health visitors, leisure centre staff, and so on. In some cases this is an acknowledged part of their role: for example, in health visiting and practice nursing it is accepted that part of the role is to work one to one with people to increase their knowledge and skills to enable them to improve their own health. However, in some cases the potential for a health promotion role may not be so easily recognised: for example, a community police officer walking the local streets will frequently come across groups of young people who might be smoking and/or intoxicated, which clearly presents a health promoting opportunity that the officer may not appreciate or be trained to deal with effectively.

There are also more developed models of health education, which see health education as

1	Preventive services	Immunisation, cervical screening, developmental surveillance
2	Preventive health education	Substance use education in schools
3	Preventive health protection	Fluoridation of water supplies
4	Health education for preventive health education	Lobbying for fluoridation or seatbelt legislation
5	Positive health education	Work with young people to develop positive self-esteem
6	Positive health protection	Smoking bans in public places
7	Health education aimed at positive health protection	Lobbying for a ban on tobacco advertising or smoking bans in pubs

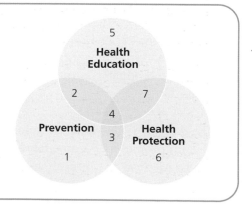

FIGURE 3.8 *Tannahil's model of health promotion*

raising critical consciousness (amongst key policy makers and members of the community), testing values and attitudes and empowering communities to address local health issues. In this model it also operates as a two-way process, informing policy makers as well (as members of the local community), raising their appreciation of the concerns of local people.

In this type of model, service users are not empty vessels waiting to be filled with the right health knowledge, i.e. people do not change their behaviour once they are in receipt of the right knowledge or skill. Health education is fraught with ethical considerations. Two of the most important issues here would be the right to self-determination of the service users and the need for the service providers to remain non-judgmental. Ethics plays an important part for health educators, as they draw out the needs of the service users and work with them towards an informed choice; this may turn out to be a health-damaging choice for the service users. Can the professionals now accept and respect that decision and not coerce or persuade them to adopt a different choice, when that would be neither effective nor ethical? Clearly health education can present serious challenges to the educators.

Think it over...

In a small group you might want to discuss:

* Should health educators tell people what is best for them?
* Do health educators fail if they accept the service user's health damaging behaviour?
* Who determines what is a healthy lifestyle, service user or educator?
* Should health behaviour be a matter of personal choice or is too important to leave to the individual?

The danger with health education activity is that health promoters become fixed on the goal of improved medical or physical health to the detriment of other aspects of holistic health. It is too easy for professionals to adopt a judgmental approach, deciding what is best for the individual to the exclusion of that person's right to self-

autonomy. It is important to remember that empowering people is an integral part of effective and ethical health-promotion work. To enable health promoters to make ethical judgments about the work they undertake, the following questions can be considered:

* Will service users be able to choose freely for themselves?
* Will I be respecting their decision, whether or not I approve of it?
* Will I be non discriminatory – respecting all people equally?
* Will I be serving the more basic needs before addressing other wants?
* Will I be doing good and preventing harm?
* Will I be telling the truth?
* Will I be minimising harm in the long term?
* Will I be able to honour promises and agreements I make?

These points are as equally applicable for a one-to-one service user/professional scenario, or a planner considering alterations to local roads in a housing estate. Here, for example they might be asking themselves whether they have adequately involved the local people in the decision-making process and if they have respected their input, not valuing it differently to that of other professionals.

Another example might be a midwife discussing smoking with a pregnant woman; here

FIGURE 3.9 *Service providers respect the service user's right to choose*

the midwife has considerable knowledge about the potential damage to the unborn child and the possibility of further health damage if the mother continues to smoke after the birth. However, to be an ethical health promoter she must respect the service user's right to choose whether to continue smoking and not allow the decision to continue smoking (should that be the case) to change the relationship.

Midwives are not alone in facing this problem. Many women resume smoking after the birth, meaning that the health visitor may also face the challenge of how to sensitively discuss possible harm to the children without damaging the relationship she has with the mother. If you were that health visitor:

* Think of three things you would most wish to convey to the mother.

* What would you have to be mindful of when having this discussion?

* Would having this conversation in the mother's home present any difficulties/opportunities for you?

* Why is it appropriate for you to have this discussion with the mother?

This task is further complicated by the changing nature of health messages as the knowledge base for health education develops. This can lead to confusion within the general population: for example, the change in alcohol safe drinking limits, which recently moved from a weekly guidance to daily levels, to reflect the shift towards binge drinking patterns.

---

* DID YOU KNOW?

Currently the Department of Health advises that:

* men should not drink more than 3–4 units of alcohol <u>per day</u>

* women should drink no more than 2–3 units of alcohol <u>per day</u>.

Daily benchmarks apply whether you drink every day, once or twice a week, or occasionally.

Research has suggested that the majority of health professionals are not clear what advice to give people and are not aware of the change.

Think it over...

Review with a family member or friend an aspect of their health-related behaviour which they know is damaging to their health: for example, continuing to smoke or not taking sufficient exercise. Try to find out:

* The extent of their knowledge about that health issues. Do they know and understand the relevant health messages?

* Why they continue with that behaviour if they know it harms them?

* How they feel when people ask them about it, as you are doing?

* What their expectations of health professionals are. Do they expect to be asked about it each time they visit their GP, for example?

Prevention

It is all too easy to see health promotion as solely focusing on preventing people from becoming ill. This is, indeed, an important part of the span of health promotion, but it also includes two other categories of health-promoting activity which deal with people who are already ill in some way: these three tiers of health promotion activity are primary, secondary and tertiary prevention.

Primary prevention

This is an attempt to eliminate the possibility of getting a disease. The childhood immunisation programme is an example of a health protection activity under this heading. Other examples include smoking education as part of personal and social health education in schools, and leaflets and posters for use in promoting healthy eating.

Secondary prevention

This addresses those people identified as being in the early stages of a disease, usually through early detection of symptoms. Action focuses on addressing the underlying causes, in order to alleviate any further symptoms. Examples might include action to address raised blood pressure taken by a doctor, who identified those symptoms as part of a routine check-up for a patient. This action might be drug therapy but equally could be a referral onto a physical activity scheme for promoting regular exercise, in collaboration with the local leisure services departments (usually referred to as an 'exercise on prescription' scheme). This sort of scheme might also be used for people who are overweight, or for people with mild depression. Therefore, a range of secondary prevention issues can be addressed through one scheme. Alternatively, a 'stop smoking' group would be a secondary prevention initiative for someone who is already suffering from respiratory problems such as repeat infections, bronchitis and so on.

FIGURE 3.10 *Secondary prevention may include support groups*

* What do people gain from support groups that they cannot get from one-to-one counselling?

* What do one-to-one sessions provide that groups can not?

* How do you think the two can compliment each other?

Tertiary prevention

This refers to the control and reduction (as far as possible) of an already established disease. This is not easily distinguishable from medical care, but it is possible to consider issues such as increasing the capacity of individuals to manage their

condition and their own health. An example might be supporting and enabling people with a history of heart attacks to regain their confidence, enabling them to live a more fulfilling life and be in control of their own destiny, as far as is possible. It could also apply to someone suffering from Parkinson's disease being supported in learning about and managing his or her condition as independently as possible. A more common and less obvious example might be the provision of dentures to people who have had teeth extracted.

Think it over...

The following are examples of tertiary prevention services:

* an 'exercise on prescription' scheme
* a coronary rehabilitation scheme
* a stroke rehabilitation service
* a community drugs service.

  1. Find out if you have any of these services operating in your area.

  2. If you were a potential service user, how would you gain access to the service? What sources of information did you use to find out about them?

  3. What do the services offer to the people using them?

Health protection – screening

Screening was defined by the American Commission on Chronic Illness in 1957 as 'the presumptive identification of unrecognised disease or defect by the application of tests, examinations and other procedures which can be applied rapidly. Screening tests sort out apparently well people who may have a disease from those who do not.'

However, screening a well population can be a contentious issue, with many attendant problems: for example, are we right to be medicalising a well population in this way? In almost all cases the majority of people screened will not be ill with the condition screened for. Also, screening for some conditions remains an imprecise science. To help with deciding if a screening programme is

| WILSON AND JUNGNER'S CRITERIA FOR SCREENING PROGRAMMES |

1. The condition to be sought should be an important public health problem
2. There should be an acceptable intervention for a patient identified as having the condition
3. Effective facilities for diagnosis and treatment should be in place
4. There should be a period when early symptoms can be identified
5. There should be a suitable test or examination
6. The progress of the disease or defect should be understood
7. There should be an agreed definition for the condition so that a diagnosis can be made against clear criteria
8. Early treatment should have favourable results
9. The cost of screening should be favourable against treatment of people who develop the condition
10. Any repeat screening should be clearly justified

FIGURE 3.11 *Criteria for screening programmes*

Think it over...

Health workers sometimes use the two terms 'screening' and 'surveillance' interchangeably to talk about the same thing. Divide a page in two with a line: place one word on each side of the page and then quickly write down all the things that word makes you think about. Do not leave out things which do not appear to be about health. Try to capture all the feelings and thoughts that this word conjures up for you.

* Can you see any differences between the way in which you think about these two words?

* What messages might we be sending out to people through use of terms like screening and surveillance?

appropriate Wilson and Jungner (1968) set out a list of criteria against which screening programmes could be evaluated. See Figure 3.11.

Cervical screening

The NHS Cervical Screening Programme was set up in 1988. The programme screens almost four million women in England each year. Cervical screening – including the cost of treating cervical abnormalities – has been estimated to cost around £150 million a year in England, or about £37.50 per woman screened.

Cervical screening is not a test for cancer. It is a method of preventing cancer by detecting and treating early abnormalities that, if left untreated, could lead to cancer in a woman's cervix (the neck of the womb). The first stage in cervical screening is either a smear test or **liquid-based cytology** (LBC). A sample of cells is taken from the cervix for analysis. A doctor or nurse inserts an instrument (a speculum) to open the woman's vagina and uses a spatula to sweep around the cervix. The sample of cells is 'smeared' onto a slide, which is sent to a laboratory for examination under a microscope. Early detection and treatment can prevent 80–90 per cent of cancers developing, but like other screening tests, it is not perfect. It may not always detect early cell changes that could lead to cancer. The programme aims to reduce the number of women who develop invasive cervical cancer (incidence) and the number of women who die from it (mortality). It does this by regularly screening all women at risk so that conditions, which might otherwise develop into invasive cancer, can be identified and treated.

All women between the ages of 25 and 64 are eligible for a free cervical smear test every 3–5 years. In the light of new evidence, the NHS Cervical Screening Programme will now be implementing screening at different intervals depending on age.

AGE GROUP (YEARS)	FREQUENCY OF SCREENING
25	First invitation
25–49	3-yearly
50–64	5-yearly
65+	Only screen those who have not been screened since 50 years old or who have had recent abnormal tests

FIGURE 3.12 *The NHS Cervical Screening Programme*

The NHS call and recall system invites women who are registered with a GP. This also keeps track of any follow-up investigation, and, if all is well, recalls the woman for screening in 3–5 years time. Women who have not had a recent smear test may be offered one when they attend their GP or family planning clinic on another matter. Women should receive their first invitation for routine screening at 25. Women under 25 and women over 65 are not invited because cervical cancer is rare in women in these age groups. Also, young women may get an abnormal smear result purely because this is the time when the female body is still developing – particularly the cervix, where cell changes may be the result of growth. This could lead to unnecessary treatment so screening young women might do more harm than good.

Breast screening

The NHS Breast Screening Programme provides free breast screening every three years for all women in the UK aged 50 years and over. Around one-and-a-half million women are now screened in the UK each year. Women aged between 50–64 years are routinely invited for breast screening every three years, and work is being carried out to extend the programme to women up to and including the age of 70 by 2004.

Breast screening is a method of detecting breast cancer at a very early stage. The first step involves an X-ray of each breast – a **mammogram** – which is taken while carefully compressing the breast. The mammogram can detect small changes in breast tissue, which may indicate cancers that are too small to be felt either by the woman herself or by a doctor. There are over 90 breast screening units across the UK, each currently inviting an average population of around 45,000 women. Women are invited to a specialised screening unit, which can either be mobile, hospital based, or permanently based in a convenient location, such as a shopping centre.

The NHS Breast Screening Programme was the first of its kind in the world. It began inviting women for screening in 1990, and national coverage was achieved by the mid–1990s. The rate of cancers detected per 1,000 women screened and the standardised detection ratio has risen steadily. In 2001/2002, statistics showed that for every 1,000 women screened, 6.8 cancers were detected. In England, the budget for the Breast Screening Programme, including the actual cost of screening, is approximately £52 million. This works out at about £30 per woman invited, or £40 per woman screened.

Women under 50 years are not offered routine screening. Mammograms seem not to be as effective in pre-menopausal women, possibly because the density of the breast tissue makes it more difficult to detect problems and also because the incidence of breast cancer is lower. The average age of the menopause in the UK is 50 years. As women go through the menopause, the glandular tissue in the breast 'involutes' and the breast tissue is increasingly made up of only fat. This is clearer on the mammogram and makes interpretation of the X-ray more reliable. Breast cancer is also far more common in post-menopausal women and the risk continues to increase with rising age.

Infant screening

Some defects in young children are unlikely to be recognised by even the most astute of parents. In these situations, only a trained health professional may identify potential problems if specific screening tests are carried out. Good examples here would include: high frequency hearing loss, before an age when a child would normally be expected to start to talk; or congenital dislocation of the hip, before the age at which a child would normally walk. From the moment of birth, young children are routinely screened for specific conditions. A newborn baby will be screened for:

* height, weight and head circumference
* birthmarks
* heart defects
* congenital dislocation of the hips
* eye defects
* hearing
* a range of metabolic disorders.

Some or all of these tests are repeated at 2 weeks, 6–8 weeks, 3–4 months, 6–9 months, 18–24 months, 3–3½ years and at 5 years. This will involve a range of health personnel including the midwife, health visitor, family doctor and school nurse who must all liaise effectively to track the health record of the one child. This is usually through a 'patient held record', which is left with the parents or guardian.

Health protection – immunisation

Conquering infectious diseases has led to the most significant reductions in mortality. It is possible to make people immune to certain diseases by challenging their immune system with a weak or inactivated version of the disease organism to stimulate the person to create antibodies to the disease. This will enable their immune system to respond quickly should they contract the disease later on, resulting in no more than mild symptoms instead of experiencing the worst aspects of the disease.

The Immunisation Programme (see Figure 3.13) creates what is known as '**herd immunity**': that is, if enough people within the population are immunised the likelihood of any epidemic is greatly reduced. For this reason the government sets targets for immunisation rates for local health services to meet. Any regular fall below these levels signals a potential epidemic and becomes a serious cause of concern.

Routinely, children are immunised for diphtheria, typhoid, polio, measles, mumps and rubella. These last three are particularly contentious because some parents believe there

may be a link between the MMR (measles, mumps and rubella) vaccine and autism. Whilst there is, as yet, no strong supporting evidence it has undermined public confidence in the vaccine and reduced the uptake by parents. This in turn risks the herd immunity and consequently an epidemic of measles or rubella, for example.

WHEN TO IMMUNISE	WHAT IS GIVEN	HOW IT IS GIVEN
2, 3 and 4 months old	Diphtheria, tetanus, pertussis (whooping cough), polio and Hib	One injection
	Meningitis C	One injection
Around 13 months old	Measles, mumps and rubella (MMR)	One injection
3⅓–5 years old	Diphtheria, tetanus, pertussis (whooping cough) and polio	One injection
	Measles, mumps and rubella (MMR)	One injection
10–14 years old (and sometimes shortly after birth)	BCG (against tuberculosis)	Skin test, then, if needed, one injection
13–18 years old	Diphtheria, tetanus, polio	One injection

FIGURE 3.13 *The NHS Immunisation Programme*

Significant educators for health and well being

If you use a social model of health it is possible to see how the promotion of health will involve a wide range of possible interventions, which influence the so-called determinants of health. With this in mind it is possible to see that a wide range of people and agencies, therefore, have the potential to promote the health of the local population. See Figure 3.14.

Think it over...

It is possible to routinely screen for many other conditions: for example, there are many screening tools available to assess a person's alcohol use and identify those who are hazardous or harmful drinkers and at risk of damaging their health. However, it is not ethical to use population-screening approaches when the relevant treatment is not available, as in the case of alcohol use.

1. What reasons might lead to treatment not being available?

2. What challenges do you think this ethical dilemma might present for healthcare professionals who are not able to treat because of this situation?

3. How would you feel as a patient if this affected you?

FIGURE 3.14 *A local health-promoting network*

Health services

The health inequalities we see in society today can, to some extent, be explained by the wide variations in access to high quality health care. In the 1970s, a GP (Tudor Hart) coined the term the 'Inverse Care Law' to describe the way in which the quality of health care provision was often directly inverse (opposite) to the local need. That is, services are usually poor in the areas with most sickness and death: for example, in these areas GPs often have larger lists, more work, less hospital support and poorer premises.

An understanding of the health care professional/patient relationship can help understand one aspect of the 'inverse care law', specifically the way in which people engage with local health services. Tudor Hart suggested that this relationship is often at its least effective in these disadvantaged communities. In 1994 Baldock and Ungerson attempted to summarise people's attitudes to community care services using a simple model which described four roles that people can adopt when services are made available to them in a free market format. This is illustrated in Figure 3.15.

This model is just that – a means of helping us understand how real world systems operate. It does not mean that people have to rigidly fit one role; they may move between roles depending upon their circumstances. However, it will explain why people will have different experiences of using the same health services.

The primary function of the NHS is to treat sick people. Although health promotion activity could and should be a feature of many health service roles, in practice this aspect of health activity is the poor relation to the primary goal of treating the sick. The recent government reorganisation of the NHS has emphasised its health improvement role, specifying that Primary Care Trusts have a primary function of 'improving the health of their local population'. There are key personnel within the NHS who can contribute to this end including those outlined opposite.

The public health department

This will usually now include both specialist public health practitioners and the health promotion service.

The public health team has a key role in assessing the patterns of ill health locally and identifying what types of health care provision and health promoting activities are required to

THE FOUR ROLES OF BALDOCK AND UNGERSON'S MODEL	
Consumers	People who expect nothing form the State and set out to arrange the necessary care by buying it themselves. They believe that using the market in this way gives them control and autonomy, much like buying a car or any other kind of consumer goods. These people know about the services but prefer to purchase their own care for a variety of reasons, including convenience and perceived quality.
Privatists	People who have learnt to manage alone. A group associated with the growth of home ownership and the increasing emphasis on home and family, as opposed to wider sociability. Adapting to being cared for in later life can mean leaving the family home and increased dependency, which they find hard to come to terms with because it means having to ask for help. They can become isolated and fail to access the necessary healthcare. Generally, they do least well of the four in accessing services.
Welfarists	People who believe in the Welfare State and their right to use it: they expect and demand their rights to relevant services. The attitudes that underpin this mode are based on a strong sense of citizenship and welfare rights. They have both the understanding and the know how to make sure they get the most from the system and use it effectively to access both public and voluntary provision.
Clientists	People who accept passively what they are offered without demanding or expecting more. Neither do they expect services to be flexible in being able to respond to their specific needs. This is commonly seen in older people and low income groups, explaining how people in disadvantaged communities will often accept the poor state of their local health services and not challenge and demand better provision.

FIGURE 3.15 *Roles that people adopt when services are made available to them in a free market format*

Source: Baldock and Ungerson (1994)

improve health locally. The activities provided through the public health team can be seen through the areas of competence which public health practitioners are able to demonstrate:

* surveillance and assessment of the population's health and well-being

* promoting and protecting the population's health and well-being

* risk management and evaluation of activity

* collaborative working for health and well-being

* developing health programmes and services and reducing inequalities

* policy and strategy development and implementation

* working with and for communities

* strategic leadership for health and well-being

* research and development

* ethical principles for health promotion and public health.

Specialist health promotion services

These are now usually located within, or alongside, the public health team. They are a small, specialised service which supports the development of the health promoting role of others, the development of new services and policies which can promote health locally. The role of these services has grown and developed over time, the flexibility to do this being largely due to the fact that it is not a profession governed by a professional body, thus enabling local teams to grow and develop into new areas of practice in response to local need. However, there is a national set of competencies for health promotion practice, which identifies the degree of overlap with public health practice, recognising that health promotion specialists are a part of the wider public health specialism. Their role is best illustrated by the example of the activities a service might offer in the school setting, as shown in Figure 3.16.

Improving health and preventing disease is also the responsibility of those working to provide health care – especially those with community-based roles (as opposed to hospital-based workers). Their health promotion role dates back to two key NHS papers, *Prevention and Health: Everybody's Business* (DHSS 1976) and the later *GP (family doctor) Contract* (1990), which emphasised the importance of risk factor reduction, screening and lifestyle advice in a primary health care setting.

Community nursing

Nurses are one professional group that has a long history of working in a primary and community care setting. Community nurses also contribute to public health practice, working with communities as well as providing care to individuals. The public health contribution of nurses, health visitors and midwives was outlined in *Making it Happen* (DOH 1995). This emphasised that nurses, midwives and health visitors were not only 'hands on'

HEALTH PROMOTION: CORE COMPETENCIES IN ACTION — THE SCHOOL SETTING	
Raising public awareness	Direct campaigning within schools, e.g. national days such as No Smoking Day or World Aids Day. The organisation of events such as sex education conferences or the supporting the school celebrations of achievements within the Healthy School Programme, linking with and involving the media in these types of events.
Advice and consultancy	The support by specialists offered to schools participating in the Healthy School Programme, facilitating training and policy development, advising on the submission and the particular topics the school is working on.
Service development	The 'health-promoting school award' provides a framework for schools to incorporate health issues into their development plans in terms of training, policy development, finance and so on. The extended schools programme also provides opportunities for developing school-based health services, e.g. School Nurse drop-in sessions. The health promotion specialists would provide a leading role for coordinating the development of these types of service-based initiatives.
Policy development	Supporting schools in the development of a wide range of specific policies including sex education, smoking, substance use, and nutrition.
Project planning	The management of specific projects, e.g. working with local parents on how to discuss difficult issues, such as sex and drugs.
Research	Undertaking research, e.g. health surveys to establish what young people's health behaviours are in the locality, or consulting young people about specific issues.
Training and education	Providing in-service training on health education, co-facilitating classes to offer models of good practice for health and health-related subjects.
Resources	Specialists both advise on purchases of new materials for the resource centre, and recommend resources and appropriate methods of use.
Challenging prejudice, and discrimination	Specialists encourage the development of policies and work practices that challenge the root causes of ill health, e.g. policies around equal opportunities, and ensuring that equal opportunities strategies are included in all policy documents and subsequent strategy initiatives.

FIGURE 3.16 *Example of a specialist health-promotion service in a school setting*

NURSE	TYPE OF ACTIVITIES
Community nurses	Carry out nursing care, e.g. bandaging and care of wounds in the patients' homes
Community midwives	Monitor and support expectant mothers, pre- and post-birth, outside the hospital; in some cases carry out home deliveries
Health visitors	Primary role is to monitor child development from first week after birth, carry out regular assessment tests and advise on parenting. However, they are also often referred to as public health nurses, able to respond to a diverse range of local community needs, such as establishing mother and toddler groups; providing a range of training and development groups for parents (e.g. on effective parenting, baby massage); or supporting local community activity such as food cooperatives.
School nurses	Carry out routine screening of school-age children and support administration of vaccination programme. They can also be involved in school-based PSHE programmes (personal and social health education).
Occupational health nurses	Provide nursing support on site for larger employers, which can include health-promoting activity, such as health check-ups and stop smoking advice.

FIGURE 3.17 *Diverse roles of nurses*

professionals, delivering care to individuals, but also had an important role to play in the development and implementation of local health improvement initiatives (see Figure 3.17).

Examples include:

* the school nursing role in supporting the implementation of the National Healthy School Standard, working with teachers, governors, parents and pupils to develop a healthy policy and practice in the school environment, across a range of issues.

* the role of the health visitor, profiling and then responding to local health needs, possibly by supporting groups of young parents, or volunteers trying to set up a food coop.

General practitioners (GPs)

GPs are independent practitioners; that is they are, in effect, small businesses that contract with the NHS in the shape of the local primary care trust to provide a range of services. GPs have a practice population, or list, which may be widely dispersed. This is because people who register with a GP may build up a relationship with them over many years and choose to remain with the

practice even when they move away from the area. GPs form the hub of a primary health care team that is itself the backbone of the local medical services. The World Health Organisation (WHO) defined primary health care in 1978 as being:

'Essential health care made universally accessible to individuals and families in the community… It forms an integral part of both the country's health system, of which it is the central function and main focus, and of the overall social and economic development of the community.'

Primary health care teams are the first point of contact for people who are unwell, and act as the gatekeeper to more specialised or secondary services in hospital settings. The operation of the GP services is governed by the new General Medical Services contract (nGMS contract)

The GMS contract aims to provide GPs with greater flexibility in determining the range of services they provide. It creates the possibility of opting-out of some provision, such as out-of-hours care, and providing others at a more enhanced or special interest level. The GMS contract is inspired by the government's NHS

SERVICES PROVIDED BY GPs	
Essential Services	All practices must provide a full range of essential services, covering the day-to-day work of general practice (for example, chronic disease management).
Additional Services	Most practices will offer a range of additional services like contraceptive services, maternity services, cervical screening and some minor surgery.
Enhanced Services	These are optional (other than Direct Enhanced Services which must be provided in every locality), and involve either the provision of essential or additional services to a higher standard, or more specialist interventions not provided by most GPs. Enhanced services can be negotiated at a local level, though for a small number of treatment areas there are national specifications and benchmark pricing.

FIGURE 3.18 *Clinical services provided by GPs under the GMS contract*

modernisation agenda, which has also informed the NHS Plan, the National Service Frameworks and the Priorities and Planning Frameworks.

The new contract will be between primary care organisations (PCOs) and practices, rather than GPs and health authorities. It compartmentalises clinical work into three service categories as shown in Figure 3.18.

Environmental health personnel

The environmental health service has a broad public health role covering housing, food safety, water supply, refuse disposal and pollution control. Increasingly, the emphasis on the key statutory duties of surveillance and enforcement, have frequently left little scope for developing a

SERVICES PROVIDED BY ENVIRONMENTAL HEALTH OFFFICERS	
Food safety	The food safety team is responsible for ensuring that all food produced or sold locally is safe. Complaints are investigated and food samples taken for examination. Diseases which could be food or water borne are also investigated.
Health and safety	The commercial safety team are responsible for enforcing health and safety legislation in the majority of work places including offices, shops, places of entertainment, consumer and leisure services. All premises allocated to the local authority for enforcement are regularly inspected and action taken, be it advice and education or formal enforcement action (including prosecution). It is a legal requirement that many workplace accidents are reported to the local authority and these are investigated to determine the cause and to prevent a repetition. Additional inspections are carried out at premises, which require special licences, including places of entertainment and skin piercers.
Environmental protection	The Environmental Health Department also has a role in investigating complaints from the public about a range of environmental nuisances which can affect people's health: this includes noise, smoke, fumes, odour and dust, all of which are investigated and minimised wherever possible.
Pest control/ Dog control	The pest control team treats rodent infestations in domestic and commercial premises throughout the district, as well as other public health pests, such as fleas, cockroaches and wasps. They also undertake an annual programme to control rats in the sewage system. The dog control team enforces the Dog Fouling Laws, provides advice and education on responsible dog ownership and removes stray dogs from the street.

FIGURE 3.19 *Some of the core statutory functions of Environmental Health Departments*

broader, comprehensive approach to the improvement of the public's health, such as the role it adopts in home safety promotion and food safety training. Environmental Health Departments have, therefore, tended to focus their activities around the core statutory functions which includes those listed in Figure 3.19.

FIGURE 3.20 *Environmental Health Officer monitoring noise pollution*

Think it over...

Noise nuisance is the most common form of complaint in neighbourhood disputes.

✴ What types of noise pollution do you experience in the place where you live?

✴ How might you be contributing to the noise pollution in your neighbourhood?

✴ Contact your local Environmental Health Department and find out what constitutes a noise nuisance

✴ How can people complain and what steps can the department take to control that pollution?

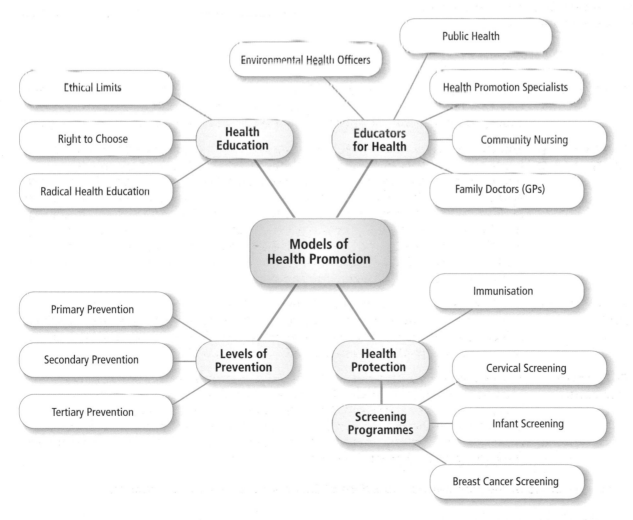

- Ethical Limits
- Right to Choose
- Radical Health Education

Health Education

- Environmental Health Officers
- Public Health
- Health Promotion Specialists
- Community Nursing
- Family Doctors (GPs)

Educators for Health

Models of Health Promotion

- Primary Prevention
- Secondary Prevention
- Tertiary Prevention

Levels of Prevention

Health Protection

- Immunisation
- Cervical Screening
- Infant Screening
- Breast Cancer Screening

Screening Programmes

Summary

There are many models of health promotion but one of the most widely accepted is Tannahil's (Naidoo and Willis, 2000), which breaks health promotion into three areas of work:

* Health education – communication to improve health
  * Ethical behaviour is a challenge for health educators when considering the service user's right to choose

* Health protection – population measures to safeguard health
  * Prevention is split into three levels, primary secondary and tertiary prevention

* Prevention – reducing or avoiding the risks of disease
  * Health protection includes national screening programmes, such as those for breast cancer and cervical cancer, and immunisation programmes

Consider this

The role of the Environmental Health Department is described in this section.

1. What aspects of the service might be classified under the three aspects of health promotion: education, protection and prevention?

2. Think of an example of activities they might undertake which could be classed as primary and secondary prevention.

3. Of the other health educators described in this section, who could help you with your role in the Environmental Health Department and what activities would they contribute?

4. The incidence of food poisoning has been rising steadily in recent years. Find out what the position is in your district and what the likely causes are of this national problem

5. How could environmental health contribute to a radical health education approach to empower a local community? What types of issues might local people wish to work with this department to address? You might want to check with your local department to see what types of complaints they routinely deal with.

Section 3: Factors affecting health and well-being

Dahlgren and Whitehead (1995) mapped these fields as layers of influence, referring to them as the determinants of health, which can be modified to improve health expectancy:

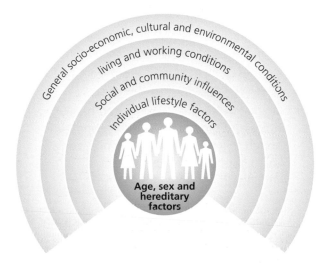

Their work is now widely used to understand the broad range of influences on health, and more importantly how best to promote it. In this section we will look at a few of these factors from across their model including attitudes to health and their link to lifestyle choice, social factors including social class and culture income and disability.

Attitudes and prejudices

Lay perspectives can determine our attitudes to health and have a significant impact in determining how we respond to the challenge of managing our own health and well-being. However, of increasing importance has been the growing distrust by the general public of health professionals and the health advice they provide. This has been most graphically illustrated through the recent collapse of public confidence in the MMR vaccine as a result of one dissenting voice in the health establishment.

A research paper by Andrew Wakefield suggesting that MMR vaccination in young children might be linked to **autism** sparked a controversy, which was swept up by a media storm and went on to heavily influence the UK's Department of Health, the World Health Organization, and most broadcast and print media for several days either side of its publication. The ensuing media storm, in many cases adopting Wakefield's stance as a *cause célèbre*, flew in the face of all existing scientific evidence.

Findings from many other researchers provide no support for an MMR-associated form of autism. Despite this there has been significant damage to the public confidence in the vaccination, leading to a reduction in coverage and an increase in the associated deaths from these diseases. (Deaths from measles are common in some European countries, and this is directly related to poor vaccine coverage.) Measles has almost been eliminated in Britain, but high levels of population immunity (greater than 90 per cent) are needed to prevent the recurrence of epidemics.

This collapse in confidence might also be linked to the MMR vaccine becoming a victim of its own success. When disease elimination is close, attention inevitably shifts to the side-effects of the vaccine.

The latest findings from the Health Education Authority, which has been tracking a random sample of mothers with children aged 0–2 years since 1991, found that 8 per cent of mothers now consider that the MMR vaccine presents a greater risk than the diseases it protects against and that 20 per cent consider the vaccine to have a moderate or high risk of side-effects.

In October 1994, just before the national immunisation campaign against measles and rubella, 55 per cent of mothers considered measles to be a very serious illness; now only 20 per cent do so. This mirrors the problems experienced with the whooping cough vaccine, where a sustained, misinformed media campaign against the vaccine throughout the 1970s saw vaccine coverage drop from 81 per cent to 31 per cent.

Worryingly, 67 per cent of people knew that some scientists had linked the MMR vaccine with autism; however, they also thought that the

FIGURE 3.21 *The MMR vaccine is given at around 13 months of age*

Think it over...

You might want to think about some of these issues in a group:

* Is it the duty of the press to provide balanced reporting? If, as in this case, the evidence is overwhelmingly one way, should the reporting still be balanced?

* How can the public differentiate between personal standpoint of the reporter and the factual reporting?

* The politicians involved at the time refused to tell the public whether their children had been vaccinated. Should they have done so to restore confidence in the vaccine?

* Should the NHS have recognised patient choice and provided a single vaccine, even though there was strong evidence that this would harm children by reducing immunisation levels?

evidence in favour of such a link was evenly balanced, or that the evidence even favoured a link. The long-term media coverage of controversy over the vaccine appears to have led the public to associate MMR and autism, despite the overwhelming evidence to the contrary. The public also thought the take-up of the MMR vaccine had fallen by more than 25 per cent since 1998, when, at the time of the survey, it was down by only 6 per cent.

The fears and concerns of parents are best seen through comments by one researcher who said: 'They [parents] wanted to trust their doctor and health visitor, but they felt they were being spun a political line', thus identifying the increasing politicisation of health practitioners and the erosion of public trust in their advice. Despite the huge amounts of scientific evidence to back up its policy, the government's medical advisors could not convince the public to simply accept their advice.

Lifestyle

As we have already seen it is too simplistic to see health as simply a matter of lifestyle choice as emphasized in this extract from *Choosing Health* (2004)...

'On paper, the answers can look deceptively simple – balance exercise and how much you eat, drink sensibly, practice safe sex, don't smoke. But knowing is not the same as doing. For individuals, motivation, opportunity and support all matter... Healthy choices are often difficult for anyone to make, but where people do not feel in control of their environment or their personal circumstances, the task can be more challenging. People who are disabled or suffer from mental ill health, stretched for money, out of work, poorly qualified, or who live in inadequate or temporary accommodation or in an area of high crime, are likely to experience less control over their lives than others.'

In a recent survey, 46 per cent of respondents agreed that there are too many factors outside of individual control to hold people responsible for their own health. Differences in responses for different groups suggest that people in lower socio-economic, socially excluded or black and minority ethnic groups may see health as being further beyond their individual control than others do.

The problem is not lack of information on what is good for you and what is not – people receive new 'facts' from all sides. The messages about health, however, are sometimes inconsistent or uncoordinated and out of step with the way people actually live their lives. It is a common assumption that lifestyle choices are simply a product of our attitudes to health. As a consequence, people routinely make judgements about the behaviours of others; statements such as 'that woman should not be smoking when she is pregnant' or 'that person who is overweight should go on a diet or take more exercise' might be typical examples of what is termed 'victim blaming' , i.e. lifestyle as a choice we all make. But there is now considerable evidence that choice is quite limited in many cases. For example, the vast majority of people who smoke are first recruited at a very young age, before they are mature enough to make an 'adult choice'. The complex nature of the environment and its impact on health choices is also important. For example, choosing healthy nutritious food is as much a feature of availability in the shops and access to the shops that provide it, as it is of personal choice. Therefore, it is unfair to make simple assumptions about people's health behaviours; lifestyle choice is often a more complex mix of issues. Several examples, including nutrition, smoking and substance use, are considered in more detail below.

Diet and nutrition

In the early parts of the 20th century the overwhelming focus of national food policy was that of securing enough food, as opposed to improving the diet of the population. This policy had its origins in the Boer War but became firmly established during the global conflicts of World War 1 and World War 11. Malnourishment, in terms of insufficient fat and protein in the diet, was widespread at this time and remained this way throughout the war years until the end of rationing. The current Western dietary problems are frequently traced back to this point as the origin of the range of choice and widespread availability of food, which we take for granted today. It is this shift to malnourishment in the form of over-consumption that now characterises the major dietary problems of the developed world.

Nutrition has recently become a high profile health issue, particularly in light of the way in which obesity has risen up the health agenda (as

illustrated by its prominence in *Choosing Health*, 2004). This is particularly because of startling recent trends in young children, where among 3–4-year-olds there has been a 60 per cent increase in the prevalence of being overweight and a 70 per cent increase in rates of obesity. Most adults in England are now overweight and one in five (around 8 million) are obese (Body Mass Index in excess of 30) with 30,000 deaths a year linked to obesity and an estimated cost to the NHS of £500 million a year.

If trends continue obesity will become, if it is not already, a major public health concern contributing substantially to:

* type 2 diabetes
* coronary heart disease
* hypertension
* depression
* cancers
* high blood pressure
* stroke.

As well as its role in tackling obesity, diet also has a major part to play in managing the current trends in cancers. Over the past 25 years the

---

* DID YOU KNOW?

The Body Mass Index (BMI) is a reliable indicator of total body fat, which is related to the risk of disease and death. BMI can be calculated using weight and height with the following equation:

$$BMI = \frac{\text{Weight in kilograms}}{(\text{Height in metres}) \times (\text{Height in metres})}$$

The score is valid for both men and women but it does have limits. It may overestimate body fat in athletes and others who have a muscular build, and it may underestimate body fat in older persons and others who have lost muscle mass.

	BMI
Underweight	Below 18.5
Normal	18.5–24.9
Overweight	25.0–29.9
Obesity	30.0 and above

---

incidence of all cancers has risen by 8 per cent in men and 17 per cent in women. Up to 80 per cent of bowel and breast cancer may be preventable by dietary change. These trends in diet-related cancers and obesity have occurred, despite the main elements of the dietary message remaining the same for many years:

* eat plenty of fruit and vegetables
* eat plenty of cereal foods
* eat red meat and processed foods in moderation
* avoid high doses of vitamin supplements
* avoid highly salted foods
* drink alcohol in moderation.

If the message remains straightforward, why is it that 4 per cent of young people aged 4–18 years still eat no vegetables at all and an average 10-year-old will eat his or her own weight in chips over a 9-month period? One reason why people fail to act on this widely known information is that healthy eating messages carry too many negative and constricting associations. That is, the public view healthy eating as being part of a boring lifestyle, as the government states in the 2004 white paper: 'Alcohol and fast food are portrayed as offering excitement, escape and instant gratification.' Therefore, it raises a need to develop positive images of healthier lifestyles for people to aspire to.

It is all too easy to view public health issues, such as obesity, in simplistic ways; nutrition inequalities mirror those of other issues, for example:

* poorer groups eat the least quantities of fresh fruit and vegetables
* dental caries are more common in children from lower socio-economic groups – due to higher levels of sweet consumption
* households in the bottom 10 per cent of income distribution spend an average of 29 per cent of their disposable income on food, compared to 18 per cent for those in the top 10 per cent.

Assumptions about the buying patterns of the less well off are often flawed: people in the low socio-economic groups buy more efficiently than those in high income brackets, obtaining more grams of food per pound spent. However, that often requires spending more on high calorific value foods, such as those rich in sugar and fat and therefore little in the way of fruit and vegetables; this also leads to lack of choice and variety to avoid risking waste. The food budget is also liable to squeezing by other demands, which impacts less in higher income households, a particular issue when healthy baskets of food can cost more in disadvantaged areas than in affluent.

The advent of large scale out-of-town supermarkets has enabled these stores to drive down cost through bulk purchasing but, as a consequence, led to a reduction in availability of healthy nutritious food locally on some estates.

FIGURE 3.22 *Local traders cannot compete with prices at the out-of-town supermarkets*

This creates difficulties in terms of travel and additional expense for these families, leading to the creation of so called food deserts on some estates, described as being 'populated urban areas where residents do not have access to affordable healthy food'. The charity 'Sustain' identifies that only 14–46 per cent of households on a £60–150 income per week have a car, often making larger out-of-town supermarkets inaccessible. People in deprived areas have to travel at least one mile to be able to access shops with a wider stock range, often requiring an expense of £2–3 in fares, both facts being compounded by the frequent shopping patterns of these households because of limited cash flow and storage. The issue is made worse by the fact that stores that do remain in deprived areas are frequently high cost and often offer poorer quality produce.

Therefore, it is highly unlikely that simplistic messages to eat the recommended five portions of fruit and vegetables a day will succeed in reversing the steady increase in the numbers of people who are overweight and obese. This problem is clearly as much to do with planning of supermarket developments, travel plans, the length of the working day, cooking skills, and a whole host of other larger societal issues, as to do with individual choice.

> **Think it over...**
>
> Promoting better diet is clearly a complex issue.
>
> Go back to the Dahlgren and Whitehead (1995) model of health inequalities; now break down the issue of nutrition using the layers this suggests. Use a single issue to consider it. For example, why are young children increasingly overweight and obese?
>
> 1 For each issue in each layer ask, how does this issue relate to the problem?
>
> 2 Write your observations down for each layer.
>
> 3 Now work back through the layers and try to suggest a couple of actions for each layer that would improve things
>
> The result is what would be called a 'whole system' approach, one which starts with the individual and works its way out to include national and international actions.

Smoking

The link between smoking and ill health is now well documented. 'Smoking is the single most important modifiable risk factor for CHD in young and old.' (*Our Healthier Nation*, 1997) A lifetime non-smoker, is 60 per cent less likely to have CHD and 30 per cent less likely to have a stroke than a smoker. Smoking mirrors other patterns of ill health, in that the highest levels are in the lowest social groups. Although the proportion of young people who smoke is similar across all social groups, by their mid 30s, 50 per cent of young people from higher social classes have stopped, as opposed to only 25 per cent from the lowest income groups. The result is that about one third of the smokers in the population are concentrated in only the lowest 10 per cent of earners in the country.

> **✳ DID YOU KNOW?**
>
> ✳ Tobacco smoking causes most lung cancers.
>
> ✳ It is implicated in a wide range of other cancers including those of the nose and throat but also cervical cancer.
>
> ✳ Overall, about one third of cancer deaths can be attributed to smoking.
>
> ✳ Smoking also contributes to CHD and stroke rates.

This reflects evidence that campaigning measures to reduce smoking levels have compounded this problem by encouraging those in higher social groups to quit, whilst having minimal effect on those in the lowest income brackets. Therefore, some health promotion campaigning can compound health inequality. In their response to the problem the government released a white paper, '*Smoking Kills*', in 1998. This outlined funding for a nationwide network of smoking cessation services to support smokers who wished to quit.

Substance use

In recent years there has been growing public concern over the levels of illegal drug use amongst young people. Data published by the Home Office (2002) shows that rates have been rising consistently over several decades and are now stabilising at an all-time high. Using the indicator of declared misuse, the percentage using any drug rises slightly from 23 per cent in 1994 to 25 per cent in 2000. Most of this use is **cannabis** (10 per cent using in the last year) or amphetamine (2 per cent). Much of this use is clearly not very regular because there is a significant difference between use in the last month (cannabis 14 per cent, amphetamine 2 per cent) and lifetime use (cannabis 44 per cent, amphetamine 22 per cent). Drug use rises to be most widespread in the 16–25 range before gradually declining, as illustrated by the 1998 figures for all drug use (See Figure 3.23).

Age range (in years)	11–15	16–25	16–29
Drug use in last year	11%	29%	25%

FIGURE 3.23 *Figures for all drug use*

Source: Home office (2002)

The cost to society of drug misuse is well documented. In the criminal justice system each crime costs on average £100 to record, (a cost of £2 million to the North West in 1998). On average, users spend £200 each week on drugs, amounting to an annual spend of £89 million per year in the North West. Approximately half this amount will be raised through acquisitive crime, burglary, shoplifting and muggings, where the depreciation in value of the stolen goods could mean a true figure for the goods stolen is nearer £134 million. Society also pays a high cost in terms of illness and deaths, with 2,117 drug-related deaths in 1997 alone, although this figure is widely acknowledged as being under-reported.

Recognising the growing concern about this widespread use of illegal substances the government of 1995 introduced the first national drugs strategy, *Tackling Drugs Together*, which set out three key aims:

✳ 'Increase the safety of communities from drug related crime

✳ Reduce the acceptability and availability of drugs to young people

✳ Reduce the health risks and other damage related to drug misuse.'

(HM Government, 1995)

This also created an infrastructure to drive forward the drugs strategy through a network of strategic Drug Action Teams (DATs) and their implementation counterparts, Drug Reference Groups. Multi-sectoral partnerships with key roles within these groups were taken up by criminal justice and treatment agencies such as the police force, probation service, prisons and the NHS.

Social factors

Social class has long been used as the method of measuring and monitoring health inequalities. Since the Black report of 1988, it has been clearly identified and acknowledged that those from the lowest social groupings experience the poorest health in society. Traditionally, inequalities reporting has used the following categories:

SOCIAL CLASS GROUPING		EXAMPLES
1	Professional	Doctors, engineers
11	Managerial/ technical	Managers, teachers
111N	Non manual (skilled)	Clerks, cashiers
111M	Non manual (unskilled)	Carpenters, van drivers
1V	Partly skilled	Warehouse workers, security guards
V	Unskilled	Labourers

However it has been accepted more recently that these groupings are no longer representative of the population. Therefore, for the 2001 census the Office of National Statistics (ONS) reclassified the population into eight layers as shown in Figure 3.24; specifically picking out the long-term unemployed as a separate group for the first time.

The unemployed are amongst the most socially disadvantaged and as a consequence experience significant inequalities in health. For a small minority, unemployment actually leads to an improvement in health, but for the vast majority being unemployed leads to significantly poorer health. The unemployed have higher

SOCIO-ECONOMIC CLASSIFICATION	
ANALYTIC CLASSES	**EXAMPLES**
1 Higher managerial and professional occupations	
1.1 Large employers and higher managerial occupations	Chief Executives of major organisations
1.2 Higher professional occupations	Doctors, lawyers
2 Lower managerial and professional occupations	Middle management in bigger organisations, departmental managers or customer services, teachers, physiotherapists
3 Intermediate occupations	lerks and bank workers
4 Small employers and own account workers	Painters and decorators, or small manufacturing company owners
5 Lower supervisory and technical occupations	Builders, joiners
6 Semi-routine occupations	Unskilled labouring jobs
7 Routine occupations	Assembly line workers
8 Never worked and long-term unemployed	

FIGURE 3.24 *Socio-economic Classification of the Office of National Statistics (2001)*

levels of depression, suicide and self harm and a significantly increased risk of **morbidity** and **mortality** across all causes. Men unemployed at both census dates in 1971 and 1981 had mortality rates twice that of the rest of other men in that age range, and those men who were unemployed at one census date had an excess mortality of 27 per cent. Adverse effects associated with unemployment include:

* increased smoking at the onset of unemployment – the prevalence of smoking is considerably higher among those who are unemployed

* increased alcohol consumption with unemployment, especially in young men

* more weight gain for those who are unemployed

* reduced physical activity and exercise

* use of illicit drugs in the young who are without work

* increased sexual risk-taking among unemployed young men

* reduced psychological well-being, with a greater incidence of self-harm, depression and anxiety.

Race is also another factor to affect life expectancy, particularly because of the differences in culture this may bring. Black and minority ethnic groups have higher risks of mortality from a range of diseases such as diabetes, liver cancer, tuberculosis, stroke and heart disease. Infant mortality and mental illness have also been highlighted as problems amongst African-Caribbean men. However, establishing the cause of these variations has proved difficult. Medical interventions have tended to concentrate on cultural practices, but this does not acknowledge the compounding factors of poverty and low employment levels in these groups. However, racism must play a part in the experiences of minority ethnic communities in contact with health services and, as a causative factor, in leading to a higher than average experience of poverty and unemployment in these groups.

> **✳ DID YOU KNOW?**
>
> In this country 67 per cent of people from ethnic minority backgrounds live in 88 deprived areas, which receive targeted neighbourhood renewal funding, compared with 40 per cent of the total population – i.e. people from ethnic minorities are more likely to live in poor/disadvantaged communities.

However we choose to classify the different social strata, most recent research suggests that it is the countries with the smallest income *differences* rather than the richest countries that have the best health status. Where income differences remain great, as in this country, health inequalities will persist; for example:

✳ children in the lowest social class are five times more likely to die from an accident than those in the top social class.

✳ someone in social Class 5 is three times more likely to experience a stroke than someone in Class 1

✳ infant mortality rates are highest amongst the lowest social groups

✳ the difference in life expectancy between a man from one of the most affluent areas in this country and a man living in Manchester is 6 years.

Environmental issues

The impact of the environment on health can be seen from two perspectives – the capacity to provide benefits to health and the capacity to do harm. Benefits to health are provided, for example, in that parks and recreational spaces can encourage us to participate in regular exercise or even just allow us the opportunity to experience time away from the stresses and strains of everyday life. On the other hand, the impact of the environment through pollution, or through poor housing which it is now well documented, can lead to chest illnesses such as asthma and bronchitis. There is also some argument as to whether landfill sites do have the potential to harm those people who live close to them and, of course, the argument still rages as to whether mobile phones and their masts have the potential, through the microwaves emitted, to cause cancer and possible brain damage in the people who use or live near them. Friends of the Earth (FOE) would argue that phone masts are often situated in built-up areas close to schools and on top of blocks of flats, thus having the potential to harm many people.

Pollution

Pollution can be said to have occurred when the environment is negatively affected in some way. It arises in many ways, from air pollution to land, water and aesthetic pollution (visual). Many of these forms of pollution have the potential to effect long-term damage on both the environment and human health and well-being on a global and national scale. It is argued that pollution should be monitored and measured to allow action to be taken to reduce the amount of all kinds of pollution.

Work environment

All companies in the UK with five or more employees have a legal duty to maintain and implement safe systems of work under the 1974 Health and Safety at Work Act. Occupational health services in the UK are an integral part of this process. They work within the spirit of the Act with the task of meeting the specific subordinate regulations relating to occupational health.

The Health and Safety at Work Act 1974 (HSWA) places a wide ranging duty on employers to protect the safety, health and welfare of their employees. Regulations made under the HSWA and other legislation place specific duties on employers relating to risk assessment, health surveillance, managing health, fitness for work, protecting the vulnerable and employing the disabled.

Home environment

The home environment links very closely with the local environment to the extent that, in some cases, they cannot be easily separated. For example, when we talk about the home we include all the internal and external factors, such as gardens, driveways and garages. The interior of the home usually consists of a number of rooms designed for specific purposes. Each room has the potential to create negative or positive effects on health. In fact, there are aspects of the entire house that could affect well-being. Think about the electricity supply, the wiring systems, electrical appliances, gas appliances, roof space and wall cavities. We also need to remember that in the home we often store cleaning materials that have the potential to harm our health and we also need to consider the environmental effects of food preparation, cooking and storage. Again, food safety forms an important part of our environment.

We can also include indoor air pollution in an exploration of the home environment; for example, inhaling other people's tobacco smoke (passive smoking) is clearly a risk to health. There is also a risk to health in some homes from **radon gas**, which is naturally occurring in many areas

> **Think it over…**
>
> Carry out an environmental audit of your own home or immediate locality.
>
> Make a note of the factors that have the potential to affect health and well-being and then explain in what ways each could affect the health of a range of service-user groups, i.e. older people, children and adults.

Health practices

To understand what is meant by health practices it is probably best to consider some examples of specific activities that can protect our health. A good example might be to practice safe sex by using a condom. This practice protects both people not only from a range of sexually transmitted infections but also unplanned pregnancy. Another example might be to practice

safer injecting if you are an intravenous drug user (IDU). Intravenous (IV) drug users are at risk from a range of blood-borne viruses, most notably **HIV**, **hepatitis** C and B and a range of other diseases if they share needles, syringes or the paraphernalia associated with their drug use. Therefore intravenous drug users are encouraged to use safer injecting practices, such as, for example, not sharing paraphernalia (spoons, cotton wool, and so on.) and not sharing needles or syringes. This is known as a '**harm reduction**' approach since it acknowledges that the associated behaviour (IV drug use) is self-damaging but accepts that there is no need to compound the problem by adding additional risks through sharing needles. As part of this philosophy, most districts will have a needle/syringe exchange service, where IV drug users can exchange used needles and syringes for clean 'works'. This protects both the drug users and the rest of the population by reducing their risk of contracting a blood-borne virus. It takes their spent needles and syringes out of circulation safely, thereby reducing the numbers of discarded needles, and controlling the levels of blood-borne viruses in the population at large.

There are other simpler forms of health practice, which are equally important, such as, for example, simply washing your hands. This might seem like a basic practice but it is central to the government's recent initiative to reduce hospital-acquired infections. This recognises that basic hygiene practices must be maintained to prevent patients from acquiring infections like **MRSA** in hospital. MRSA is an antibiotic-resistant form of *Staphylococcus aureus*, a micro-organism which most people carry without symptoms. However, the resistance to antibiotic treatment can make this a potentially life-threatening condition, particularly for vulnerable people who are, by definition, already ill if they are admitted to hospital. If you observe nurses whilst they work today, it is highly likely that they will have a small bottle of cleansing solution attached to their uniform, which they use to wash their hands after dealing with a patient to avoid transferring any micro-organisms to another patient. This is supported by training in effective hand-washing techniques, strict cleaning rotas and promotional materials, urging people to remember to wash their hands and showing them how best to do it.

Recreation

What we do with our spare time in terms of recreation can have a significant influence on our health. Recreational pursuits can contribute to a wide range of health benefits such as promoting physically active lifestyles, weight management, stress release and promoting a sense of well-being, leading to improved mental health status. In 2004 the Health Development Agency published a review of how people use their leisure time, which found that:

* those who participate in sporting activities are also more likely to participate in cultural activities, and vice versa

* for both sport and culture, the biggest single groups were of people who tend to do very little of anything

* higher levels of household income, education and social class usually predicted higher rates of participation in most cultural and sporting activities

* after accounting for household income and social class, not having access to a vehicle was important in determining the amount of sporting and cultural activity that individuals are able to participate in

* there were no especially marked regional differences in participation in culture and sport.

ACTIVITY	PERCENTAGE OF RESPONDENTS WHO CARRIED OUT ACTIVITY IN PAST FOUR WEEKS	AVERAGE TIME SPENT ON ACTIVITY IN PAST FOUR WEEKS (MINUTES)
None	17	0
Walking or hiking (1 hour/2+ miles)	12	108
Swimming indoors	9	34
Keep-fit, aerobics, yoga, dance exercise	7	49
Cycling	7	26
Snooker, pool, billiards	6	26
Football outdoors	4	no data
Jogging, cross-country, road running	3	6
Weight training	3	no data
Golf	3	no data
Swimming outdoors	2	no data
Tenpin bowling	2	no data
Darts	2	no data
Football indoors	2	no data
Tennis	2	no data
Darts	2	no data
Badminton	2	no data

FIGURE 3.25 *Physical activities carried out in the past four weeks – all persons aged 8 years and over*

Source: ONS (2002)

In terms of participation in the last 12 months the five most popular sports, games or physical activities among adults were:

* walking (46 per cent)

* swimming (35 per cent)

* keep-fit/yoga – including aerobics and dance exercise (22 per cent) cycling (19 per cent)

* cue sports – billiards, snooker and pool (17 per cent).

Men were found to be more likely to participate in sports activities than women (either including or excluding walking). Active forms of recreation were found to be in decline. In 1996, 54 per cent of men and 38 per cent of women had participated in at least one activity, excluding walking, but by 2002 participation had fallen to just over half (51 per cent) of men and 36 per cent of women. Participation rates also decreased with age. In 2002, 72 per cent of young adults (aged 16 to 19 years) compared with 54 per cent of adults aged 30 to 44 years and 14 per cent of adults aged 70 years and over had participated in at least one activity (excluding walking) in the last four weeks before interview.

Whilst the levels of participation shown in Figure 3.25, at first glance, appear to be encouraging, it is important to reflect on the amount of time people spent on this activity in the last month. The longest average time spent was 108 minutes walking in a month, with most others being 20–30 minutes (where information was available). Therefore, this does little to dispel the concern that as a wealth of surveys now demonstrate we are becoming an increasingly sedentary (inactive) population that increasingly does not participate in active forms of recreation which would improve our heart health, or cultural activities which might benefit other aspects of health, such as our mental well-being.

Housing

Public health campaigners have been advocating for improvements in housing to better the public's health since the middle of the 19th century. For example, Edwin Chadwick's (an active campaigner on a number of public health issues, including poor housing), *Report on an inquiry into the sanitary conditions of the labouring population of Great Britain* (1842), resulted in the first national Public Health Act (1848).

The link between housing and health remains true to this day, the Office for National Statistics Longitudinal Study showing that between 1971 and 1981 age-standardised mortality rates for social tenants (those in rented accommodation) were 25 per cent higher than for owner-occupiers. Although death rates have declined since that time, the gap between these groups has widened. Owner-occupiers have seen greater reductions in death rates than those living in rented accommodation.

This link between housing tenure and health status is probably best explained by considering housing as an indicator for income deprivation, or social class. Those on low incomes are more likely to live in poor housing conditions, experience overcrowding, poor washing and cooking facilities, damp and disrepair. Children who live in such houses with damp are known to have higher than usual rates of respiratory conditions like asthma, and **communicable infections**, which are transmitted more easily in overcrowded conditions. Childhood accident rates are also highest in areas of high-density housing, where play facilities are limited and it is difficult for parents to supervise children at play outside.

The patterns of housing tenure are changing due to the introduction of the 'right-to-buy' scheme in the early 1980s, and the transfer of housing stock from local authorities to housing associations (or Registered Social Landlords [RSLs]), during the 1990s. The result has been an increase in home ownership from 49 per cent to 69 per cent, between 1971 and 2002, with most of the increase occurring in the 1980s, the increase levelling off since then.

Corresponding to this, the percentage of households which are rented council homes increased from 31 per cent in 1971 to 34 per cent in 1981, but then gradually declined during the 1980s to 24 per cent in 1991. The percentage continued to decrease so that by 2002 only 14 per cent of all households were rented from the council. The percentage of households renting from a housing association increased from 1 per cent in 1971 to 3 per cent in 1991, continuing throughout the 1990s to 7 per cent in 2002.

How these changes influence the health of the population is not yet apparent, but it may not be as simple as saying that the numbers of home owners has risen, therefore the health of those people will also improve. Right-to-buy schemes allowed people to purchase their home at heavily discounted rates, therefore it does not necessarily represent an increase in the income of those people. Indeed, the additional responsibilities of maintaining their own home may act as a drain on their limited resources in some cases, making them less well off with the attendant health problems this may bring.

Workplace health

Sickness absence costs employers at least £11 billion each year, a staggering 16 per cent of their total salary costs. Research has found that 90 per cent of employers believe sickness costs can be significantly reduced, yet very few employers monitor sickness absence or take active steps to reduce it. Indeed, 55 per cent of employers do not even measure the cost of sickness absence and only 49 per cent of employers have set targets to reduce sickness absence. However, despite this apparent indifference 60 per cent of employees do want their employers to take some responsibility for their health at work.

Two million people suffer an illness they believe has been caused by, or made worse by, their work. Forty million working days are lost each year to occupational ill health and injury, where stress-related conditions and **musculoskeletal** disorders are now the commonest reported causes of work-related sickness absence. Stress is commonly linked to long working hours; this country has the longest working week of any European country, with 3.74 million workers clocking up more than the 48-hour-limit under the Working Time Directive – 423,000 more than in 1992 when there was no protection against long working hours.

This illustrates the potential for improving health through the workplace and possible financial rewards for employers who are prepared to invest in their workforce's health. Reflecting on this information it should be apparent that workplace health promotion is not just about promoting healthy eating and physical activity it covers a wide range of issues, such as:

* health promotion policies for smoking, alcohol, transport and nutrition
* access to health care services, including occupational health
* good human resource approaches
* flexible working arrangements
* helping employees achieve a work life balance
* fostering good employer/employee relations
* staff benefits, e.g. discount arrangements with local shops or leisure providers.

Effective workplace programmes, which address these aspects, can provide real benefits for employers in terms of reduced absenteeism, increased productivity, improved staff attitude and morale and reduced staff turnover.

For example, the government introduced the Work–Life Balance Campaign in 2000. The campaign aims to help employers recognise the benefits of adopting policies and procedures that enable employees to adopt flexible working patterns. This helps their staff to become better motivated and more productive because they will be better able to balance their work and other aspects of their lives. There is now evidence that employers that offer flexibility in working arrangements are experiencing an increase in recruitment and retention, employee commitment and productivity, and a decrease in staff turnover and sickness absence. A report by the Institute for Employment Studies (IES) shows some small businesses save up to £250,000 on their budget, simply by using family-friendly work policies. One company claimed profitability was up by 37 per cent.

Family

Our family can play a significant part in determining our health status in a variety of ways.

The genes we inherit can determine our future health status; for example, the risk of developing coronary heart disease is linked to family history, as are certain types of breast and other cancers. These are aspects of our health that we have little control over (although the possibilities raised by genetic engineering may change this in the future).

The health behaviours of adults in key positions in the family can have a major impact on the health of young people. For example, an estimated 920,000 children are currently living in a home where one or both parents misuse alcohol, with 6.2 per cent of adults having grown up in a family where one or both of their parents drank excessively. Serious problems are experienced by children as a result of the drinking behaviour of their parents. An analysis of NSPCC helpline calls showed parental alcohol misuse to be a factor in 23 per cent of child neglect cases, and parental alcohol misuse was also reported in 13 per cent of calls about emotional abuse, 10 per cent of calls about physical abuse and 5 per cent of calls about sexual abuse. Children of problem drinkers have higher levels of behavioural difficulty, school-related problems and emotional disturbance than children of non-problem drinking parents, and higher levels of dysfunction than children whose parents have other mental or physical problems.

Another aspect of family life is the way in which we are socialised, i.e. the types of behaviours we are raised to accept as normal. This can involve our ethnicity, the region we live in, or our religious beliefs, for example. However, family health behaviours are also invloved; it is now well evidenced, for example, that young people are more likely to engage in sporting activity if their parents are also active.

We know that 42 per cent of British children live in a household where at least one person smokes. Smoking levels are often high amongst families and within friendship groups in the most income-deprived households. Here smoking is accepted as the norm; in these families many people started smoking regularly in their early teens, and there is considerable evidence that because smoking is very much the norm, parents are willing to accommodate their children's smoking (either actively or passively). In a recent piece of research by the Health Development Agency, a sample of young people from disadvantaged backgrounds were asked about their experiences of smoking and few said they encountered any pressure from parents or partners to quit smoking, usually because they themselves smoked.

This illustrates another aspect of family influence which is important – the link between family health and disadvantage. For example, people are more likely to smoke if:

* they have no educational qualifications/early school-leaving age

* live in rented accommodation

* do not having a car and/or phone

* the adults in the household are traditionally involved in manual labour

* they live off means-tested benefits (especially income support).

These are just some of the markers for predicting whether someone is more or less likely to smoke. No one chooses to be born into a disadvantaged family, but clearly the material wealth of the people in that family will play a major part in determining the health of its members. This fact is repeated through a range of the wider determinants of health. For example, the level of a mother's education correlates particularly strongly with her children's success at school.

In general, children from low-income households go on to leave full-time education much earlier, and with fewer formal qualifications than their more affluent counterparts. Of children born in 1970, for example, some 24 per cent failed to achieve any formal qualifications by the age of 30, whilst 23 per cent went on to get a degree. Among children from low-income households, however, only 11 per cent went on to get a degree and 38 per cent achieved no formal qualifications. Illustrating the cyclical nature of disadvantage, that once born into disadvantage, a person is likely to remain disadvantaged throughout life and consequently suffer poorer health.

Physical factors (disability as an example)

Disability is the consequence of impairment or other individual difference. The disability a person experiences is determined by the way in which other people respond to that difference. It can have serious social consequences, which in turn can harm that person's health. In the past, being left handed was considered a disability and left-handed people were banned from certain jobs. Today we are more accepting of that difference, but this does not apply for all such differences; for example, people with a disability are three times more likely to be unemployed with all the attendant health impacts described below. As a means of addressing some of these inequalities the Disability Discrimination Act 1995 (DDA) requires employers with 15 or more employees to treat disabled persons equally with non-disabled persons in all employment matters and make any reasonable changes to the premises, job design, and so on, that may be necessary to accommodate the needs of disabled employees.

Think it over...

Look at the Dahlgren/Whitehead diagram of the determinants of health. Using the categories in the layers of this diagram and the examples below, try to plot the issues which might impact on the health of the following two case studies.

But first consider all the factors which impact on your own health. Start at the centre with the issues that you can least influence and work outwards to think about issues like the work environment and local neighbourhood, before thinking about more national issues like our long working hours and high car dependency. Then you can begin to explore the case studies of people who might figure in socially excluded groups; for example:

* a woman aged 65 years, living alone and whose family has now moved abroad. She has arthritis and can only walk a short distance

* a gay man, living with his partner 'out' to close friends, but not 'out' to work

Summary

* People's attitudes to their own health and the advice of health professionals can significantly affect their behaviour.

* Lifestyle is both a product of our own lay beliefs about health and environmental influences; key lifestyle issues considered here include:

  * nutrition – and its links to rising obesity levels in all age ranges

  * substance use where young people's use (illicit substance use being predominantly an activity for under 25s) has stabilised in recent years

  * smoking – which is a major contributor to levels of cancers and coronary heart disease.

* Social factors are also an important contributor to health inequalities with the unemployed being amongst the least healthy people, as are other disadvantaged groups like ethnic minorities and those with a disability.

* Environment plays a both a negative and positive part in promoting health.

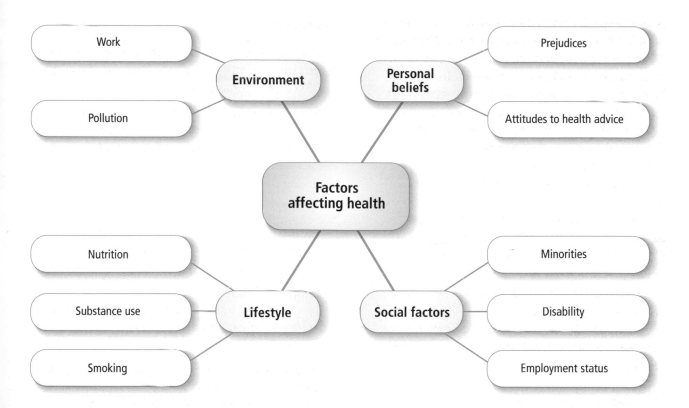

Consider this

Young people are a key group for addressing many of the health issues dealt with in this chapter:

1   Research suggests that young people often over-estimate the numbers of people who smoke in the population. Make an educated guess about the proportion of people in college who smoke. Then design and carry out a piece of research to check how accurate your assessment was.

2   How would you have to change your research design if you were trying to do the same exercise for a range of illicit substances including cannabis, amphetamine and Ecstasy?

3   Does substance use mirror other health inequalities? I.e. Does it impact most on the poorest groups in society and, if not, why

not? If you are unsure, begin to find out by looking on the Home Office website, where this data is routinely published.

4   If you were planning a health education campaign to warn young people about the dangers of drug use, you need to know the age at which people start to experiment and the age that it becomes regular use? Which type of use is most dangerous and why? What messages would be appropriate for these two differing types of use?

5   How might public opinions and attitudes about drugs impact on the type of information you would like to get across to young people? How could it limit or moderate your ideas?

Section 4: Health promotion

Approaches to health promotion

The term health promotion covers a wide range of different activities, all of which have a part to play in promoting health. None of these differing approaches is essentially the right way; they are simply different aspects which complement each other. The balance between them is very much a choice based on personal perspective, influenced by our own life experience, personal standpoints and values, as illustrated in the wide range of differing lay perspectives on health. Health promotion is commonly characterised as having five differing approaches:

* the medical approach
* the behaviour change approach
* the educational approach
* the service-user-centred approach
* the societal change approach.

However, these are by no means the only approaches within this field of practice and, confusingly, people can refer to the same approach using differing terminology. Figure 3.26 identifies the most commonly identified five approaches and other terms used to describe those approaches. The issue of smoking is used to illustrate the varying aims and activities of each approach.

Approaches, methods and materials

There are many ways in which you can communicate health-promotion messages to your local community.

Interaction

It is hard to quantify the extent to which individual face-to-face interaction can contribute to health campaigning. However, it is clear that the general public hold certain groups within society in high regard and, therefore, respect the information they obtain from their doctors,

nurses, teachers and environmental health officers; this creates considerable potential for promoting key health messages simply through the day-to-day routine of work. It might mean a doctor suggesting to people that they consider giving up smoking when they attend for a health check, or a district nurse suggesting that moderate activity is still possible and potentially beneficial for an older service user whilst visiting them at home. It is quite normal for key health campaigns to engage these health promoters in the communication of a key message: for example, National No Smoking Day, for which many health practitioners plan specific events to link with the national campaign and offer support to people wishing to quit smoking.

Leaflets

Leaflets are the backbone of health education activity. They can serve a wide variety of purposes such as informing people about local services, providing information about specific health conditions, giving advice about specific health-promotion issues or engaging people in thought about broader health considerations. In many cases leaflets are designed to support specific health campaigns such as those for immunisation and National No Smoking Day. However, it is important to remember that for many people a leaflet will not be a useful means of communication. It was identified in a 2003 national research study for the Department of Education and Science (DfES) that:

* 5.2 million adults in England could be described as lacking basic literacy (that is, they were at entry level 3 or below according to National Standards for Literacy and Numeracy)
* more than one third of people with poor or very poor health had literacy skills of entry level 3 or below
* low levels of literacy and numeracy were found to be associated with socio-economic deprivation
* 53 per cent of all adults surveyed had entry or lower level practical skills in using information and communication technology (ICT).

APPROACH	AIM	HEALTH-PROMOTION ACTIVITY
Medical model (Interventionist)	To be free from medically defined disease and disability	Using a medical treatment either to prevent or reduce the effects of ill health
E.g. smoking	To remain free from diseases associated with smoking, e.g. lung and heart diseases	Encouraging people to seek early detection and treatment of smoking-related disorders
Behaviourist (Preventive/ Persuasive)	To promote individual behaviours in the population which keep people free from disease	Encouraging adoption of 'healthier' lifestyle by changing attitude and therefore behaviour
E.g. smoking	To change people's smoking behaviour	Persuading people either not to start smoking or to stop smoking, and if they have already started, to stop
Educationalist (Informative)	To provide people with the necessary knowledge and skills to them to make well-informed decisions	Launching educational activity to disseminate information about health and maintenance of good health. Development of skills required for healthy living
E.g. smoking	To develop people's understanding of the effects of smoking on health and their decision-making skills	Giving information to service users about the effects of smoking. Developing their skills in quitting smoking or resisting enticement to start smoking
Service-user-centred (Empowerment)	To work on health issues on the service user's terms, not your own	Allowing the service user to identify health issues, choices and actions which they choose and thereby empowering the service user
E.g. smoking		Here the smoking issue would only arise if the service user selected it. Any further discussion would be led by the service user's willingness to address the topic
Working to change society	To change the physical and social environment to enable healthier lifestyles	Working within the political or social system to change the physical/social environment
E.g. smoking	To make smoking socially unacceptable, i.e. to change the way in which society as a whole views the behaviour – making it more difficult to smoke	Increasing the number of public spaces covered by no smoking policies, making non-smoking the norm in society, making cigarette sales to children more difficult, banning tobacco advertising and sports sponsorship
Fear	To frighten people into adopting a healthier lifestyle	Launching educational activity to disseminate information about the effects of unhealthy lifestyles
E.g. smoking	To make the effects of smoking so frightening as to prevent people taking up smoking or to encourage those who do smoke to quit	Using real-life patients talking about their experiences of lung cancer brought on by smoking

FIGURE 3.26 *Commonly used approaches to health-promoting activities*

Clearly many agencies still do little to take account of people's literacy levels. Another survey of the readability of patient information produced by hospices and palliative care units showed that 64 per cent of leaflets were readable only by an estimated 40 per cent of the population.

Therefore, a leaflet on first appearance is a relatively simple tool, but it is important to consider a range of questions when designing or using one:

* Who is this leaflet for? A drugs leaflet appropriate for secondary school children will not be appropriate for use in primary schools.

* Who produced the leaflet, will they have an interest in the information? If a commercial organisation, such as a drug company, produced the leaflet will this mean they have been selective in their reporting of the information?

* How long ago was it first produced? Is the information still relevant or accurate? For example, information on drug-related harm changes very rapidly.

* Is the language level used appropriate to the target audience? Is it too adult? Does it include abbreviations or technical terms?

* Is it well designed, i.e. will it grab the attention of the reader from amongst the other leaflets and posters? Will it connect specifically with the target audience?

* Are the key messages clearly identified, or are there too many other distractions?

* For the particular leaflet and target audience, where is the best place to display it?

Posters

Posters provide an excellent tool for catching the attention of the target audience and supporting the key broad messages you might then develop in more detail within a leaflet. The factors which draw attention to a poster can be divided into two groups – physical characteristics and motivational characteristics (see Figure 3.27). Clearly these summarise the key points of a poster: to be eye catching and big enough to attract attention. It will need to be in colour, or, if in black and white, to use this for impact or dramatic effect. Wording should be minimal and very bold. Posters need to be placed carefully in positions where the target audience will see them, and routinely changed after a short period so the information is never out of date.

PHYSICAL CHARACTERISTICS	MOTIVATIONAL CHARACTERISTICS
Size: the whole of the poster as well as parts within it like key lettering	*Novelty:* unusual features or surprising objects
Intensity: bold headings	*Interest:* items of interest to the target audience
Colour: use of primary colours such reds, greens and orange	*Deeper motivations:* fashion and sex
Pictures: use of photographs and drawings	*Entertainment or humour:* i.e caricatures, cartoons

FIGURE 3.27 *Factors that draw people's attention to a poster*

The role of the mass media

Many people would view the use of the media as the most effective means of reaching the population to promote health, probably assuming that because it reaches a large number of people its effect will be correspondingly great. However, there are other considerations to take into account.

The success of a health message conveyed by the media will be dependent upon the attitudes

Think it over...

Consider the lay models of health. What types of message about moderating your drinking might appeal to the following lay perspectives:

* the robust individual account?
* the willpower account?

How different are these messages?

What does this tell you about the effectiveness of broad-based health messages in national campaigns?

and viewpoint of the individual receiving the message. Therefore, it is not surprising to find that many research studies have now shown that the direct persuasive power of the media is very limited. Expectations that the media alone will produce dramatic long-term changes in health behaviour are doomed to disappointment.

Realistic expectations of using mass media in health promotion work

Appropriate aims when using the media in health promotion work might include using it to:

* raise awareness of health and health issues – for example, to raise awareness about the link between over-exposure to the sun and the risk of skin cancer

* deliver a simple message – for example, that babies should sleep on their backs not their tummies; that there is a national advice line for young people wanting information about sexual health

* change behaviour if it is a simple one-off activity – for example, phone for a leaflet) which people are already motivated to do and which it is easy to do. (Phoning for a leaflet is more likely if you are at home with a phone than if you are at a friend's house or if the nearest phone is a broken public one a few streets away.)

The use of the media should be viewed as part of an overall strategy, which includes face-to-face discussion, and personal help, and attention to social and environmental factors that help or hinder change. For example, media publicity is just one strand in a long-term programme to combat smoking.

The media cannot be expected to:

* convey complex information (for example, about transmission routes of HIV)

* teach skills (for example, how to deal assertively with pressure to have sex without a condom or take drugs)

* shift people's attitudes or beliefs. If a message challenges a person's basic beliefs, he is more likely to dismiss the message than change his belief (for example, 'My grandad smoked sixty cigarettes a day till he died at 80, so saying I should stop smoking is rubbish')

* change people's behaviour unless it is a simple action, easy to do, and people are already motivated to do it (for example it will only encourage those people who are already motivated to be more active to start walking because this is an easy and accessible form of exercise, it will not do this for those who are not motivated to be more active).

Planning a campaign

To plan effectively requires a clear understanding of what you are trying to achieve. A health promoter should define clear aims and objectives before commencing any form of action. Planning should provide you with the answer to three questions:

* What am I trying to achieve?

* What am I going to do?

* How will I know whether I have succeeded?

Aims and objectives

Identifying the target audience for a campaign starts with the question, 'what is the health need which I should be addressing?' The need for a campaign will usually come from the types of sources discussed in Sections 1 and 2, where target setting for health and the collection of epidemiological data were covered. Having done this it is important to translate the idea of how to meet these needs into aims and objectives. It is important to start by differentiating between an aim and an objective.

| **Aim** | A broad goal |
| **Objective** | Specific goal to be achieved |

Any one *aim* may have several supplementary objectives within it, whilst *objectives* are usually defined as being SMART (see Figure 3.28). The objectives that do not fulfil the criteria cannot be effective aids to planning. They may be aims which require breaking down further into specific objectives. Without this level of detail an objective becomes immeasurable and therefore evaluation of the work is undermined.

Specific	Are defined in terms which is clear and not too vague
Measurable	When the work is finished we can see whether the objective has been achieved or not
Achievable	The target is realistic, i.e. within our power to change
Relevant	Is focused on addressing the issue within our broad aim
Timed	We have agreed a timescale by which we expect to have delivered this objective.

FIGURE 3.28 *SMART characteristics of objectives*

For a Theatre in Health Education project, for example, one objective might be:

'Engage young people in an accessible, fun but rigorous discussion about the legal, health, personal and social consequences of decisions made in relation to drugs, sex and crime.'

Identification of target audience

Identifying your target audience for a campaign starts with the question 'what is the health need which I should be addressing?' The need for a campaign will usually come from one of four sources as shown in Figure 3.29.

Think it over...

If you were to undertake a piece of health promotion activity locally, how would you start to identify local needs that would frame the aims and objectives of your work?

∗ List possible sources of useful information.

∗ What information might they provide for you?

∗ How would you decide whether this information is a reliable basis for your decision-making?

∗ What felt or expressed needs are you aware of within the student body of your college?

Therefore, as a health promoter the first action in undertaking any campaign is to identify the source of the need we are considering and this will identify who we are targeting.

Liaison with other agencies

Health promotion is rarely effective when the activity is focused within one organisation. The causes of ill health are so broad that it requires a wide-ranging response across agencies to influence health for the good. This is reflected in current government thinking through statutory duties to work in partnership on planning mechanisms such as the local community plan, HImP, community safety strategy, and so on. When working with other agencies it is important to know who you need at what stages of the

DIFFERING NEEDS FOR CAMPAIGNS	
Normative need	Defined by experts or professionals according to their own standards, where something falls short of this standard then a need is identified. For example, the percentage of people who are overweight or obese
Felt need	Needs which people feel, i.e. things we want. For example, people might want their food to be free of genetically modified products
Expressed need	A felt need which is voiced. For example, the felt need to have genetically modified free food becomes an issue of public debate with pressure groups focusing public debate on the issue
Comparative need	Arises from comparisons between similar groups of people, where one group is in receipt of health promotion activity and the other is not. Examples here might be one school having a well thought out and planned PSHE curriculum and another not

FIGURE 3.29 *Sources of campaigns*

work, to make sure you do not miss them out of your planning and then find that they are either unable or unwilling to support the work, or cannot fit in with your timescale.

Milestones

These are steps along the way to delivering the outcome or objective; they are useful for helping you to plan the work effectively. For example, the milestones towards an objective which involved recruiting people from local voluntary agencies, to participate in a focus group about support for carers, might include:

* design publicity materials including leaflets, posters and press adverts
* order sufficient stationary to support the mailing of these materials
* compile a circulation list for the mail
* arrange for materials to be printed
* mail to relevant people
* visit local community groups to raise awareness about the project.

Milestones can also contribute to the evaluation process for a piece of work; they can be documented as a series of process-related targets, which can be easily measured in terms of achievement – 'that milestone was met on time'.

Evaluation and outcome measures

Evaluation is something which we actively engage in on a daily basis. If evaluation is judging the worth of an activity, then questions to ask ourselves would be:

* Do I enjoy my job or should I apply for another one?
* Will I use that restaurant again?

Or on a professional footing:

* How did that session go?
* Did I achieve what I set out to do?
* Did that patient or service user really understand my explanation or was she just being polite when she said she did?

In the context of evaluating health-promoting activity we are probably considering something of a more formal approach to evaluation. An approach that is more public or open to scrutiny by an outsider and therefore capable of being made public. In this type of evaluation there are two key aspects:

* defining what we hope to achieve, i.e. aims and objectives
* gathering information to assess whether we have met these.

The question of when to evaluate is closely bound up with the purpose of the evaluation. Is it to be a final *summative* assessment of what has happened? Evaluation of this type, which seeks to establish the worth of work when it has reached its conclusion, is termed an *outcome* evaluation. Or is it an ongoing appraisal of the progress made? Evaluation that involves feedback during the course of a project, when things are still taking shape, is termed *formative* or an evaluation of *process*.

An outcome measure is the end point of the piece of work a health promoter undertakes. This can be a target as challenging as those seen in *Our Healthier Nation* (1997) which refer to reductions in disease but reflect national policy, and require coordinated action at that level to deliver them. Conversely, it could be something quite small-scale such as creating and improving the knowledge and skills of people from a specific geographical community about healthy cooking skills. There will be considerable overlap with objectives here, but it is important not to confuse the two.

Objectives refer to the work required to deliver the outcome. In this example, an objective might be to develop a model training programme for delivery to a group of women from the identified community. Outcomes refer to the product of the work; the health promoters will have to identify the desired outcomes in advance of the work, to ensure that they design into the process ways of measuring whether the product is delivered. That is, if the knowledge and skills were successfully developed in the community and people then went on to alter their diet and eating behaviours. It is not always possible to predict the outcome of a piece of work. It can create unintended or unexpected outcomes which are a bi-product of the work; for example, in this situation the bi-product might be better community relations due to the sustained programme of group activities during the cooking skills course, or the establishment of local community market gardening initiatives to grow local fresh produce.

For your assessment activity you need to ask yourself, how will I know that this has been a worthwhile activity? The key things to look at here are: what information will you need to enable you to state categorically that this has been achieved? You might want to scale down some of your objectives and outcomes when you begin to do this and realise how ambitious you have been!

Establishing clear objectives for your own work

If you have been working on your assessment activity you have probably tried to do this already as part of your original project proposal. For each

Objective

State your objective here (use a separate sheet for each objective).

Engage young people in an accessible, fun but rigorous discussion about the legal, health, personal and social consequences of decisions made in relation to drugs, sex and crime.

> One objective from a Theatre in Education project with Year 7–9 students.

Key tasks/activity

Briefly describe what service or activity you will be providing, and evaluating, that supports the achievement of this objective.

* Interactive theatre performances by a team of actors with groups of 60–90 students, lasting 90 minutes

* Students will receive preparatory and follow-up work in the school

* Some preparatory and follow-up work will be done with school staff

> Each Year group has a session on a different theme, watched by form tutors and other pastoral staff **Year 7: Bullying; Y8: Drugs; Y9: Sex and Relationships**

Results

What do you hope will change as a result of this activity?

* Students will show a greater repertoire of behaviours, enabling them to make informed and safe decisions

* Students and staff will feel more confident and informed when discussing the issues raised in the performances

* Staff will feel able and confident to follow up this work

* Students and staff will feel that the interactive theatre experience can make this learning enjoyable and memorable

Measures

How will you measure if the described change is occurring/has occurred?

* Access student attitudes before and after the performances

* Access staff attitudes and confidence before and after the performances

* Observe and evaluate the performances

* Follow up after 6 months to review progress

FIGURE 3.30 *An example of an Objective Sheet for a project*

objective, try and complete an Objective Sheet. The more carefully you describe your objectives and hoped-for outcomes, the easier it is to evaluate the effectiveness of your programme. An example of an Objective Sheet worked up in this way is shown in Figure 3.30.

Standard

Is it possible to define levels of success? It can be helpful to describe these at three levels (see Figure 3.31).

Changing behaviour

Activities in the health education arena focus on the need to motivate individuals to change their health-related behaviours, most commonly in areas such as increasing physical activity, quitting smoking, adopting a healthier diet, and adopting safe sex messages. It is not easy to monitor the changing behaviour of a group of people, possibly over many months, to assess how successful a health-promotion activity has been. This is exactly the problem faced by the smoking cessation services, set up with the support of government funding in each health district in 1999/2000. The services must report how many people referred to them: set a quit date; went on to quit smoking; were still not smoking after one month. To assess the effectiveness of the services in this way requires a considerable investment in administration to track the patients, collect the necessary information and collate it for the returns to the Department of Health.

In the case of behaviour change, outcome measures are often difficult to assess in a real-life situation, being time-consuming and expensive to observe systematically. In the case of provision of fruit to all schoolchildren the goal would be to increase their consumption of fruit and

What will be the best you could hope for?
(A great result!)

A highly enjoyable experience with high levels of satisfaction; students much more confident in discussion and feedback, staff very pleased, and happy to continue and develop the work; school uses some interactive techniques in its PSHE; we get to do more work with them!

What will you be happy with?
(A satisfactory result)

The students and staff enjoy the day; there is evidence of some change in student knowledge and attitudes, and some staff express interest in continuing the work. Some follow-up takes place in school and there is evidence of links to the PSHE curriculum.

What will you be unhappy with?
(A disappointing result)

Preparatory work is not done, or done badly; feedback from students and staff is only satisfactory; there is little evidence of increased knowledge or changed attitudes in the students. Staff don't attend the performances and show little interest in following up the work, or using or developing the techniques as part of their curriculum.

Start to think about what some of these mean in quantitative terms; for example, does 'high level of satisfaction' mean 100 per cent were very satisfied, or 90 per cent, or less?

FIGURE 3.31 *Levels of success*

vegetables, clearly not an easy outcome to monitor systematically. Therefore, instead of trying to observe the eating patterns of the children directly, an indirect indicator using the children's self reporting of changes to their own eating patterns might be used, or changes in purchasing patterns in local shops as a 'proxy indicator'.

Therefore self-reported change (i.e. change people perceive they have made and are willing to report) is a very popular measure in health-promotion evaluation, because it allows evaluation to take place without adding significantly to costs. Sometimes a project's aims and objectives are framed in terms of self-reported changes in knowledge, attitudes and behaviour. For instance, an HIV educational programme for young adults might aim to:

* increase knowledge

* generate positive attitudes towards condom use

* increase self-reported safer sexual practices involving condom use.

This illustrates a particular difficulty facing health promoters. It is difficult to see how information about sexual behaviour can be reported other than by those actually involved. (Routine observation of sexual activity is unlikely to be acceptable to subjects in the study!) Therefore, the health promoter is reliant upon the subject's honesty in self-reporting, an issue which is equally important in less private aspects of health-promoting activity.

FIGURE 3.32 *Collecting data on sexual behaviour*

If self-reported behaviour change is not considered a robust enough measure, then this must be externally verified in some way. In the Allied Dunbar Fitness survey of 1995 a large sample of the population were asked to self-assess their fitness. To gauge the accuracy of their assessment a smaller sub-sample were invited for a full fitness assessment and the results were compared against their self-reporting estimates. The results demonstrated that people routinely over-estimate both their level of activity and their level of fitness. This information became invaluable for informing the goals of future promotional activity.

An alternative to behaviour change is the use of knowledge and attitudes. However, it is not possible to bring about behaviour change directly through changes in knowledge or attitude change, since other factors can act to resist that change. A good example here is the fact that, at any time, over half the adult population who smoke would like to quit, but only a small proportion are ready to try at any one time. This reflects the fact that your health beliefs are also affected by other issues, such as moving house, getting divorced or being made unemployed, which would all act against a person's desire to quit smoking. However, changes in knowledge or attitude can mean that people are better informed and have attitudes that predispose them towards a particular line of action. A success here might be moving some one from the pre-contemplative phase (I am OK with my smoking) to contemplating quitting (thinking about quitting).

Cost effectiveness

Whilst much local health-promotion activity may be viewed as being relatively cheap in relation to the illness it seeks to prevent, it is also hard to measure the precise outcome of the work. Therefore, the investment of 2 or 3 hours of a practice nurse's time in helping someone to quit smoking is considerably less expensive than the cost of extensive treatment for lung cancer. However, it is impossible to state categorically that the nurse's time led to that individual quitting, since many other factors might have influenced the outcome; i.e. it is not an attributable outcome.

During recent years, questions about the relation between costs and effectiveness in the field of health promotion have become important. In a world of limited resources costs clearly have to be taken into account. If, for instance, a health education programme is entirely effective in changing the health behaviour of a small group of people but achieves this success through enormous financial and human resource investment, it is important to acknowledge that in the evaluation process. Without this information it is not possible to make comparisons between differing health-promotion activities, which achieve the same outcome, or health-promoting activities and medical interventions.

Cost-effectiveness analysis (CEA) compares the costs of similar interventions that achieve a specific objective (for example, the cost of the new smoking cessation services compared with GPs providing routine advice on giving up smoking). If different interventions meet with similar success then it becomes important to know which is cheaper. This is useful if the success is the same in each case but becomes difficult when there are differing degrees of success or costs are different. Therefore, the ability to measure the cost-effectiveness in health-promotion activity is fraught with difficulties, particularly when you take into account the range of issues it has to address, and the local flexibility to design individual responses to health challenges. It is precisely this problem which the HDA was set up to address by assessing the weight of evidence for specific interventions nationally and then informing local practitioners. This will be a work-in-progress because historically little investment has been made in assessing the cost-effectiveness of health promotion activity.

Deciding what will be an appropriate and feasible measure of effectiveness or change is a crucial step in planning and carrying out an evaluation. Where it is difficult to gather information directly about the outcome of an activity and where it is not possible to demonstrate a direct link between health promotion activities and the desired outcome, intermediate and indirect indicators are often used. For example, HIV/AIDS health promotion's ultimate aim is to reduce the incidence of infection, but trying to measure change along the way and, in particular, identifying changes that are directly linked with the activity being evaluated involve choosing intermediate and indirect indicators as well as lower-level outcome indicators. The choice of indicators will depend on the objectives of the activity as well as on an understanding of the relationship between health and factors influencing behaviour.

Disease reduction

It is virtually impossible to attribute the most important outcome (reduction of a specific disease) specifically to a health-promotion intervention. The range of other influences which impact on a person's life make this impossible. If we are not able to state categorically that smoking causes lung cancer (the appropriate terminology is that there is a very strong association between the two), how can we say that the 5 minutes spent with this person in counselling them on quitting smoking led to a reduction in lung cancer?

Therefore targets for disease reduction are usually set at national, regional or district level (as we have seen with the two national health strategies) but are rarely used as health promotion success indicators. Even national health-promotion initiatives, such as the introduction of smoking cessation services, use short-term measures which are more easily attributable to the intervention; for example, the number of people setting a quit date, the numbers still stopped at one month, and the numbers stopped at 3 and 6 months.

It must also be recognised that some disease patterns can take several years to change even if the health promotion intervention succeeds. For example, the smoking cessation service can reduce the numbers of people smoking. For many people, however, their cancer may already be established but undiagnosed; therefore, it will take time for the impact of reducing smoking levels to take effect. Some health-promotion interventions can actually lead to a rise in the incidence of disease, screening campaigns being a particularly good example. Whenever campaigns are undertaken to encourage uptake of screening it is inevitable that the numbers of additional patients seen will lead to an increased number of diagnoses.

Think it over...

Imagine you are the project lead for the local stop smoking service. A variety of local practitioners refer people who wish to stop smoking to your service for one-to-one and group support.

* What measures could you use to show that the service was having the desired effect on the participants?

* What tests would you have to do to collect this information?

* How often would you need to collect it to monitor changes effectively?

* How practical is all of the above likely to be?

* What benefits, other than changes to physical health, might participants experience by being involved in the scheme?

Evaluating personal practice

An essential part of being an effective health promoter is to be a reflective practitioner, that is:

* to review your practice

* identify any areas of weakness or improvement

* to identify what would improve your practice in the future

* to build that into future work.

This is an essential part of adult learning as described by Kolb (1975).

The model of experiential learning

This model has four elements: concrete experience, observation and reflection, the formation of abstract concepts and testing in new situations. Kolb represented these in the experiential learning cycle. See Figure 3.33.

Kolb and Fry (1975) argue that the learning cycle can begin at any one of the four points – and that it should really be approached as a continuous spiral. However, it is suggested that

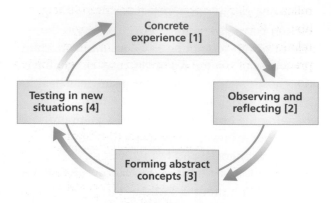

FIGURE 3.33 *Kolb's experiential learning cycle*

the learning process often begins with a person carrying out a particular action – in this case your health-promotion activity – and then seeing the effect of the action in this situation.

Following this, the second step is to understand these effects in the particular instance so that if the same action was taken in the same circumstances it would be possible to anticipate what would follow from the action.

In this pattern the third step would be to understand the general principle under which the particular instance falls. An educator who has learnt in this way may well have various rules of thumb or generalisations about what to do in different situations. So you will begin to develop both confidence and competence to deal with managing health-promotion activities (see Section 2 for detail about health promotion competencies).

When the general principle is understood, the last step is its application through action in a new circumstance within the range of generalisation. In some representations of experiential learning these steps, (or ones like them), are sometimes represented as a circular movement. In reality, if learning has taken place the process could be seen as a spiral.

Reflective practice is about taking time out to carry out steps 2 and 3 and using other people to discuss how you are performing within a role so you can begin to generalise about your future practice to change and improve it. This could cover any aspect of the areas of competence in health promotion in Section 2, be it acting ethically (e.g. not using inappropriately sponsored materials) managing projects (e.g. keeping to timescales in the milestone plan), or working in partnership (e.g. how well you maintain effective working relationships with your colleagues or other practitioners you are depending upon to get the job done).

Summary

The following key areas of theory have been covered in this section.

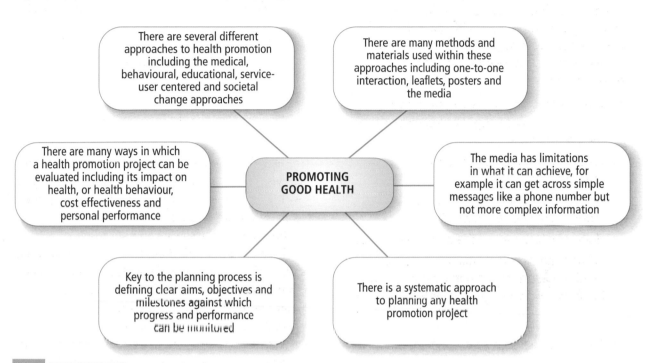

There are several different approaches to health promotion including the medical, behavioural, educational, service-user centered and societal change approaches

There are many methods and materials used within these approaches including one-to-one interaction, leaflets, posters and the media

There are many ways in which a health promotion project can be evaluated including its impact on health, or health behaviour, cost effectiveness and personal performance

PROMOTING GOOD HEALTH

The media has limitations in what it can achieve, for example it can get across simple messages like a phone number but not more complex information

Key to the planning process is defining clear aims, objectives and milestones against which progress and performance can be monitored

There is a systematic approach to planning any health promotion project

Consider this

Imagine you are a health promotion worker who has been asked to develop a local programme to raise awareness of HIV risk amongst older people. This request is based on recognition of the large number of older people who are leaving failed marriages without having the benefit of good health education on HIV risk, which many young people now receive in school. These people require some specifically targeted information that will meet the above criteria to help them manage their risk as they embark on life as a single person again.

1 First of all, describe an aim for the campaign.

2 Now establish 3–4 key objectives you could use to monitor the effectiveness of the programme. One of these should be to develop new leaflets and posters for the target group – but you will need to word that appropriately.

3 Now design a leaflet which would give the correct information, reach the target group specifically and be culturally appropriate for the group.

4 If people fail to take this advice they are likely to have to access their local genito-urinary medicine department (GUM clinic) to have their sexually transmitted infections treated. Find out where your nearest service is and when it operates. Think about the stigma which might be attached to attending this service – particularly for this age group. What actions could the service take to address them?

5 Write down a list of possible actions or activities which might form a part of your programme – to raise awareness of HIV with the target group. Next to each action, record any potential cost. Try to find out what the annual cost is for maintaining someone who is HIV positive on **combination therapy**. Prevention routinely has to compete with treatment for limited resources; this therapy is not cheap but can save someone's life. How would you argue for investment in this health promotion programme?

UNIT 3 ASSESSMENT

How you will be assessed

This unit is assessed through a portfolio of work, with the mark you gain for that assessment being your mark for the unit. As part of the portfolio you will be required to produce a report which describes the planning of, and your participation in, a small-scale campaign to promote good health in a care setting (or your own centre if you prefer).

Any materials you use for the campaign should be published by an existing agency, as opposed to produced by yourself. This will save you time, which can be spent more effectively on the other aspects of planning and delivering the campaign and documenting it accurately for your portfolio. There may be little time for them to produce posters and leaflets which are generally already available. Therefore, where possible, use existing campaigning materials, which for the most part, can be readily obtained from health-promotion departments, health centres, social services, and shops. Your evidence will include:

✳ Evidence that you understand the models and concepts of health and well-being, including ill health, and the implications of government initiatives

✳ Applying knowledge and showing understanding of the job roles of key workers who promote health, including information about two preventative measures

✳ Relevant research and analysis of two factors that can affect health and well-being, giving an analysis of their effects on service users

✳ Evidence of your own performance when planning, and participating in, a small health-promotion campaign, evaluating your own performance.

To help you understand how your work will be assessed, guidance on what you need to do to achieve the highest marks for each AO section have been included in the table at the end of the unit.

Key things to bear in mind

You will need to undertake some consultation activity with both service users and service providers about any planned activity which may affect them. Review your findings according to the theories of the social and medical models. Some of these people may be workers you cover in the course, such as health visitors, school nurses, community nurses, environmental health officers and GPs, so it will be important to either use opportunities with visiting speakers, or to go out to visit these workers to test out your ideas for the campaign and find out about their roles.

You can find information about government initiatives on most government department websites. Examples include the Department of Health (DOH) and Department for Education and Skills (DfES), whilst you can find information about the effectiveness of health-promotion activity on the (HDA) web site.

Both primary (your own) and secondary (review of other people's) research would be useful to enable you to develop an understanding of the different factors affecting health and well-being, and the effects of ill-health on service users in various settings. You will not be expected to give detailed information about substance abuse; the focus needs to be on how this can affect health and well-being.

In the assessment, you will be expected to provide an explanation of the health-promotion approach you have adopted in the planning and implementation of the campaign. It will be important to have a sound understanding of these approaches before you attempt any detailed planning, you will not be expected to have an in-depth knowledge of each approach that could be used, but to demonstrate a good understanding of the applied approach.

Most commonly, people use the educational approach which seeks to inform and educate to promote healthy practices, but the preventative approach is also frequently utilised. Increasing in popularity is the use of fear as an approach, particularly when used on television; for example, using vivid images of people suffering the consequences of unhealthy lifestyle choices, such as smoking, to instil fear into those who watch.

It is important to set clear aims and objectives in the plan for the campaign. These will vary with the intended outcomes. For example, improving health and well-being may be the aim of a campaign provided for people who are overweight and inactive and thus at risk of coronary heart disease. Alternatively, a campaign to promote safe sexual practices to young adults may have two aims, firstly to reduce the number of sufferers of sexually transmitted diseases, and secondly to reduce the number of unplanned pregnancies.

The objectives of the campaign will link directly to the different stages and tasks which need to be completed, to ensure the campaign takes place as efficiently as possible. You also need to consider the intended outcomes of the campaign so that effectiveness can be measured accurately. Try to identify the skills you use, such as, for example, practical skills, organisational skills and communication skills.

The evaluation needs to include evidence of reflective practice, where you make judgments about your performance and the success of the campaign against the pre-set criteria stated. Higher marks are dependent on demonstrating analytical skills and the ability to make reasoned judgments together with consideration of both the intended and unintended outcomes; for example, a campaign which encourages counselling may result in long waiting lists.

You may wish to work in groups to collect materials and when participating in the health-promotion campaign, however, for all other aspects of this unit, you are required to produce your own individual portfolio of evidence.

ASSESSMENT OBJECTIVE	MARK BAND 1	MARK BAND 2	MARK BAND 3
AO1 *evidence that you understand the models and concepts of health and well-being, including ill health and the implications of government initiatives*	You show a basic understanding of the concepts and models of health and wellbeing from **two** different perspectives, including the effects of ill health, and how they relate to service users, including the implications of **one** government initiative **[marks available 0–5]**	You show a sound understanding of the concepts and models of health and well-being from **two** different perspectives, including the effects of ill health, giving a detailed description of how they relate to service users, including the implications of **one** government initiative **[marks available 6–10]**	You show a comprehensive understanding of the concepts and models of health and well-being from **two** different perspectives, including the effects of ill-health, giving a detailed explanation of how they relate to service users, including the implications of **one** government initiative **[marks available 11–15]**
AO2 *applying knowledge and showing understanding of the job-roles of key workers who promote health, including information about two preventative measures*	You provide, with guidance, a basic account of the job roles of **two** key workers who are involved in promoting health, and you give a basic description of **two** preventative measures that they could apply; you write in a manner which is adequate to convey meaning, although it will be expressed in a non-specialist manner **[marks available 0–5]**	You provide a sound level of understanding of a range of job roles of **two** key workers who are involved in promoting health, and you describe thoroughly **two** preventative measures that they could apply; you write in a manner which conveys meaning, using specialist vocabulary with few errors/inaccuracies **[marks available 6–10]**	Working accurately and independently, you provide in-depth knowledge and understanding of a wide range of the job-roles of **two** key workers who are involved in promoting health, explaining **two** preventative measures that they could apply; you write in a manner which conveys appropriate meaning, using specialist vocabulary with accuracy – there will be no errors/inaccuracies **[marks available 11–15]**
AO3 *relevant research and analysis of two factors that can affect health and well-being, giving an analysis of their effects on service users*	You use limited sources of information to research and collect evidence about **two** factors that can affect health, giving a basic analysis of their effects on service users **[marks available 0–4]**	You use a range of sources of information to research **two** factors that can affect health, giving a detailed analysis of their effects on service users **[marks available 5–7]**	You undertake research using a range of techniques to explore **two** factors that can affect health, giving a comprehensive analysis of their effects on service users **[marks available 8–10]**
AO4 *evidence of your own performance when planning and participating in a small health-promotion campaign, evaluating your own performance*	You produce a plan for a small-scale health-promotion campaign and records to show how it was implemented, including a basic evaluation of your own performance **[marks available 0–4]**	You produce a plan for a small-scale health-promotion campaign and records to show how it was implemented, including an evaluation that draws valid conclusions about your own performance **[marks available 5–7]**	You produce a plan for a small-scale health-promotion campaign and records to show how it was implemented, including an evaluation that makes reasoned judgments about your own performance **[marks available 8–10]**

References

Acheson, D. (1998) *The Independent Inquiry into Inequalities in Health* (The Stationery Office)

Benzeval, M., Judge, K., Whitehead, M. (1995) *Tackling Inequalities in Health, an Agenda for Action* (Kings Fund Publishing)

Dawson, D. (1990) *Women's Cancers, The Treatment Options, Everything You Need to Know* (Piatkus Publishing)

Department of Health (1992) *Immunisation against Infectious Disease* (The Stationery Office)

Department of Health (2000) *The NHS Cancer Plan* (The Stationery Office)

Department of Health (2001) *The National Strategy for HIV and Sexual Health* (The Stationery Office)

Department of Health (2001) *Involving Patients and the Public in Healthcare* (The Stationery Office)

Downie, R. S., Tannahill, C., Tannahil, A. (1996) *Health Promotion Models and Values* (Oxford University Press, Oxford)

Draper, P. (1991) *Health Through Public Policy* (Green Print)

Ewles, L. and Simnett, I. (1999) *Promoting Health – A Practical Guide* (Bailliere Tindall, London)

Hall, D. (1996) *Health for all Children* (Oxford University Press, London)

HM Government (1992) *The Health Of the Nation* (The Stationery Office)

HM Government (1997) *The New NHS: Modern Dependable* (The Stationery Office)

HM Government (1997) *Saving Lives – Our Healthier Nation* (The Stationery Office)

HM Government (2004) *Choosing Health – Making Healthy Choices Easier* (The Stationery Office)

Jones, L. and Sidell, M. (1997) *The Challenge of Promoting Health – Exploration and Action* (Open University Press)

Jones, L. and Sidell, M. (1997) *Promoting Health – Knowledge and Practice* (Open University Press)

Moonie, N. (2000) *Advanced Health & Social Care* (Oxford, Heinemann)

Naidoo, J. and Wills, J. (2000) *Health Promotion – Foundations for Practice* (Bailliere Tindall, London)

Useful websites

http://www.cieh.org
The website of the Chartered Institute of Environmental Health Officers for information about their role and training to be one

www.quick.org.uk
Quality information checklist for young people to assess the quality of information they find on the Internet

http://www.hda.nhs.uk/index.asp
The home page of the Health Development Agency giving information about effective health promotion interventions

www.ohn.gov.uk
Gateway for the *Our Healthier Nation* website – original document, technical data and regular progress updates

www.wiredforhealth.gov.uk
Wired for Health provides teachers with access to relevant and appropriate health information

www.mindbodysoul.gov.uk
Provides accurate and up-to-date health information for young people

http://www.bhf.org.uk
Heart health information from the British Heart Foundation including information about activity and nutrition

http://www.homeoffice.gov.uk/drugs/index.html
Information about the National Drugs Strategy and links to information about current drug use trends and patterns

http://www.drugscope.org.uk
National Drugs Agency which provides advice to drugs treatment and prevention services, includes high quality information about patterns of use, information about specific drugs and advice on how to prevent use.

www.doh.gov.uk
Main Department of Health website – search here
for links to *Choosing Health* (public health white
paper) and health statistics

http://www.nhs.uk/england
This site connects you to local NHS services in
England and provides national information about
the NHS

www.givingupsmoking.co.uk
The NHS quit smoking website, information
about smoking, how to quit and where to access
local services

www.cancerscreening.nhs.uk
NHS screening programmes website, provides
good quality information about both Cervical and
Breast Cancer Screening programmes

www.nhlbisupport.com/bmi/bmicalc.htm
Calculate your own BMI using the information on
this site

www.who.int/en
The website of the World Health Organisation

http://www.surestart.gov.uk
The SureStart website for information about the
programme including its aims

http://www.immunisation.org.uk
Information about immunisation programmes

http://www.mmrthefacts.nhs.uk
Government website specifically set up to provide
quality information abut the MMR vaccine for
parents to counter the fall in public confidence in
the vaccine

Answers to assessment questions

Unit 1

1. Two from:
   * Gender socialisation/being a boy or girl
   * Language acquisition
   * Saying please and thank you/manners
   * Behaviour (e.g. hitting)
   * Eating habits.

2. Three from:
   * Peers
   * Media/TV
   * Education/teachers
   * Religion
   * Advertising.

3. Basic needs:
   * Giving and receiving attention – human beings are social animals designed to live in groups and have intimate relationships and social connections with others.
   * Care of the body/physical care – need for food, rest and exercise in sufficient amounts to maintain health.
   * Stimulation/challenge – human brain needs external stimuli to provide interest and prevent boredom or mental health is at risk.
   * Meaning and purpose – humans need to achieve things (aims and goals) and contribute to the group in order to feel valued as individuals.

4. An individual's identity and sense of self-esteem or self-worth is shaped through interaction with the wider world, therefore the more positive experiences an individual has, the higher their self-esteem is likely to be. If the individual belongs to a minority group which is under-represented and/or undervalued within society, this is likely to lead to low self esteem and feelings of marginalisation or *not belonging*.

4. Three from:
   * **Devaluing people** – treating other people's needs and interests as being of less value than those of others, including oneself.
   * **Making assumptions** – about people's needs, preferences and abilities, e.g. that it is acceptable to predict someone's needs without consulting them. Assuming that everyone should be treated the same, given the same experiences and responded to in the same way.
   * **Negative non-verbal communication** – such as not making eye contact when speaking to someone, walking away without waiting for a response or speaking to someone else, such as a colleague, whilst carrying out care activities with a client. All these actions make an individual feel invisible and unimportant, invalidating their existence.
   * **Avoiding people** – because they are different to you or what you are accustomed to, or because you do not know how to speak to them, or do not want to interact with them. This includes ignoring requests for help from clients, if you are a care worker.
   * **Excluding people from activities or opportunities** – for example, assuming someone does not want to join in an activity, deliberately leaving someone out of the team or group exercise and failing to make appropriate arrangements, so that everyone can participate.

6. Types of abuse:
   * **Physical** – slapping, hitting, burning, scolding, pushing, inappropriate restraint, inappropriate use of medicine, withholding medicine as punishment, lack of consideration, roughness when handling or treating people, e.g. helping them to the toilet or when changing dressings.
   * **Psychological** – including shouting, swearing, frightening someone,

threatening someone, withholding or damaging something with emotional importance to someone, and failing to deal with people with respect and dignity.

* **Financial** – stealing and fraud, especially from elderly people.
* **Sexual** – including inappropriate touching, unwanted sexual attention, making sexual remarks designed to make someone feel uncomfortable, and rape.
* **Neglect** – such as failure to provide food, heating, adequate care or attention to hygiene, such as helping with bathing; neglecting treatment, e.g. prevention of pressure sores.

7   Direct discrimination is when a person is treated less favourably because of a certain characteristic (e.g. skin colour, age, marital status). Indirect discrimination is when criteria are applied that only some people can meet, preventing them from accessing the same opportunities as the majority. Direct discrimination is usually deliberate and intended; indirect discrimination is often unintentional.

8   The main duties of the CRE are:
* to work towards the elimination of discrimination
* to promote equality of opportunity and good relations between different racial groups
* to review the implementation of the Race Relations Act and make proposals and recommendations for amendment to the Home Secretary (or government).

9   New laws proposed by parliament must ensure they are compatible with the articles in the European Convention on Human Rights detailed in the Human Rights Act 1998.

10   Three strengths from:
* Provides protection for people who might harm themselves or others.
* There is a right to appeal to a Mental Health Tribunal for a decision on discharge.
* There is a right to receive information (orally and in writing) explaining why they have been detained and that they have a right to appeal.
* The Act makes provision for aftercare services.

11   Three weaknesses from:
* The Act is out of date and does not match present day mental health care practice
* It does not make provision for those whose condition is untreatable, e.g. severe personality disorder.
* Compulsory detention may be incompatible with the Human Rights Act
* It does not address discrimination (stigma) against people who are or have been suffering from mental illness.
* It makes no provision for the prevention or treatment of less severe mental ill health/mental health conditions such as anxiety/depression and diverts resources away from community treatment.
* It may focus too much on control and containment of mentally ill people instead of treatment, reinforcing the perception of all mentally ill people as dangerous.
* It does not cover the needs of people with dual diagnosis – substance abuse and mental illness.

11   Four from:
* The welfare of the child is paramount (the most important consideration).
* Children should be cared for and brought up within their own families wherever possible.
* Local Authority Social Services Departments have a duty to safeguard the welfare of children in need and support them and their parents.
* Children should be protected and kept safe if they are in danger.
* Courts should ensure that delays in the decision making process are kept to a minimum and should only make a care order if it is better for the child than not doing so (not making a care order).
* Children should be kept informed about what is happening and should participate in the decisions affecting them.
* Parents continue to have parental responsibility for their children even when they are not living with them and should therefore be informed and included in decision-making.

12   Physical barriers, e.g. stairs, narrow doorways, no disabled toilet. Geographical barriers, e.g.

uneven distribution of services nationally, rural locations with poor transport.

Psychological barriers e.g. stigma, fear, guilt. Financial barriers, e.g. childcare services and insufficient NHS dentists, prescription charges. Cultural and language barriers, e.g. no available translation service, health professionals of opposite gender, food and dietary requirements unable to be met.

13 The key values of care are:
  * promoting equality and diversity by treating everyone impartially and fairly
  * promoting individual rights and beliefs, especially for people who are vulnerable and unable to exercise their rights independently
  * maintaining confidentiality in relation to the personal and private information in order to promote trust and confidence between care workers and service users.

14 The regulatory framework consists of:
  * the professional councils responsible for registering and regulating practitioners and producing codes of professional practice, e.g. Nursing and Midwifery Council
  * the regulation and inspection bodies that monitor service providers, e.g. The Commission for Social Care Inspection
  * the National Minimum Standards for Care (NMS) and the National Service Frameworks (NSF) which set the basic standards of care (NMS)and evidence based treatment (NSF).

15 An Equal Opportunities Policy should contain:
  * a statement of the organisation's commitment to equality of opportunity
  * details of who is managerially responsible for implementing the policy
  * an explanation of how the policy will be monitored and reviewed
  * a list of the discriminatory treatment covered by the policy, e.g. harassment/bullying
  * guidelines for how to make a complaint or take out a grievance using the appropriate procedures.

16 If care workers are not trusted then service users are unlikely to share confidential information with them that may be important to their care and treatment.

17 The Children Act 2004 is intended to maximise opportunities and minimise the risks for all children by focusing services on the needs of children and young people. This means that health services, social services, education services and child care organisations must work together to plan, commission, fund and deliver services for children and families. Three key features from the following:
  * The appointment of a Children's Commissioner to represent children's views
  * Local Authorities to appoint Director of Children's Services and Lead Member for Children's Services
  * Information sharing across agencies
  * Local Safeguarding Children Boards to be set up to co-ordinate child protection procedures
  * Local Authorities to produce plans for children and young people in their area
  * New inspection arrangements across the integrated services.

18 Parents are experts on their own children and know them better than anyone else. They are central to children's well-being, so information on children's development, progress, behaviour and daily activities should be shared with parents.

19 Because childcare workers are part of the socialisation process, they can help to shape and expand the child's understanding of the world outside home, including differences and similarities between people.

20 Child protection policies enable childcare workers to fulfil their legal duty to protect children. The policy should outline the reporting procedures and lines of accountability within the organisation and externally between organisations concerned with child protection in cases of suspected abuse. The policy will detail how the different organisations work together and the responsibilities of each, including the Area Child Protection Committee (Local Protecting Children Boards).

Glossary

A

active listening: more than just hearing, this involves building an understanding of what a person is saying and demonstrating that you have understood what he or she intends.

Acheson Report (1998): a major milestone report, which outlined the current state of health inequalities in the country and set out a programme to address them; this later influenced many areas of government policy.

advocacy: a person or agency with a role in defending or promoting a cause or a person's rights.

African-Caribbean: people with ethnic origins in the African sub continent or the Caribbean Islands

aim: the 'aim', or outcome, is the broad goal for a piece of work. Usually a project has only one or two aims.

amphetamine: a stimulant drug that increases the activity of certain chemicals in the brain. Street names for amphetamines include *uppers, go fast, zip,* and *whizz.*

assertion: this is different from both submission and aggression. It involves being able to negotiate a solution to a problem.

attributable outcome: an outcome which can be directly related to a piece of health promotion activity, i.e. the cause and effect can be linked.

autism: a condition whereby a person cannot develop social abilities, language and other communication skills to the usual level.

B

barriers: barriers to communication can exist at a physical and sensory level, at the level of making sense of a message and at a cultural and social context level, where the meaning of a message may be misunderstood.

behavioural norm: behaviour which is accepted as usual by the majority of people in a society.

Black Report (1980): a milestone report which clearly described the health inequalities in Britain – viewed as too politically sensitive by the government of the day, the report was suppressed and its distribution strictly limited

Braille: a system of raised marks that can be felt with fingers. It provides a system of written communication based on the sense of touch for people who have limited vision.

British Medical Association: the professional body for the medical profession, representing their interests at a national level, for example in negotiations with the government over changes in management of the medical profession.

British Sign Language: this is a real language in the same way that English or French is a language. BSL is not a signed version of the English language. BSL has evolved in the UK's Deaf community over hundreds of years.

C

cancer: a term which covers a wide variety of diseases caused by uncontrollable growth of a particular body tissue, for example, lung and bone.

cannabis: a drug made from the dried leaves and flowers of the hemp plant, which produces a feeling of relaxation when smoked or eaten.

care values: occupational standards and codes of practice identify a framework of values and moral rights of service users that can be referred to as care values. These values include promoting equality and diversity, maintaining confidentiality, and promoting individual rights and beliefs.

caste: a form of social ordering through which an individual's position in society is fixed at birth and cannot be changed (e.g. through marriage).

code of practice: a set of statements describing the standards of conduct and practice required of professional workers (e.g. the General Social Care Council Code of Practice describes the standards expected in care work).

combination therapy: usually refers to treating a single disease with two or more medications at the same time (e.g. for HIV, triple therapy is the most commonly used). The term is also used when other types of therapy are used at the same time.

communicable infections: any infection that can be transmitted from one person to another.

communication cycle: a process of listening to and interpreting other people's responses to check your communication has been understood, building up an understanding through clarifying oral messages.

community strategy: a planning document led by the local authority and owned by key partner agencies locally known as the Local Strategic Partnership. This sets out the way in which the partnership will improve the local community across all issues, such as health, environment, crime, transport employment and housing.

comparative need: identified from comparisons between similar groups of people, where one group is identified as having poorer health as a consequence of an identified difference.

Council for Voluntary Services: an umbrella organisation for a wide variety of local voluntary sector organisations.

confidentiality: this is an important moral and legal right, promoting safety and security of service users and their property. The maintenance of confidentiality is vital in order to maintain a sense of trust.

cultural variation: communication is always influenced by cultural systems of meaning. Different cultures interpret systems of communication such as body language differently.

D

dental decay: usually recorded as DMF (decayed, missing filled teeth), the DMF ratio for an area is one of the best indicators of health inequality (high DMF = high levels of ill health).

disability: the consequence of impairment, or other individual difference. The disability a person experiences is determined by the way in which other people respond to that difference.

discrimination: activities that prevent members of a certain group from accessing the same benefits and rewards as others.

Drug Action Team (DAT): a local partnership responsible for planning the local delivery of the government's drugs strategy.

drug prevention initiatives: a range of Initiatives which aim to discourage young people from using drugs.

Drug Reference Group: a local partnership which is tasked to deliver the DAT strategy.

E

Ecstasy: medically referred to as MDMA (methylenedioxymethamphetamine), this is a synthetic drug that acts simultaneously as a stimulant and a hallucinogen. Users take it for the sense of well-being or the sensory distortions it induces, or to stay awake.

empathy: the ability to enter into and understand the world of another person and communicate this understanding to him or her.

equity: the principle of social justice – directing resources to those who need them most.

ethics: acting in a principled fashion – to act ethically.

ethnic group: a group that shares a common origin, culture or language (e.g. black or ethnic minority groups).

evaluation: to judge the worth of something.

evaluation of process: to establish the benefits delivered through the process of implementing a piece of work (e.g. the new partnerships it creates).

evidence-based practice: to base your practice on evidence of what works best.

Exercise on Prescription: supervised series of exercise sessions provided to patients at a reduced rate, or free, in response to an identified condition such as high blood pressure or mild depression.

expressed need: a felt need that is voiced by a person or community.

F

felt need: needs which people feel, i.e., things we *want*.

Fluoride: an inert substance which when added to the water supply can reduce the level of tooth decay.

Food Deserts: populated urban areas where residents do not have access to affordable healthy food.

food safety: the practice of storing and preparing food safely.

formative evaluation: feedback during the course of a project, when things are still taking shape.

G

gender socialisation: learning the socially acceptable behaviours for boys and girls, which may be different.

General Practitioner: the family doctor, who is an independent contractor funded through the NHS but not employed by it.

H

harm reduction: defines the policies, programmes, services and actions that work to reduce health, social and economic harm to individuals, communities and society.

health authorities: an arm of the health service whose role is to monitor the performance of PCTs, support public health practice and develop local health partnerships and networks.

Health Development Agency (HDA): a national health agency set up in 2000 to provide information about what works in terms of health promotion activity – to enable evidence-based practice in health promotion.

health education: an aspect of health promotion which largely relates to educating people about good health and how to develop and support it.

Health Education Authority (HEA): a special health authority that existed to co-ordinate national campaigns and provide the government with specific advice about health-promoting activity. This was replaced by the Health Development Agency (HDA) in 2000.

Health Improvement Programme (HimP): a local health document for each PCT that sets out plans for meeting both national and local health targets in partnership with other local agencies. Renamed the Health Improvement and Modernisation Plan as a result of the NHS Plan 2000.

health promotion outcome: the result of a piece of health promotion work – a reduction in a particular disorder or an uptake in screening, for example.

health protection: population measures to safeguard health, such as through legislation, financial or social means (e.g. using legislation to govern health and safety at work or using taxation policy to reduce smoking levels or car use by raising the price of cigarettes or petrol).

health visitors: a specific branch of the nursing profession with a key public health role in local communities, working at a neighbourhood level to identify local health need and support community activity to address those needs.

hepatitis: a serious disease of the liver. There are three main types of hepatitis: hepatitis A, B and C.

herd immunity: when a certain percentage of a population is vaccinated, the spread of a disease can be stopped. The critical percentage depends on the disease and the vaccine, but 90% is not uncommon.

holistic health: recognises that there are different dimensions – physical, mental, emotional, social, spiritual and societal health – that together build a holistic concept of health.

Human Immunodeficiency Virus (HIV): the virus that, when acquired, leads to the breakdown of the body's immune system, leading to the syndrome known as AIDS.

I

immunisation: the process of making people immune to certain diseases by challenging their immune system with a weak or inactivated version of the disease organism to stimulate the person to create antibodies to the disease.

injunction: a court order imposing a ban on certain actions by individuals, making these illegal and punishable by law.

interaction analysis: a method of analysing how far group members are focused on a group task or on the social maintenance of the group.

intervention: to intervene or take action in order to effect a change, for example to intervene by helping someone quit smoking.

L

lay models of health: the term 'lay' refers to a non-professional viewpoint, i.e. the models of health held by the public at large as opposed to professionally or scientifically phrased perspectives.

learning cycle: a theory proposed by David Kolb that learning often involves a four-stage process of experience, reflecting on experience, theorising and experimenting.

liquid-based cytology (LBC): a new way of preparing cervical samples for examination in the laboratory. Rather than smearing the sample onto a microscope slide, the head of the spatula (where the cells are lodged) is broken off into a small glass vial containing preservative fluid, or rinsed directly into the preservative fluid.

local authorities: the local organisations responsible for environmental health, building control, leisure facilities, refuse collection and street cleaning.

Local strategic partnership (LSP): a single body that:

* brings together at a local level the different parts of the public sector as well as the private, business, community and voluntary sectors so that different initiatives and services support each other and work together

* is a non-statutory, non-executive organisation

* operates at a level which enables strategic decisions to be taken and is close enough to individual neighbourhoods to allow actions to be determined at community level

* should be aligned with local authority boundaries.

M

Makaton: a system for developing language that uses speech, signs and symbols to help people with learning difficulties to communicate and to develop their language skills.

mass media: an umbrella term for a range of media conveying information to the general population including radio, television, newspapers and magazines.

mammogram: an X-ray photograph of the breasts taken to help discover possible cancers.

medical model: probably the most widely known model of health and the one that has come to dominate all others in the Western world, this adopts a scientific view of health and body functioning.

Methicillin Resistant Staphylococcus Aureus (MRSA): a bacterium that is resistant in differing degrees to antibiotics.

micro skills: the non-verbal components of caring behaviour (a term used by Gerard Egan).

milestones: major points along a the course of a project by which its progress can be monitored.

MMR vaccine: vaccination against measles, mumps and rubella.

morale: the level of confidence, hopefulness and purpose within a group. A group with low morale may be depressed or lacking in direction. A group with high morale may be co-operative, optimistic and eager to work together towards agreed goals.

morbidity: the rate of illness caused by a particular condition.

mortality: deaths due to a particular condition.

musculoskeletal: the complex system involving the body's muscles and skeleton and including the joints, ligaments, tendons and nerves.

myalgic encephalopathy: an illness, sometimes lasting for several years, in which a person's muscles and joints hurt and they are generally very tired (also known as chronic fatigue syndrome).

N

National Healthy School standard: a national initiative that uses an organisational approach to health promotion. This provides schools with a framework they can work within to develop their health-promoting capacity.

National Service Framework: a mechanism for unifying standards of care within the NHS. These set out in quite practical terms what health districts must provide in key areas such as coronary heart disease, mental health, diabetes.

nGMS: the new contract negotiated by the government with family doctors to govern the delivery of General Medical Services.

NHS Plan (2000): government document which outlines a ten-year plan for modernising the NHS.

normative need: where an expert or professional identifies that something falls short of a standard they have set and a need is identified.

norms: the expectations that people have of other people within a particular group or culture – what people regard as normal.

O

obesity: a Body Mass Index in excess of 30.

objective: the specific goal to be achieved in delivering the stated aim or outcomes.

offending background: history of illegal behaviour.

Office of Population Censuses and Surveys (OPCS): national body which compiles information on the UK population, responsible for carrying out the census every ten years.

Ottawa Charter for Health Promotion (WHO 1986): defined the role of health promotion as being (Author query)

outcome evaluation: seeks to establish the worth of work when it has reached its conclusion.

outcome measures: indicators of success for health-promotion activity.

P

paraphrase: to put what you think a person has said into your own words.

postcode rationing: describes the variations in the availability of treatments and services in different areas of the UK. This variability may be deliberate, in an attempt to conserve resources for certain priority groups or unintentional, as a result of poor planning.

prevalence: a measure of how many people are suffering from a particular condition or behaving in particular way at any one time.

prevention: reducing or avoiding the risks of diseases and ill health primarily through medical *interventions*. There are several approaches and levels for health promotion activity to take place within.

Primary Care Trust (PCT): new NHS organisations, which have three key responsibilities to:

* improve the health of their local population
* develop local primary health care services
* commission other local health services in line with local health needs.

primary group: a collection of people where members know and recognise each other personally (e.g. a family or a class of students).

primary health-care setting: usually a term used to refer to the GP surgery or health centre.

primary prevention: an attempt to eliminate the possibility of getting a disease.

primary socialisation: the process through which babies and young children learn the cultural norms of society through the family.

probes and prompts: a probe is a very short question that is used to *dig deeper* or probe into a person's answer. Prompts are short questions or words, which you offer to the other person in order to encourage them to answer.

professional relationships: these are different from ordinary social relationships and friendships because professionals must work within a defined framework of values. Their work always involves a duty of care and professional relationships involve working within appropriate boundaries.

public health specialism: held by workers with expertise in assessing the patterns of ill health locally as well as identifying what types of health care provision and health promoting activities are required to improve health.

R

race: a large group of people with common ancestry and inherited physical characteristics.

racism: discrimination against people on the basis of their race background, usually based in the belief that some races are inherently superior to others.

radon: a radioactive gas produced through the natural decay of uranium that is found in nearly all soils.

reflective practice: a methodology commonly used by healthcare practitioners to improve their practice. It involves thinking about a recent experience in their work in order to decide what can learned from it and identify how the learning can be applied to future practice.

restriction order: command preventing free movement by a person being treated under the Mental Health Act 1983.

role model: someone who demonstrates exemplary behaviour.

S

SOLER: an acronym formed from the words Squarely, Open, Lean, Eye Contact, Relaxed. These words are drawn from a theory of non-verbal supportive behaviour identified by Egan.

schizophrenia: a mental illness where the relation between thoughts, feelings, and actions breaks down, usually with a withdrawal from social activity and the occurrence of delusions and hallucinations.

school nurse: a specialist branch of community nursing, historically with a key role in screening programmes within schools, but increasingly they are involved with other health promoting activity, such as drop-in sessions on school premises offering advice about drug use or sexual health.

screening: identification of unrecognised disease or defect by the application of tests, examinations and other procedures which can be applied rapidly. Screening tests identify people who appear well but may have a disease.

secondary group: a general category of people, such as motorists, where an individual may identify with other motorists but will not know them personally.

secondary prevention: activity to improve the health of those people identified as being in the early stages of a disease.

secondary socialisation: the process of learning behavioural codes that continues throughout life, influencing and changing perceptions, attitudes and behaviours through interaction with others.

sectioned: subjected to an order for compulsory treatment under the Mental Health Act 1983.

settings-based approach: a way of organising health-promoting activity, a setting might be school, hospital, primary care or workplace, for example.

sexually transmitted disease: can only be passed by sexual activity.

SMART: an acronym for effective objective setting; objectives should be Specific, Measurable, Achievable, Realistic, and Time specific.

social model of health: this emphasises that to improve health it is necessary to address the origins of ill health, which make it more prevalent in some groups than others.

socialisation: the process through which children learn the behavioural codes (i.e. how to behave acceptably) of the society they are born into.

societal change: attempts to elicit health improvement by radically changing society, for example by reducing tolerance to drink driving.

speech communities: evidenced by their own special words, phrases and speech patterns, these might be based on people who live in a certain geographical area, a specific ethnic group, or different professions and work cultures.

specialist health promotion services: a small specialised service which supports the development of the health-promoting role of others, the development of new services and policies which can promote health locally.

stereotyping: a fixed way of thinking, involving generalisations and expectations about an issue or a group of people.

summative evaluation: an assessment of what has happened.

Sure Start/Sure Start Plus: local programmes concentrated in neighbourhoods where a high proportion of children are living in poverty and work with parents and parents-to-be to improve children's life chances through better access to, family support, advice on nurturing, health services and early learning.

synopsis: a summary or overview.

T

Tackling Drugs Together: first national drugs strategy launched in 1993.

target audience: the group an activity is aimed at, be it research, marketing, or health education material, for example.

tertiary prevention: the control and reduction, as far as possible, of a disease or disability that is already established.

transgender: a man or woman who believes they belong to the opposite sex (i.e. 'born into the wrong body')

transsexual: a man or woman who has physically changed their sexual characteristics to those of the opposite sex, usually involving medical and surgical treatment.

The Health of the Nation (1992): the UK's first national health strategy.

V

vaccination: to challenge a person's immune system to produce antibodies by Injecting a dead or weakened version of the disease organism.

value judgments: to judge someone or something from a standpoint based on your own values (e.g. 'because I don't smoke and believe it to be bad for you, I you are a bad person').

victim blaming: people frequently simplify health choices by blaming the person who chooses to adopt an unhealthy behaviour for making that choice. In reality, things are rarely that simple; for example, people site lack of time due to work pressures as the major cause of taking too little exercise.

voluntary sector: agencies which obtain their funding from charitable giving, specific funding from public sector organisations such as PCTs or through the National Lottery.

W

Water (Fluoridation) Act 1985: an act that did not make all water companies fluoridate their water but enabled them to if they so chose.

World Health Organisation: established on 7 April 1948, it was a response to an international desire for a world free from disease, and since then 7 April has been celebrated each year as **World Health Day**.

Index

If you liked this, you'll also like...

YOUR REF. NO.
S 666 CAR A

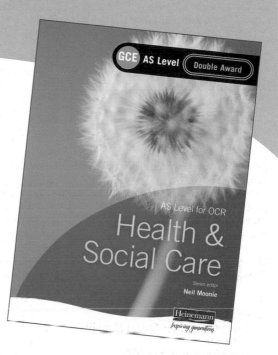

AS Level GCE Health and Social Care Double Award for OCR

This book contains all the units that you need to complete the Double Award.

◆ Packed full of activities and case studies relating to Health and Social Care.

◆ Written by an expert author team to ensure that everything you need to know is covered.

◆ Full colour and easy to read with useful assessment guidance.

Why not place your order today?

AS Level GCE Health and Social Care Double Award for OCR
0 435 45358 0

Visit your local bookshop or call our Customer Services Department quoting the following promotional code – S 666 CAR A

Contents

Unit 1 Promoting quality care

Unit 2 Communication in care settings

Unit 3 Promoting good health

Unit 4 Health and safety in care settings

Unit 5 Caring for people with additional needs

Unit 6 Working in early years care and education

Unit 7 Health as a lifestyle choice

Unit 8 Complementary therapies

Unit 9 Caring for older people

 01865 888068  01865 314029 (e) orders@heinemann.co.uk (w) www.heinemann.co.uk

Heinemann
Inspiring generations

K556